The Fishermen

and Women of the Firth of Forth

is dedicated, with respect, to the original authors

Mr David Octavius Hill RSA and

Mr Robert Adamson

Hill and Adamson's

THE FISHERMEN AND WOMEN OF THE FIRTH OF FORTH

Sara Stevenson

SCOTTISH NATIONAL PORTRAIT GALLERY
MCMXCI

First published 1991 by
The Trustees of the National Galleries of Scotland
for the exhibition at the Scottish National Portrait Gallery, Edinburgh
21 November 1991 — 18 January 1992

ISBN 0 903598 15 9

The publisher acknowledges subsidy
from the Scottish Arts Council towards the publication of this volume

Copy photography by Antonia Reeve
Designed & typeset in Monotype Bell by Dalrymple
Printed by Lecturis, Eindhoven on Mellotex 135gsm made in Fife
by Tullis Russell

The National Galleries of Scotland gratefully acknowledge
the generous support the Nancie Massey Charitable Trust has given to this exhibition
and the co-operation of the Photography Collection,
Harry Ransom Humanities Research Center, The University of Texas at Austin,
in allowing the reproduction of calotypes from the Clarkson Stanfield album
from the Gernsheim Collection

Contents

Foreword

The intention to publish this work, *The Fishermen and Women of the Firth of Forth*, was first announced by David Octavius Hill and Robert Adamson in 1844. It is a surprising piece of publishing history that it is only in 1991, 147 years later, that the book has finally appeared. We are indebted to the Nancie Massey Charitable Trust, the Scottish Arts Council and Tullis Russell for the support which has made this possible.

The Scottish Photography Archive was prompted to undertake this unfulfilled project by the generous gift to the nation of the Edinburgh Photographic Society's collection in 1987. When the most valuable part of the collection, which included eighty-seven of Hill and Adamson's paper negatives, emerged from the bank vaults into the light of day, it provided a startlingly new insight into their original idea. These negatives, which were technical 'failures', when added to the existing, well-known images, make up a whole-hearted account of fishing life, which places the origins of the photographic social documentary survey in Scotland in the 1840s. The entire project was a co-operative one, a social engagement between the artists and the subjects, in which the results are powerful, beautiful and true.

The intention of this publication is to present the motivation behind the survey; to give an understanding of the social and cultural life of the fishing village of Newhaven (where most of the photographs were taken); and to attempt to come close to the photographers' own thoughts and ideas.

Timothy Clifford
Director of the National Galleries of Scotland

Duncan Thomson
Keeper of the Scottish National Portrait Gallery

Acknowledgements

This book has been made possible by the personal and institutional generosity of the following: James Brownlee Hunter, Dr A. M. Elliot, Mrs Peggy Notman, Mrs Ann Riddell, Mrs Eleanor Robertson, the Edinburgh Photographic Society, Glasgow University Library (Special Collections), the Harry Ransom Humanities Research Center, University of Texas. I am also indebted to the enthusiastic encouragement and help of my colleagues, most especially to Janis Adams, Keith Bell, David Bruce, Robert Dalrymple, Roy Flukinger, Barbara Gray, Michael Gray, James Lawson, Julie Lawson, Alison Morrison-Low and Naomi Tarrant.

Sara Stevenson
Curator of Photography

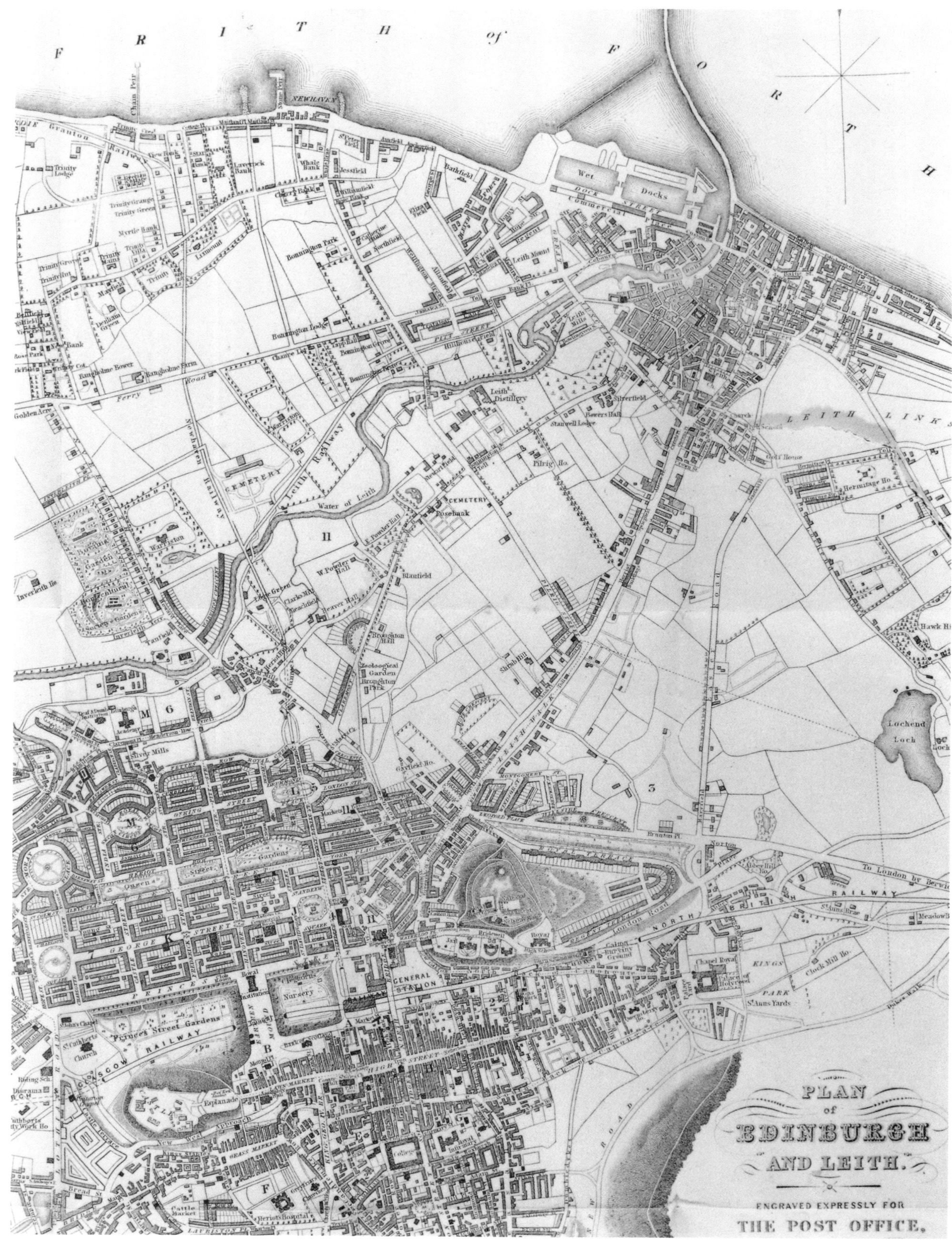

F R I T H of F O R T H
NEWHAVEN
Wet Docks
Commercial
Trinity Lodge
Laverock Bank
Whale Bank
Bonnington Park
Bonnington Lodge
Ferry Road
Leith Distillery
Stanwell Lodge
Pilrig Ho.
LEITH LINKS
Hermitage Ho.
CEMETERY
Water of Leith
Leith Railway
Rosebank
Inverleith Ho
Warriston
Blandfield
Broughton Hall
Zoological Garden
Lochend Loch
3
To London by Berwick
RAILWAY
London Road
Clock Mill Ho.
St. Anns Yards
Chapel Royal
GENERAL STATION
Nursery
Princes Street Gardens
RAILWAY
St. Cuthberts Church
Esplanade
GRASS MARKET
HIGH STREET
Cattle Market
Heriots Hospital
F
B
M 6
PLAN
of
EDINBURGH
AND LEITH.
ENGRAVED EXPRESSLY FOR
THE POST OFFICE.

'Mr. D. O. Hill ... is on the Eve of Entering into Partnership with Mr. Adamson.'

THE Scottish judge, Lord Cockburn, wrote a letter to the editor of the *North British Review* in November 1847, recommending that he publish a review of the progress of the art of photography. '... certain artists here,' he said with mild irony, 'hold that this is the Paradise of Calotype.'[1] The calotype process—a rich and subtle form of photography—had been brought to a state of technical brilliance and exploited with such intelligence and invention within the four preceding years, that this affectionate opinion was justified. In these four years, the City of Edinburgh had seen one of the most exceptional partnerships made in art.

The first public announcement of the invention of a negative / positive process of photography was made by the inventor, William Henry Fox Talbot, in 1839. Talbot worked on improving the process, which he finally succeeded in doing with the discovery of the latent image and the use of gallic acid as a developer in the autumn of 1840. One of his most interested correspondents was the physicist, Sir David Brewster, who lived in the university town of St Andrews. Brewster and his friends experimented with Talbot's 'calotype' process of photography and, after lengthy trials, his colleague, Dr John Adamson, succeeded in taking a portrait photograph in May 1842.[2] Thereafter, Adamson taught his young brother, Robert, and between them they mastered the process and devised improvements of their own (fig. 1). At the beginning of 1843, they were sufficiently confident to propose that Robert should take it up as a career and, with Talbot's permission, Robert Adamson left for Edinburgh in May. He set up his calotype studio in the highest private house on the Calton Hill at the east end of Princes Street—a house with a sheltered, south-facing garden which would catch the best of the sun (fig. 35).

Robert Adamson's arrival in Edinburgh went unremarked. In the first few weeks he was presumably setting up the studio and the only dated negative for that period is an uninspired photograph of the Royal High School taken only a hundred yards away from home.[3] Brewster, with an interested eye on his protegé, took the first opportunity of sending business his way.

Sir David was in Edinburgh for the General Assembly of the Church of Scotland which was in the throes of a violent dispute. For years the Church and the lawcourts had been caught in an irreconcilable fight centring on the right of the owners of the presentation to ministerial livings to put in ministers against the will of the Church presbyteries. The fight had finally reached deadlock and the attention of the whole of Scotland was focussed on the Assembly. On 18 May, the Assembly opened. The Moderator, the elected head of the Assembly, arose, uttered a formal protest and left. Behind him followed four hundred ministers, more than a third of the Church, who progressed through Edinburgh to Tanfield Hall, signed a Deed of Demission resigning their livings and set up the Free Church of Scotland.

This extraordinary gesture made a remarkable impact, even on those who did not agree with the dissenting ministers. It was the expression of a passionate strength of feeling that the Church had ceased to have true authority—'I felt' said the Rev. Dr Stewart of Cromarty, 'as I could imagine a child to feel hanging at the breast of its mother, if that mother had been suddenly shot through the heart. I might cling to the body but the life has gone out of her.'[4]

One of the people present, who was deeply moved, was the painter, David Octavius Hill (fig. 2). He decided to paint a great commemorative painting (fig. 3) and, with the encouragement of the leaders of the new Church, he obtained permission to take sketches during the Assembly sessions. Within six days of the Disruption, he was advertising engravings from his painting, which he calculated would take two to three years to complete.[5]

Sir David Brewster, who took a prominent role in the Free Church, was interested in Hill's painting. It occurred to him that Hill would have some difficulty securing the likenesses of all the ministers and elders he wished to include in the painting, who would soon be leaving Edinburgh and scattering throughout Scotland. Brewster wrote to Talbot on 9 June that he had talked to Hill about using photography as an aid: 'He was at first incredulous, but went to Mr. Adamson, and arranged with him preliminaries for getting all the necessary portraits.'[6]

Within a couple of weeks of meeting Adamson and experimenting with the calotype, Hill's doubts were transformed into enthusiasm. On 3 July, Brewster wrote again to Talbot: *'they have succeeded beyond their most sanguine expectations.—They have taken on a small scale, Groups of 25 persons in the same picture all placed in attitudes which the Painter desired, and very large Pictures besides have been taken of each individual to assist the Painter in the completion of his picture. Mr. D. O. Hill, the Painter, is on the eve of entering into partnership with Mr. Adamson and proposes to apply the Calotype to many other general purposes of a very popular kind, & especially to the execution of large pictures representing diff[eren]t bodies & classes of individuals.*

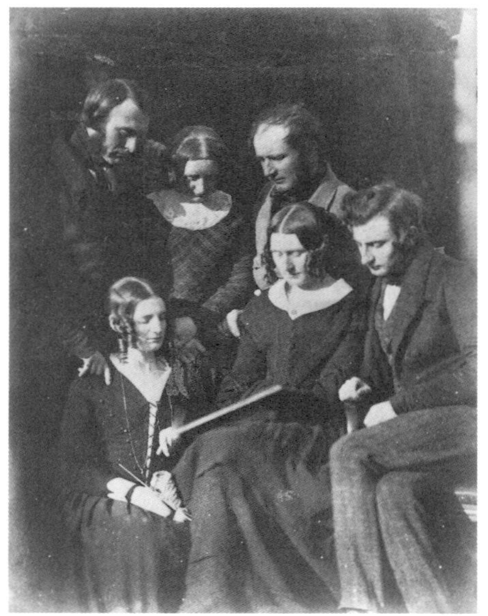

fig. 1
D. O. Hill and Robert Adamson
The Adamson family, with Dr John on the left and Robert on the right
calotype
Scottish National Portrait Gallery

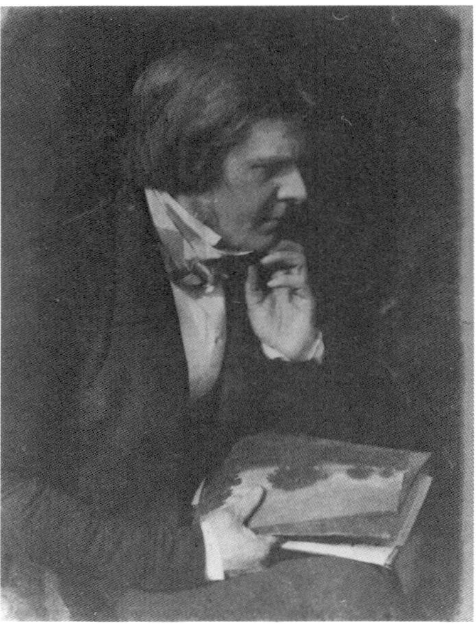

fig. 2
D. O. Hill and Robert Adamson
David Octavius Hill
calotype
Scottish National Portrait Gallery

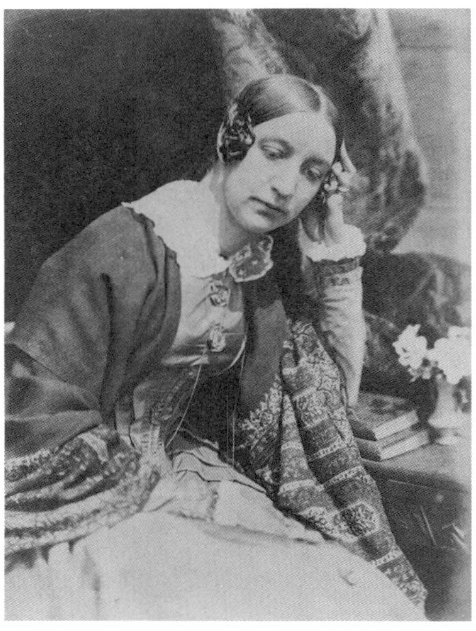

fig. 4
D. O. Hill and Robert Adamson
Elizabeth Rigby, later Lady Eastlake
calotype
Scottish National Portrait Gallery

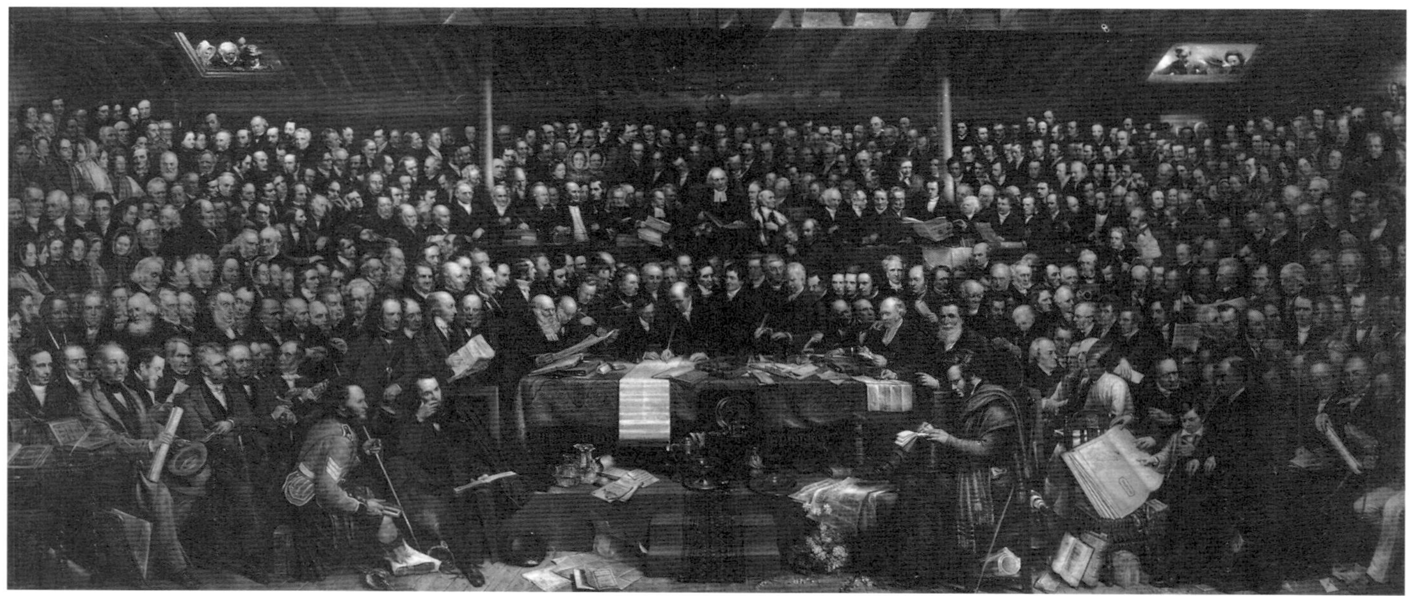

fig. 3
David Octavius Hill
The Signing of the Deed of Demission
oil painting
Free Church of Scotland

I think you will find that we have, in Scotland, found out the value of your invention not before yourself, but before those to whom you have given the privilege of using it.' [7]

Hill and Adamson's enthusiasm for the work they could do together may be measured by the fact that Hill had embarked on a most ambitious and difficult painting only weeks earlier. Hill's original discussions with Adamson were part of his preparation for that painting, but by July they had discussed and experimented with a range of ideas, which had become independently so exciting that Hill was sidetracked into a working partnership which was to take up much of his time and energies in the next three years.

Some idea of their intentions may be gathered from the first review of the calotypes, which appeared in the *Witness* newspaper on 12 July. This was written by Hugh Miller, the geologist and journalist, who had already been calotyped by Hill and Adamson. His article was partly prompted by an exhibition of studies and sketches for the Disruption picture which opened on the same day and already included 'a projected Series of Portraits of Clergymen and Laymen of the Free Protesting Church of Scotland, comprising nearly the whole of the Calotype Pictures executed jointly by Mr. Adamson and Mr. Hill.' [8] This was an extension of the idea of using photography as a source of rough sketches, and the individual prints were to be issued to the public as finished portraits independently of the painting.

Miller's article talked of the calotype as, 'A real invention which bids fair to produce some of the greatest revolutions in the fine arts of which they have ever been the subject...' He discussed the possibilities at length and suggested that it would be useful in producing improved treatises on perspective, in providing pictures for engraving—specifically for book illustration—for judging the truth of art and for investigating the psychology or physiology of perception. He concluded: 'the subject is so suggestive of thought at the present stage, that it would be no easy matter to exhaust it; and it will, we have no doubt, be still more suggestive of thought by and by.' [9] This idea of the overflowing potential of photography was clearly the basis for the partnership.

Robert Adamson's studio practice was confidential to the point of secrecy. In response to an anxiety expressed by the painter, David Roberts, in 1845, that another photographer might pre-empt their own plans, Hill responded: *'About three years ago this said process was chemically and artistically speaking a very miserable affair. Dr. Adamson of St. Andrews—brother of my friend R. Adamson whose manipulation produced the pictures now with you, took up Mr. Talbot's process as an amateur. You are aware how jealous some scientific men are, as to their rights in the paternity of inventions or improvements, therefore I say* entre nous *that I believe Dr. Adamson & his brother to be the fathers of many of those parts of the process which make it a valuable and practical art. I believe also from all I have seen that Robert Adamson is the most successful manipulator the art has yet seen, and his steady industry and knowledge of chemistry, is such that both from him and his brother much new improvements may yet be expected. I must tell you that Dr. Adamson, up to the time that his brother thought of using the art professionally, was a most liberal communicator to all and everyone, of all his improvements—and Mr. Talbot had regularly a knowledge of his results.'* He added, *'I know not the process though it is done under my nose continually and I believe I never will.'* [10]

The only eye-witness account of Robert Adamson at work was given years later by the commercial photographer, James Good Tunny: *'Hill and Adamson's calotype portraits became the wonder of every gathering of scientific or artistic men. Time after time have I gone and stood on the projecting rock below Playfair's monument on Calton Hill, and drawn inspiration from viewing Mr. Adamson placing a large square box upon a stand, covering his head with a focussing cloth, introducing the slide, counting the seconds by his watch, putting the cap on the lens, and retiring to what we now know to be the dark room. Oh! if I could only have got an introduction to these men, it would have been the consummation of my happiness! ...'* [11]

The impression we have of Robert Adamson is of an unassertive young man. It may be argued from the few photographs of him that he was modest and from Hill's friendship that he was amiable. The evidence quoted above gives a more positive view of him. His grasp of a difficult process was in itself remarkable and his professionalism enabled him to produce consistently good results. James Nasmyth referred to him in a letter to Hill as 'the authentic contriver & manipulator in the art of light and darkness,' [12] which implies that he agrees with Hill that Adamson had added effectively to Talbot's invention. Unfortunately, from the time he set up his business, he remained professionally discreet. Unlike his contemporaries, he did not treat photography as a scientific curiosity which he wished to discuss either in private or in public meetings and kept his results for his own use—it is presumably significant that Hill does not say he has been told what Adamson is doing, merely that it is done under his nose.

The studio also employed at least one assistant, who was less prominent even than Adamson. This was Miss Mann, who apparently came from Perth and may for that reason have been introduced by Hill, whose family lived there. She provides part of the explanation for the studio's exceptional output of more than 3,000 photographic images. [13] In practical terms, Miss Mann's contribution must have been considerable. James Nasmyth, who is again the only person who comments on her work, refers to her as 'thrice worthy Miss Mann that most skilfull and zealous of assistants.' [14]

Hill was the leading figure and the driving force of the partnership. It was he who communicated freely with friends and fellow artists and it is from him that we have the evidence to construct an idea of the intentions and ambitions behind their photography (the emphasis throughout this book is, therefore, on Hill's knowledge and ideas in relation to Newhaven). He was an ambitious man and he was a man who overflowed with ideas. He was sufficiently practical to understand the camera, and to understand what it could be used for and what it could be pushed to do. He was sociable and enthusiastic in a manner which could encourage not merely co-operation but inventiveness. The partnership was, as a result, one of the rare examples of intelligences linking in an active practical manner to achieve remarkable art.

During the first six months of the partnership, Hill and Adamson were able to take a second group of calotypes of the Free Church ministers at the October meeting in Glasgow. They worked with at least three painters—Sir William Allan, George Harvey and the English watercolourist, John Harden. Harvey commissioned a series of photographs in Greyfriars' Churchyard, which he planned to use as studies for a big allegorical painting. At the end of the year, David Brewster was reporting to Talbot: *'I wish I could send you some of the fine calotypes of ancient Church yard monuments, as well as modern ones taken by Mr. Adamson, and also specimens of the fine groups of Picturesque personages which Mr. Hill and he have arranged and photographed. Those of the Fishermen & women of Newhaven are singularly excellent. They have been so inundated with work that they have not been able to send me a Collection which they have promised. I think your plan of publication excellent. The same idea had occurred to Mr. Hill & Mr. Adamson, who advertised it some time ago as a plan in contemplation.'* [15]

Also at the end of the year, the calotypes were on view in the Board of Manufactures exhibition in Edinburgh. They were awarded a prize of ten pounds for 'combining in the happiest possible manner artistical freedom of excellence with scientific precision of execution.' [16]

Calotype photography, which required good light to take the negative and to print the positive, was a seasonal profession. In mid-November, Robert Adamson went back to St Andrews and apparently did not return until April, when the activities of the studio seem to have taken on new impetus. Hill, who had been living in Inverleith Row, moved into Rock House. It was at this point that they publicly declared their interest in photographing fishing life. In August, they announced their intention of producing six volumes of calotypes 'in a style of great elegance on a paper the size and quality of *Roberts' Views in the Holy Land*.' The first was to be *The Fishermen and Women of the Frith* [sic] *of Forth*, which would be followed by *Highland Character and Costume*, *The Architectural Structures of Edinburgh*, *The Architectural Structures of Glasgow, &c*, *Old Castles and Abbeys &c in Scotland* and *Portraits of Distinguished Scotchmen.* [17]

With these extensive plans in mind, they commissioned the optician, Thomas Davidson, to make them a new camera on a far larger scale. Davidson talked about this years later: 'Messrs Hill and Adamson … had also a camera, about two feet square, fitted up for taking portraits as large as life; but the imperfections in it, & difficulty of preparing paper so large, were against it. I also made a speculum of 24" diameter & 30" focus, for the aforesaid, for taking smaller portraits, or to reflect light on the object; but that was never much used.' [18] This camera was apparently adaptable—it could take photographs in three sizes, 16 x 13 inches, 11¾ x10½ or 11¾ x 9 inches. The larger size was used only for architecture, whilst the two smaller sizes were used for single portraits and groups.

In attempting the larger sizes, Hill had it in mind to compete with large-scale engravings. Despite the difficulties they experienced with the camera, they did succeed in taking several fine architectural photographs and portraits with it—including a number with Newhaven fishwives (plate 40). The idea of the speculum or mirror—used inside the camera with the lens removed from in front so that light passed by the paper and bounced back from the mirror to the other, prepared, side of the paper—was originally devised in America. [19] In theory, the fact that the mirror had only one surface rather than the two of the lens made the mirror a more reliable and perfect means of casting the image onto the paper. In practice, it proved difficult, presumably because the large size of the paper blocked out much of the light on its way to the mirror and made longer exposure times necessary.

Hill and Adamson involved Thomas Davidson in another project. He wrote in 1859: *'It is now more than sixteen years since I assisted Messrs. Adamson & Hill, photographers, Edinburgh, in taking a few copies of magnified representations of minute objects by an achromatic solar microscope, which I had made for Mr. Octavius David Hill, Calton Stairs, Edinburgh … The objects I adopted were transverse sections of wood, about ⅜" in diameter. The enlarged copies were, so far as I recollect, about 18" in diameter … as regards patents, Mr. Hill & Mr. Adamson had arranged to lodge a Caveat, but the premature & lamented death of the latter prevented it.'* [20] This was not the first time photographs had been taken through a solar microscope, which Davidson would have known, so it is not clear what Hill and Adamson were thinking of patenting—possibly again an idea about printing on a large scale. But Davidson's account is evidence of the range of interest shown by the partnership, which was not confined to a narrow definition of photography's usefulness to current practice in painting.

Examples of the calotypes taken for the Disruption series were on view in Cupar in Fife and in Liverpool at Mr Grundy's Repository of the Arts during 1844. One of the Directors of the Trustees' Academy in Edinburgh, Alexander Christie, took a large group, which presumably included examples of the Newhaven pictures, over to Paris in September. There they were shown to the Academie des Sciences where the meeting as a whole preferred the daguerreotypes although the painter Ary Scheffer *'les qualifiat de merveilleuses.'* [21]

At the end of the month, Hill received Talbot's permission to attend a meeting of the British Association for the Advancement of Science in York. This was not a happy occasion and the reaction to Hill and Adamson's work was partly hostile. Hill reported later: 'I did a few other things at York—which by the Yorkites have since been considered beastly affairs (though a few of them were among the best things I have tried).' [22] He consoled himself with William Etty's comforting remarks: 'Etty saw in them revivals of Rembrandt, Titian and Spagnoletto.' The hostility probably stemmed from a general hostility to Talbot's patent, which was blocking a number of new methods of photography described during the meeting. The calotypes they took were not as consistently good as usual, presumably because Adamson did not have the ideal conditions to work in but also because Hill did not work well in face of hostile criticism.

At the beginning of 1845, Hill determined to make a serious move to market the calotypes and sent a portfolio down to Dominic Colnaghi in London. According to David Roberts, Colnaghi kept them under the counter and he himself rescued them and carried them off to meetings at the Graphic Society and Lord Northampton's house. [23] The reaction there was so enthusiastic that Hill was once more encouraged and characteristically leapt into a further ambitious scheme to take a series of great English portraits. In a lengthy and singularly illegible letter to Roberts, he wrote: *'my ambition is to leave my name on a great and noble work worthy of England and of this* English *invention ... I, though much occupied, would have no hesitation in undertaking to conduct a work of this sort of British statesmen and others ... this first book of English Calotype* pictures *for really Talbot's examples in his Pencil of Nature are not intended to be such should be such as to make the French look only second best in their Sun Painting efforts. It should almost be a book worthy of the tables [?] of sovereigns and of the highest cognoscenti. Now there is my naked bosom in the matter, which I hope will not make you rate me as absolute and arragant as Petruccio making you exclaim. "Why! This gallant will command the sun."'* [24]

Hill wrote to Talbot in the hopes of making an arrangement with him but, despite repeated letters, Talbot never replied. This was presumably because Antoine Claudet already held Talbot's licence to take portraits but possibly also because he and Hill did not understand each other and the praise of Hill's friends was beginning to irritate him. In April 1845, the Director of the Schools of Art at Somerset House, Charles Heath Wilson, wrote to Hill, 'If I had had the calotypes I could have done a great deal, I have lately had important opportunities under very favourable circumstances, I have one friend especially who will prove an enormous puffer. I can send them to Mr. Rogers the Poet & to other people ½ doz. will answer the purpose perfectly. Mrs. Jamieson is going to take them up strong, but you should guide us what to say in case we get upon wrong ground in respect of the English patent.' [25]

These grandiose plans did not interrupt vigorous activity in the Edinburgh studio. On 26 April, Hill reported, 'We are preparing fishwives for a book, and have done some fine things lately ...' [26] He is also recorded at work again in Newhaven in July, taking a group of pictures including plate 46 (see below p.21). Between the summer and autumn Hill was apparently ill with rheumatism and unable to work, but he wrote to Roberts in December: 'I have never yet heard from Mr. Talbot—some fine things in his art have been produced by us since you last saw what we have done. Mr. Lockhart who was here lately—thinks with you that I should come to London in the Spring and I have heard from him since urging that measure—we will see.' [27]

Hill's increasing frustration may have helped to prompt the most enthusiastic review of the calotypes. This was written by Elizabeth Rigby, who was very interested in the process and often posed at Rock House (fig. 4). Her review appeared in March in the *Quarterly Review* in an attack on modern German painting. She held the Edinburgh calotypes up as a model of truth (see below, p.49). Her footnote reference to Talbot was regrettably not calculated to be conciliating: *'To Mr. Fox Talbot the happy invention is owing, but that artistic application of it, which has brought these drawings to their present picturesque perfection, required the eye of an artist, and for this the public is indebted to Mr. D. O. Hill of Edinburgh, in conjunction with Mr. Adamson, a young chemist of distinguished ability. It is to be hoped that Mr. Talbot, in justice to his own genius, will soon invite these gentlemen to London—where they would find rather more interesting, though certainly not more grotesque subjects than the fat Martyrs of the Free Kirk—as yet seemingly their favourite subjects.'* [28] John Murray, who published the *Quarterly Review*, wrote a tempered version of this suggestion to Talbot in May: *'There are points in which your Calotypes have the decided superiority over his—there are others in which I think he excels—especially in obtaining artistic effects—a combination of the two would be a step in advance.'* [29]

In April, one of Hill's friends, Dr John Brown, took up art criticism for the *Witness* newspaper. His privately expressed intention was partly 'on account of David Hill. I want to tell the truth about him to himself and the public ...' [30] The Royal Scottish Academy exhibition was showing calotypes with which Hill now proposed to fulfil another grand plan—a published album of a hundred calotypes, which he described as 'a sort of Liber Studiorum in its way,' [31] that is to say, finished examples of photography used as an art. Brown began his review of the calotypes with the Newhaven pictures: *'Mr. Hill's other works in the exhibition are his Calotypes, in which he has shown his true genius for art. What wonderful things they are! Look at these delicious fisher boys, Nature's own children painted by herself. No self-consciousness, no lay-figure attitudes: there they are lying as carelessly and as gracefully as if flung down by chance, with their impudent, dirty, knowing faces; and these clean, sonsy, caller, comely, substantial fishwives,—what a refreshing sight! As easy, as unconfined, as deep-bosomed and ample, as any Grecian matron …We are astonished this invention is not more thought of … We repeat, that in nothing has Mr. Hill shown his true love for, and his power over, the best part of his art, than in what he has accomplished in this department.*' [32]

The weather in 1846 was particularly fine and the first calotypes of the year were taken in January. Strawberries ripened near Edinburgh early in February. Hill was still keeping an eye on his original purpose in taking up photography and in May advertised for yet more of the Free Church ministers to come and be calotyped for the Disruption picture.[33] Impervious to Elizabeth Rigby's acid remark, he had since 1843 doubled the size of the painting and proposed including twice or three times as many portraits. In April, he and Adamson took groups of the soldiers at Edinburgh Castle (fig. 5) and presumably also a panoramic group of views from the Castle. The latter may have originally been intended to be sold in their own right but were technically poor.[34] Hill used them as studies for a big painting of *Edinburgh Old and New* (fig. 34), which also included one of the Newhaven groups among the foreground figures (plate 45).

Less than a tenth of the calotype negatives are dated, so that the year in which they were taken is generally a matter of speculation. But after the group photograph of Hill in discussion with his friend, Dr George Bell (fig. 13), which is dated 7 June 1846, there is a sudden stop in the flow of dated negatives. It is possible that this marks the beginning of Robert Adamson's illness, which Hill first mentions in August of the following year: 'Adamson has been so poorly for many months that our calotyping operations have gone on but slowly.'[35] This may mean that the calotype work of the partnership was substantially complete within three years.

There are a few photographs which may be dated to 1847. A letter from Hill to Lady Ruthven in December suggests that her portrait had been taken recently. He sent her a set of photographs as a gift and talked again of the volume of a hundred calotypes. 'With its publication,' he added, 'the art and I will probably part company.'[36]

Hill may not have known when he wrote this letter that Robert Adamson was mortally ill. At the end of the year, he had returned to St Andrews to the care of his family, and on 15 January 1848, he died in his brother's house.

The brief partnership of Robert Adamson and David Octavius Hill was an exceptional experiment in the art and potential of photography, based on Adamson's considerable technical skill and Hill's invention. This experiment has had a powerful impact on the history of photography, but neither the rationale behind the photographs nor the seeds of inspiration are immediately clear, because the work is very sophisticated, yet often looks simple and natural.

'The more they are seen,' reported David Roberts of the reception of the photographs, from London in 1849, '*the more the wonder grows.*'[37] And this sense of puzzlement re-surfaces at intervals. James Craig Annan, who was an excellent photographer, found himself confused by the amount of labour involved in achieving similar 'natural' effects. He thought the calotypes were 'evolved as unconsciously and directly from nature as are the trees and flowers, and constitute a pure product … To present day pictorial photographers it is extremely interesting and almost humiliating to observe that on the very threshold of the photographic era there was one doing with no apparent effort what they would fain accomplish with eager strivings …'[38]

The 'nature' in the photographs, their consistent subtlety, skill and invention, is no happy accident. The photographs were closely calculated in their physics and chemistry and intelligently constructed. They are also, and less obviously, informed by cultural sophistication. In the first half of the nineteenth century, Scottish society was still small. Practical invention may have achieved a revolutionary force but subjects had not yet broken up into mutually incomprehensible disciplines. People were still talking to each other—more or less formally over dinner or in the many societies—trying out each other's ideas in relation to their own, directly criticising and supporting one another. D. O. Hill was, for example, educated at Perth Academy under Adam Anderson, who was notable for introducing the subjects of chemistry and geometry, which he taught to a standard which challenged the universities. When Hill came to Edinburgh, as a young painter, he was part of the circle round Alexander Nasmyth, described with such affection by his son in later years, where painters, engineers, physicists, architects and geologists mixed casually and discussed their ideas. It is possible to identify a range of people Hill admired, most of whom were his friends. Leaving aside the artists, these included the evangelical leaders, the Rev Dr Thomas Chalmers and the Rev Thomas Guthrie; the engineers, James Nasmyth and John Miller; the great literary figures, Robert Burns and Walter Scott; the writer and Professor of Moral Philosophy, John Wilson; the critic, Elizabeth Rigby; the judge, Lord Cockburn; the politician and economist, James Wilson; the classicist, Professor John Stuart Blackie and the medical doctor, Dr George Bell. This loosely-knit circle provided a wide range of inspiration and stimulus—intellectual, practical and imaginative.

D. O. Hill was described in a review of his work as having, 'a rich, versatile, rapid, facile mind, crowded with thick coming fancies …'[39] His skill in invention was fuelled also by ambition.

Unravelling the threads of influence on his photographic work and even identifying his intentions depends on the premise that the work is an idea of nature based on sophistication and knowledge, which relates to the society in which he moved as a welcome guest and friend.

Most of the calotypes taken by Hill and Adamson were portraits, and a high proportion of those are understandably of men connected with the Free Church. However, a more general overview gives an excellent idea of the liveliness of Edinburgh in the 1840s—in terms of the notable people living there and the number of interesting people who visited the city—from the Methodist Red Indian, Kahkewaquonaby, to the Irish harper, Patrick Byrne, or the Afghan, Mohun Lal. The range of sitters is matched by a consistent inventiveness of arrangement and pose in the photographs, which is all the more extraordinary in view of the practical constraints of the calotype process. The generally lengthy exposure times meant that most of the subjects were propped and clamped into position, and groups especially needed careful engineering.

The photographs of fishing life on the Firth of Forth were taken mostly in Newhaven with a few pictures from Prestonpans, Leith and St Andrews, where the wide streets and the harbour were in striking contrast to the narrow lanes and poorly sheltered beach of the village. Numerically, they are overshadowed by the portraits—around 130 pictures from the whole 3,000. But their importance is out of proportion to their numbers. They were a radical experiment in the art of photography, which challenges the history of social documentary at the same time as contributing to the history of aesthetics. Hill's intentions in undertaking the project and what he may have discovered from working with the fishermen and women are both far-reaching. As a case study in Hill and Adamson's art of the calotype, the photographs are of immense importance.

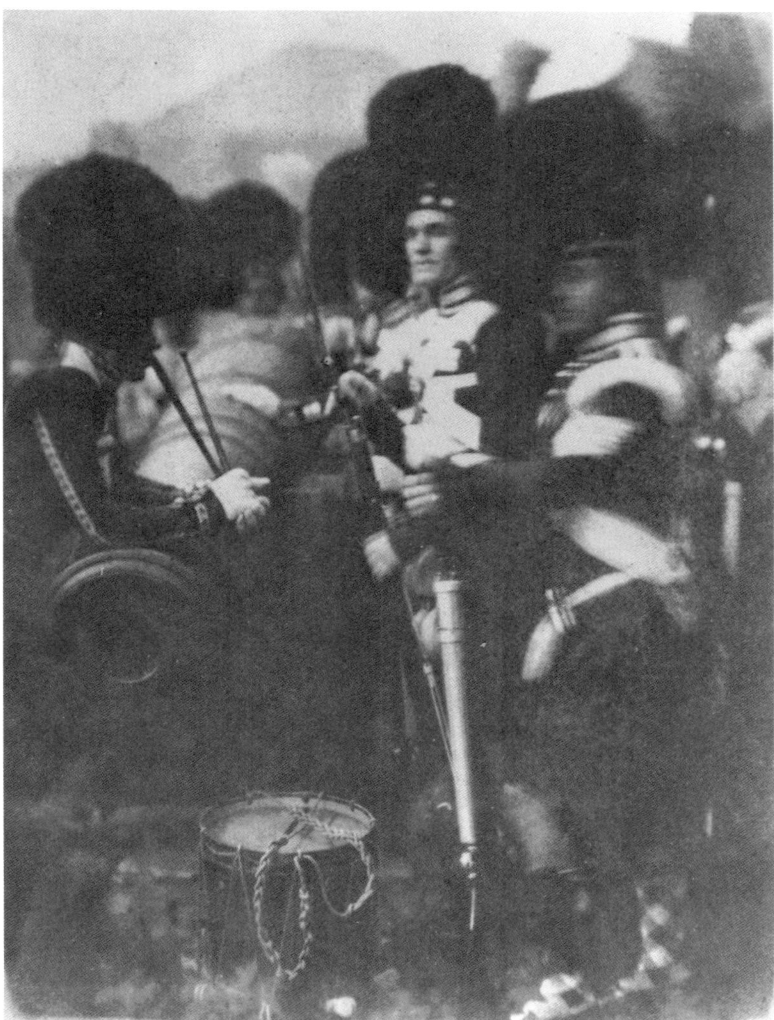

fig. 5
D. O. Hill
and Robert Adamson
92nd Gordon Highlanders at Edinburgh Castle, 1845
calotype
Scottish National Portrait Gallery

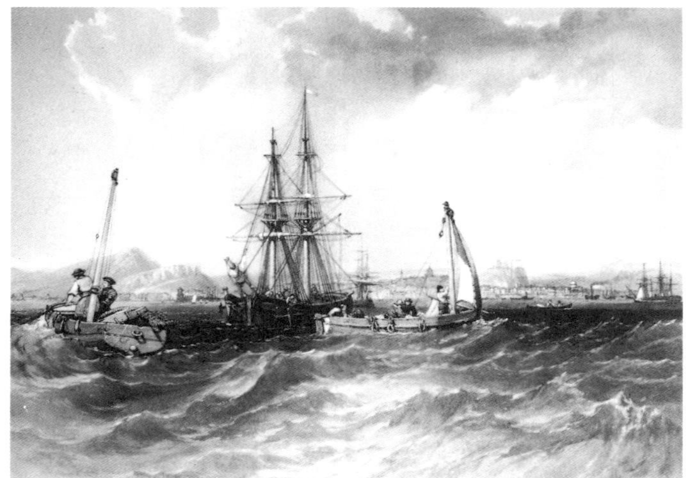

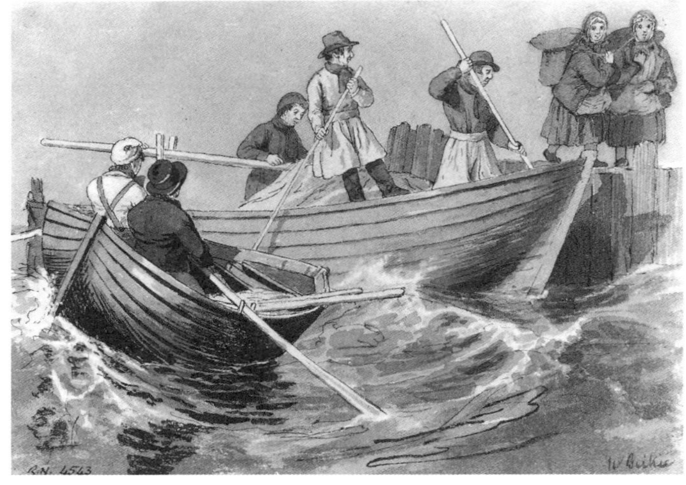

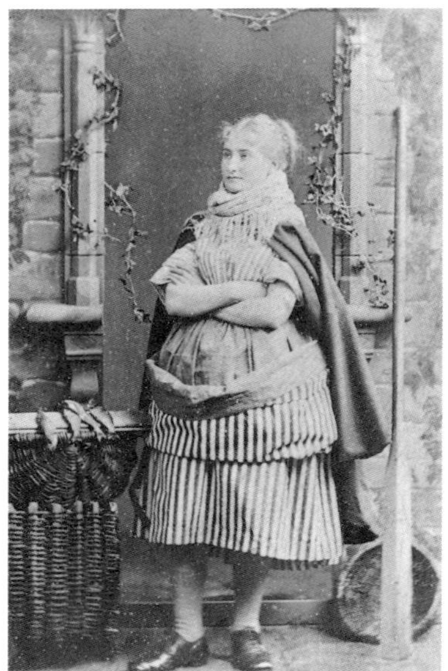

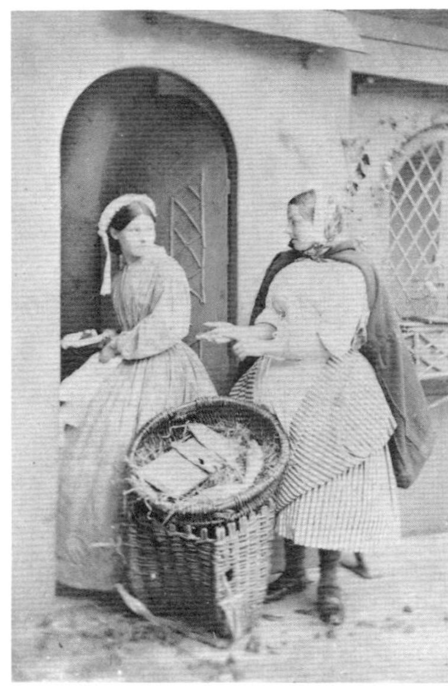

fig. 6 *above left*
Clarkson Stanfield
Edinburgh from the Firth of Forth
engraved for *Scotland Delineated*, 1847
National Library of Scotland

fig. 7 *above right*
Walter Geikie
Newhaven pier (?)
watercolour
National Gallery of Scotland

fig. 8 *below*
Diagram for a Newhaven fishing boat by Rose of Leith
published in the government report on the 1848 disaster

fig. 9 *far left*
Kyles and Moir
Portobello fishwife, about 1870
'carte de visite' photograph
Scottish National Portrait Gallery

fig. 10 *left*
James Ross
'Anither bawbee', about 1865
'carte de visite' photograph
Scottish National Portrait Gallery

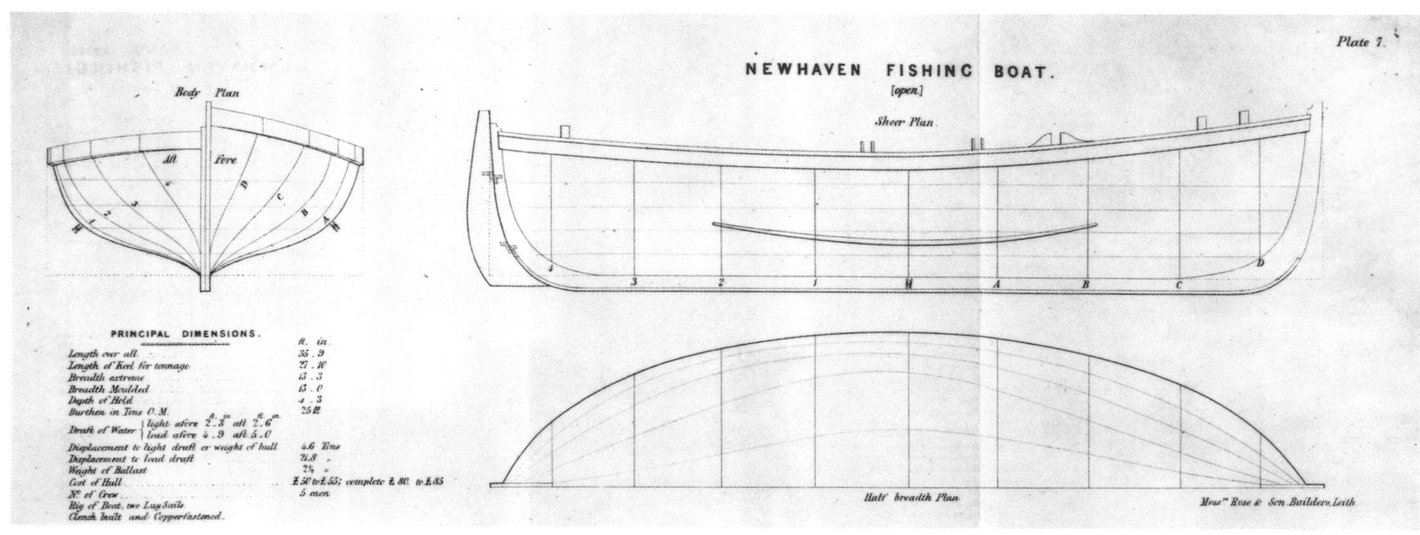

The People and Village of Newhaven

By the 1840s, the rush of summer visitors from Edinburgh down to the seaside for the therapeutic effects of dipping into the chilling waters of the North Sea, found the activities of the village of Newhaven a natural tourist entertainment. The more numerous visitors to the city encountered the fishwives, famous for their beauty and their picturesque dress, as a distinct and engaging feature of the Edinburgh scene. This mild interest in the fishermen and women is reflected in paintings, engravings, pottery figures and songs about fishing life, which were all common in the 1840s. But a better understanding of the attraction of the village comes in passages like the following from the memoirs of the young actress Fanny Kemble, herself an independent woman, describing her friendship with Mrs Sandie Flockhart whom she first met in 1828 or 1829:

'I stopped at a cottage on the outskirts of the fishing town (it was not much more than a village then) of Newhaven, and knocked. Invited to come in, I did so, and there sat a woman, one of the very handsomest I ever saw, in solitary state, leisurely combing a magnificent curtain of fair hair, that fell over her ample shoulders and bosom and almost swept the ground. She was seated on a low stool, but looked tall as well as large, and her foam-fresh complexion and grey-green eyes might have become Venus Anadyomene herself, turned into a Scotch fishwife of five and thirty, or "thereawa." "Can you tell me of anyone who will take me out in a boat for a little while?" quoth I. She looked steadily at me for a minute, and then answered laconically, "Ay, my man and boy shall gang wi' ye." A few lusty screams brought her husband and son forth, and at her bidding they got a boat ready, and, with me well covered with sail-cloths, tarpaulins, and rough dreadnaughts of one sort and another, rowed out from the shore into the turmoil of the sea. A very little of the dancing I got now was delight enough for me, and, deadly sick, I besought to be taken home again, when the matronly Brinhilda at the cottage received me with open-throated peals of laughter, and then made me sit down till I had conquered my qualms and was able to walk back to Edinburgh. Before I went, she showed me a heap of her children, too many, it seemed to me to be counted; but as they lay in an inextricable mass on the floor in an inner room, there may have seemed more arms and legs forming the radii, of which a clump of curly heads was the centre, than there really were.

The husband was a comparatively small man, with dark eyes, hair and complexion; but her "boy," the eldest, who had come with him to take care of me, was a fair-haired, fresh-faced young giant, of his mother's strain, and, like her, looked as if he had come of the Northern Vikings, or some of the Niebelungen Lied *heroes.*

When I went away, my fish-wife bade me come again in smooth weather, and if her husband and son were at home they should take me out; and I gave her my address, and begged her, when she came up to town with her fish, to call at the house.

She was a splendid specimen of her tribe, climbing the steep Edinburgh streets with bare white feet, the heavy fish-basket at her back hardly stooping her broad shoulders, her florid face sheltered and softened in spite of its massiveness into something like delicacy by the transparent shadow of the white handkerchief tied hoodwise over her fair hair, and her shrill sweet voice calling "Caller haddie!" all the way she went, in the melancholy monotone that resounds through the thoroughfares of Edinburgh,—the only melodious street cry (except the warning of the Venetian gondoliers) that I ever heard.

I often went back to visit my middle-aged Christie Johnstone, and more than once saw her and her fellow fish-women haul up the boats on their return after being out at sea. They all stood on the beach clamouring like a flock of sea-gulls, and, as a boat's keel rasped the shingles, rushed forward and seized it; and while the men in their sea clothes, all dripping like huge Newfoundland dogs, jumped out in their heavy boots and took each their way to their several houses, their stalwart partners, hauling all together at the rope fastened to the boat, drew it up beyond watermark, and seized and sorted its freight of fish, and stalked off each with her own basket full, with which she trudged up to trade and chaffer with the "gude wives" of the town, and bring back to the men the value of their work. It always seemed to me that these women had about as equal a share of the labour of life as the most zealous champion of the rights of their sex could desire.

I did not indulge in any more boating expeditions, but admired the sea from the pier, and became familiar with all the spokes of the fishwife's family wheel; at any rate, enough to distinguish Jamie from Sandie, and Willie from Johnnie, and Maggie from Jeanie, and Ailsie from Lizzie, and was great friends with them all.

When I returned to Edinburgh, a theatrical star of the first magnitude, I took a morning's holiday to drive down to Newhaven, in search of my old ally, Mistress Sandie Flockhart. She no longer inhabited the little detached cottage, and divers and sundry were the Flockhart "wives" that I "speired at" through the unsavoury street of Newhaven, before I found the right one at last, on the third flat of a filthy house, where noise and stench combined almost to knock me down, and where I could hardly knock loud enough to make myself heard above the din within and without. She opened the door of a room that looked as if it was running over with live children, and confronted me with the unaltered aspect of her comely, smiling face. But I had driven down from Edinburgh in all the starlike splendour of a lilac silk dress and French crape bonnet, and my dear fish-wife stared at me silently, with her mouth and grey eyes wide open; only for a moment, however, for in the next she joyfully exclaimed, "Ech, sirs! but it's yer ain sel' come back again at last!" Then, seizing my hand, she added breathlessly, "I'se gotten anither ane, and ye maun come in and see him;" so she dragged me bodily through and over her surging progeny, to a cradle where, soothed by the strident lullabies of its vociferating predecessors, her last-born and eleventh baby lay peacably slumbering, an infant Hercules.'[40]

Newhaven lies about a mile and a half to the north of Edinburgh on the south shore of the Forth estuary (fig. 6). In the 1841 census, the population was recorded at 2103 with 300 of the men engaged in fishing. In 1848, 380 men and boys were employed in the Newhaven fishing working from 150 boats.[41] By the 1830s, the high ground above the village had been occupied by 'a considerable number of new houses … chiefly in the villa style, or for sea-bathing quarters. The village itself, however, the nucleus of all this aggregation of families, remains in its pristine unseemly condition, and is certainly one of the dirtiest places in Scotland. As a small advance towards civilized usages, the Edinburgh magistracy have lately appointed a constable to look after the village.'[42] A stone pier provided some shelter for the fishing boats and the steam ferries which crossed to Fife. 1842 saw the opening of the railway line from Edinburgh down to Leith and Granton, with its station at Trinity a short distance from the Newhaven pier.

The Newhaven fishermen worked from small open boats (fig. 7 and plates 19 & 20), dredging for oysters, catching lobsters and crabs, and fishing for herring, cod or haddock. The normal fishing divided itself into the 'small' and 'great' line fishing. The first, for haddock, whiting and codling which swam comparatively close to the shore, could be undertaken in a few hours of daylight. The lines, usually baited with mussels, could carry from 500 to 3,000 hooks. The 'great line' fishing, using a heavier line with fewer hooks, took the fishermen out beyond the Isle of May at the mouth of the Firth of Forth to the Mar Bank for two or three days at a time. The herring fishery was seasonal depending on the migration of the shoals of fish—usually appearing first on the east coast in the spring up in Shetland and moving down the coast in summer when the main stock arrived for spawning. The herring fishery required bigger boats and about 80 to 90 travelled north to the fishing at Wick from the Firth of Forth (apparently about 40 from Newhaven)[43], 'no inconsiderable journey as it was often the custom to row the entire distance.'[44] These boats spent two months between July to September at the fishing grounds, fishing from the shore and returning every day to deliver the herring for salting. The number of herring cured in the area of Wick in 1840 was reckoned to be over 48,000,000, the catch of about 900 boats (over 53,000 fish per boat).

By the 1840s, mechanisation was moving in on the fishing industry but it was still possible to make a good living, albeit under difficulties. The movement and appearance of the herring was in itself erratic. The fishermen were inevitably dependent on the weather and driven in by storms at sea. Their boats were small. The larger Newhaven boat for fishing the herring was 35 feet 9 inches long, and unprotected. The east coast was short of low water harbours and such harbours as there were were often poorly maintained. The contrast is marked between the St Andrews and Leith harbours (plates 7 to 10), which could take in ships and the simple pier at Newhaven (fig. 7). There was, the Newhaven men laconically remarked, 'Great want of shelter.'[45] Their own defence against storm was simply to haul the boats higher up the beach (plate 2). In December 1847, a sudden gale from the north-east hit the east coast: *'The effects of the storm were particularly felt at Newhaven. On that part of the coast, about forty fishing boats were broken in pieces, being dashed against each other; and about twenty others have been more or less damaged. The tide must have deepened upon the coast, by the influence of the north wind, not less than eight or ten feet, as it came fully thirty feet farther in shore than the oldest fisherman in Newhaven recollects to have ever seen. The consequence was, that the boats that had been hauled up high and dry on the beach a considerable distance from the usual flood mark, were floated and dashed against each other. A number of boats had left Newhaven for the herring fishing up the Forth, about five o'clock in the afternoon; but seeing symptoms of the gale, they made for Granton Pier, which they reached in safety. We have also to record that five or six Newhaven fishing boats with nets on board, lying a little off the pier, foundered whilst at anchor, and the nets were washed out. The loss sustained by the poor fishermen is very great. One individual has, in the article of nets alone, lost to the value of £ 50. The amount of property destroyed belonging to the fishermen is in all, we understand, about two thousand pounds; which, we fear, will tell seriously upon the welfare of this little village.'*[46]

A worse disaster hit the summer herring fishing around Peterhead in 1848. On 19 August, a storm drowned 100 men who left 47 widows and 161 orphans, and destroyed and damaged 124 boats. This led to a parliamentary investigation which discovered the poor harbours and examined the design of the boats. The report particularly condemned the Wick boat, as the worst shape 'that could be given to a floating body for the useful purposes of a boat,' that is 'spheroidal' and liable to travel round in circles. The investigators were little more impressed by the design of the Newhaven boat: *'This boat from having a rising floor and no length of midship body, can only be considered as a slight improvement on the Wick boat … the improvement arising from the level lines being rather less rounding , and thence in a degree better calculated to prevent leeway. The character the Firth of Forth boats are said to bear, of being fine sea-going boats, must be attributable more to the skill of the crews than to the form of the boats.'* (fig. 8)[47] The final ironic comment is useful evidence of the truth of the Newhaven fishermen's reputation for skill and heroism. Many of them qualified as pilots (plate 23) and they took pride in their readiness to volunteer in times of war.

The skill of the Firth of Forth fishermen resulted from the social organisation of the fishing villages. There was a clear distinction in the early nineteenth century between the west and the east coast fisheries. In the west and in the Northern Isles, small, lonely, and often poor communities undertook fishing and farming together. On the east coast, the fishing villages tended to be distinct from the farms and pursued the fishing with a single-minded professionalism. The 1848 disaster brought out the further difference between the north and south. The seasonal herring shoals attracted unskilled labour. The agricultural reform of the 'Highland Clearances' had driven numbers of people accustomed to farming crofts out to the shores in search of work. The government report identified this as a lethal problem: *'In the greater part of the north-country-boats wrecked at Peterhead, three men out of five were landsmen, and in consequence they were not equal to managing their boat and dipping their sails in running before the storm, and thus hauled up for the harbour with their sails aback against the mast, when the boats lost their way and drove ashore, while the Newhaven and south-country boats, with properly set sails, fetched up to the pier head and were saved. Fewer boats and better manned would be a safer principle to act on, and this the thorough-bred fishermen are aware of.'* [48] The report also pointed out that the habit of paying the hired hands in advance was ill-advised, since it meant that many of the men on board the boats were not just inexperienced but drunk.

The idea of the 'thorough-bred fishermen' is not as strange as it sounds. The fishing villages built their success on a deliberate isolation; an isolation that fostered professional skill. Fishermen and wives married within the village because an outsider would probably have baulked at the dangers and labour of the work. The Free Society of Fishermen of Newhaven as late as 1845 was only accepting the lawful sons of its own members, who had learnt the craft of sailing and fishing in their fathers' boats. The sons joined the Society at the age of fourteen for a fee of 6s 8d—should they delay in entering the fee rose sharply. This separation often gave the villages a reputation as 'foreigners'. Newhaven was reputed to be Flemish in character. Mrs George Cupples, who wrote an account of Newhaven's history and origins in 1888, identified the people of Newhaven as descended from the Flemings who had fled from religious persecution. Her argument was based on a cheerfully romantic view of the village, rather than on historical evidence: *'To any one who is personally acquainted with their village ways, customs, idioms, family names, and costumes, it is often noticeable how much they resemble Flemish and Dutch fisherfolk. Even now-a-days we may observe this said resemblance in various points, such as their women's manifold petticoats, striped in contrasted colours; peculiar shortgowns, displaying bare arms with white elbow bands; bright head-shawls, or, in the case of the elder women, peculiar white linen caps; trim stockings, conspicuously shown, and neat, serviceable shoes. To these add a special household care for elaborate collections of "crockery," for furniture "made to last," and for making gradual provision against the time when their daughters shall leave home as brides. In complexion and general physique both sexes often exemplify an old Flemish descent; some being blonde, as any typical Netherlander; some dark, as any typical Spaniard; comparatively few intermediate. And among their children, any day, broad-beamed little Dutchmen toddle across the street, costumed as if fresh from Flanders itself; dear flaxen-haired wee lassies, whose doll-like cheeks and eyes carry out the picture …'* [49]

The fishermen worked mostly out of sight at sea, and it was the fishwives who were the more familiar figures. They were notably picturesque in their physical confidence and their attractive costume. Many people, like Mrs Cupples, thought of it as foreign in character, but it was based on the late eighteenth-century working dress, the short gown, a bodice which came below the waist, and short petticoats and skirts, which could be kilted up to keep the outer surface clean.[50] Independence and practical consideration—the thin 'Empire' dresses of the early nineteenth century would have been ludicrously impractical for work—kept elements of the costume fixed. A natural taste for fashion and probably an increase in prosperity ensured changes in its detail. By the 1830s for example, the fishwives normally wore shoes and stockings where they would have gone barefoot before. In the 1840s, they wore white, lace-edged caps, which were replaced later in the century by coloured shawls (fig. 9).

The art critic, Elizabeth Rigby who took an interest in costume, described the beautiful fishwife, Jeanie Wilson (plate 49), in 1843: *'Went down to look at Jinny Wilson—a tremendously hot day, and she with as heavy a load of petticoats as of fish: a lovely blooming creature, with a complexion of that transparent kind of which our aristocracy are most proud; her eye laughing, her hair, without any figure of speech, golden—such a colour as an indoor life never permits. She was laden with clothes, petticoat over petticoat, striped and whole colour, all of the thickest woollen material, and one of a kind of dreadnought frieze; also a tremendous serge coat with long sleeves, that hung flat upon her back, over it a striped butcher's apron "to wipe ma haunds"—and she made a graceful gesture over her shoulder with a fine pair, full in the palm and slender in the fingers—perfect pictures. Altogether, guessing roughly, I should say she was carrying to the amount of five ordinary box-coats, or fifteen conventional flannel petticoats. She wore, she told us "sax on common days, four at hame, and twa of a Sunday, and nae cheap, thirteen shillings the pair," and she had "sax pair." One petticoat was obviously not accounted worth the putting on or pulling off: hers were chiefly blue and white … She told me that this quantity of apparel was necessary to prevent the creel from hurting her back, and I suggested a pad for the necessary part, and a little less weight of material, and expenditure of shillings upon the rest; but Jinny had an unanswerable: "It was verra true—a piece upon the bock might be better, but ye ken it's juist the fashion o' the place."'* [51] The fishwives gutted the catch and carried it to market. Some followed the men to Wick for the summer fishing where they worked almost uninterrupted from early till late, at a rate of twenty four fish cleaned every minute, for pay of four pence a barrel. At home they carried the fish up to Edinburgh for sale 'from one to two hundredweight upon their backs, in creels or willow-baskets'.[52] *'Her labours are extraordinary. In a large wand-basket resting on her back, and slung by a strap that crosses her brow, she will carry a hundred-weight of fish from Newhaven (two miles), and sometimes from Fisherrow (six miles), yet walk the metropolis during the whole day, crying her fish, and after all go home at night, still on foot.'*[53] *'The morning's cargo being now disposed of, these industrious females return home, and by the time they have cleaned and refreshed themselves, the boat will be again seen nearing the shore with another load, not of fishes, but oysters, with which they will, on the evening of the same day, cheerfully trudge to Edinburgh or Leith, in companies of six or eight, in order to dispose of them on the streets; and few persons who have heard these sturdy amazons prosecuting this part of their duty, calling "Caller ou" in their clear, piercing, but melodious tones, although in a variety of keys, can remain insensible to the thrilling effect.'*[54] Bargaining for a good price was of obvious importance and the fishwives were known for their vigorous dealing: *'In their mercantile capacity these robust persons are not very distinguished for conscientious dealings, it being very difficult to make a proper bargain with them. They generally ask about three times the real value, and it becomes the business of the customer to bate them down to the proper price.'*(fig. 10)[55]

The notable confidence of the fishwives relied on independence, equality and social supportiveness. *'There is something delightful to contemplate in the virtuous natural independence of a young Newhaven fishwoman. After being 'red up' of an evening, she will stand under … her outside stair, with her arms akimbo, gazing abroad on the busy human fry of the village street; perfectly at ease about herself; altogether superior to the formalities of the world; blenching not, nor blushing, under the survey of the most curious or impertinent stranger; in the immemorial usage of her tribe, which allows only of alliance with her fellow villagers, exempt from every feeling of deference or regard, or even scorn, for the people of the world without …'*[56]

Because the women sold the fish at market they had an authority that comes from a control of the family money. The debate Walter Scott wrote between the servant girl and the fishwife, Luckie Mucklebackit, is a sardonic version of the relationship between the couples: *'"Slaves? gae wa', lass! Ca' the head o' the house slaves? little ye ken about it, lass. Show me a word my Saunders daur speak, or a turn he daur do about the house, without it be just to tak his meat, and his drink, and his diversion, like ony o' the weans. He has mair sense than to ca' onything about the bigging his ain, frae the rooftree down to a crackit trencher on the bink. He kens weel eneugh wha feeds him, and cleeds him, and keeps a' tight, thack and rape, when his coble is jowing awa in the Firth, puir fallow. Na, na, lass—them that sells the goods guide the purse—them that guide the purse rule the house. Show me ane o' your bits o' farmer-bodies that wad let their wife drive the stock to the market, and ca' in the debts. Na, na."'*[57]

Husbands and wives made an equal partnership (plate 33), with the men undertaking the work at sea and the women taking on most of the land work. The close family alliance was further supported by friendship: *'Both among the women and the men there is much stress laid on what may be called "chumming," or close companionship between two of the same sex; according to which, from early schooldays they pair off into a faithful copartnery, as it were, that lasts throughout life. The one girl becomes bridesmaid to the other if she gets first married; each considers it her duty to help or attend to her "chum" in time of need …'*[58] (plate 39)

Despite the individual effectiveness of both the family unit and the principle of friendship, fishing was an industry and the general affairs of Newhaven needed organising as a community to give the fishermen sufficient weight to deal with the outside world. The management of the village's affairs was largely controlled by the Free Society of Fishermen of Newhaven. This was nominally a friendly society designed to provide relief for the fishermen during sickness, infirmity and old age and for widowed fishwives. Boys joined the Society at the age of fourteen and were allowed to vote from the age of eighteen. The Society met for a general meeting every quarter and the committee was elected annually. The members of the Society paid one shilling every quarter into the Society's funds until they were 65. In case of 'sickness or misfortune not occasioned by excess or debauchery,' they were allowed four shillings a week for the first twenty weeks and two shillings thereafter. Widows were allowed £ 1 10 shillings a year for life, on payment of 6d a quarter and on condition that they should not be found 'railing, scandalising or upbraiding any of the Society concerning the regulations or management thereof.'[59]

The Free Fishermen had some political power. They owned property in the village including the two school houses. They had control of the cleaning and mending of the streets. In the 1840s, the Society was involved in considerable litigation at no little expense. This mainly related to the oyster beds or 'scalps' in the Forth which the Newhaven fishermen traditionally dredged (plate 20). A recent increase in the value of the oysters and a confirmation in law of the right to them as property, led in the first instance to the City of Edinburgh leasing its scalps out at a public roup. In 1838, the Newhaven men secured the rights for £ 75. In 1839, the rights were purchased by a George Clark from Essex, who leased the scalps for ten years at the unprecedented sum of £ 600 per annum. A legal wrangle followed and in 1845, the Society secured a City act allowing it the right to the oyster dredging under fixed conditions. The situation was further complicated by the Duke of Buccleuch who laid claim to an area of the oyster beds and secured them in 1842. In 1845, Buccleuch's agents refused to let the scalps to Newhaven to 'preserve the oysters for the season' and added the acid comment, 'We are also directed to say that the behaviour of the Newhaven Fishermen has been such as to deprive them of any claim to favour from His Grace, and that it will depend upon their conduct in time to come whether he will ever let the fishery to them.'[60] The complicated and tricky negotiations over the oyster beds involved the Society in all aspects of their management; defending them by force against unlicensed fishermen and carrying the trespassers to court, collecting and organising the payment from the fishermen, regulating the size of oyster which might be kept so that the stocks should not be damaged, keeping the beds clear of mud and predators like starfish, and negotiating the bulk sale of oysters to merchants.

The Society echoed the family life of Newhaven in the rules dictating the manners expected by the members. Fines were imposed for swearing or intoxication or for attempting to discuss church or political affairs during meetings, on boats going to sea on the Sabbath and on boats that 'drag Mussels for bait to strangers.' A socially positive rule said 'all members of twenty years of age and upwards shall attend such funerals [i.e. the funerals of members and their wives] in decent apparel under the penalty of sixpence, unless they can give a lawful excuse for their absence.'[61]

While the rules of the Society prevented the discussion of church affairs, the fishermen also took a leading role there. At the Disruption of the Church of Scotland, the congregation followed the minister, the Rev James Fairbairn, and formed the Newhaven Free Church. The Newhaven taste for independence and self-determination made this a natural move. The elders of the church were predominantly, or wholly, fishermen in the 1840s, and the senior elder, James Flucker, represented the church at the General Assembly in 1843. The evangelical character of the Free Church meant that the elders, and the deacons who were elected in 1844, took a close interest in the moral and religious development of the village. The church session acted as a moral check on the behaviour of the congregation and the elders seconded the minister in visiting and praying with individuals and families.

This close concern had its unattractive side in men like James Gall, who was an elder in the parish of South Leith but much involved in the religious affairs of Newhaven. Gall was a regrettably humourless man given to preaching humility to servant girls and gratitude to the destitute and dying. At a church session in 1840, Gall quarrelled with a fellow elder, Mr Wallace, and reported in his diary: '*"It is strange," said he, "that twelve persons should always be wrong & you only right and opposing."* .. *I said that it had before been stated at this table that Mr. Gall had the faculty of praying at, instead of praying for his Brethren."—To which Mr. Wallace replied, "The person who said so, had no doubt good grounds for his assertion before he did it."... I very meekly, & kindly endeavoured to shew Mr. Wallace, before we parted, the evil consequences which might result from making such assertions...*'[62]

Gall records few encounters with the fishermen and wives, other than the young girls, and would seem to have met with a restrainedly polite reception: '*In returning today from Leith, I entered into conversation with several of the fishermen, who were preparing to go North to the Herring fishing, & advised them next year to prepare to as a fleet, to meet altogether afloat at the pier (about 40 boats) have prayers there, & then go off in a body. They are to take it into consideration.*'[63]

James Gall and a group of fishwives appear in one of the Newhaven photographs with James Fairbairn (plate 46). The reference to this in Gall's diary, dated 16 July 1845, is uninformative: '*Today Mr. D. O. Hill was taking Groups of Fishwomen & others at the head of the Lane. Requested me to form part of a group with Mr. Fairbairn, which I did.*'[64] Since this is the only first hand reference we have to the taking of the Newhaven calotypes, James Gall's customary self-absorption has a melancholy effect.

Gall is described as a friend of James Fairbairn. He was a publisher who regularly expressed himself in print and he made handsome contributions to the Newhaven library. It may be that the link between the two men was literature. Fairbairn was an enthusiastic collector of books: '*Dr Fairbairn's library was such as few private collectors could boast of, the editions of Shakespeare forming a special feature. In the collecting of such choice specimens as he could come across, his tall, stately, and latterly, most venerable figure, might be seen bending over some bookstall in Leith Walk, or in the line of the bridges, or behind the college; and it was no unusual spectacle to behold him in the middle of town, his coat pockets stuffed with minor volumes, while a couple of larger tomes, or even a huge folio, would be at the same time stuck under his arms. On various such occasions, too, might be witnessed what was by no means uncommon with him—namely his being spied out by some stalwart Newhaven fishwives, who, regardless of passers-by, accosted the doctor with a determination to carry his books for him, which beyond question they would succeed in doing, in the bottom of their big creels, however odorous these might be of cod, haddock or herring.*'[65]

This passage implies a generous affection between the minister and his congregation. Unlike Gall, Fairbairn combined his pastoral diligence with a personal knowledge and sympathy for the population: '*he had his familiar greeting for each, could find for everyone some appropriate salutation or general remark; he would enter into their humour, did not disdain to make allowances for occasional eccentricities, and at christening or wedding he could promote innocent mirth; no less than at any occasion of disaster, or in time of sickness, or death, he was sure to bring with him the consolations, the instructions, and the spiritual counsel which the Gospel has provided, and which his own thoroughly evangelical doctrine was suited to enforce.*'[66]

The Free Church, with its emphasis on personal responsibility, was well-fitted to Newhaven. There was general agreement amongst commentators, even those who expressed reservations, for example, about the fishwives' bargaining, that the community had a high moral standing: *'they exhibit a great degree of honour in all dealings with each other, and are, on the whole, an honest and peaceful class of the community.'* [67] *'This Newhaven colony is pre-eminent over others for its sober, industrious and peaceable habits.'* [68]

The main criticism of the fishermen and women was their taste for whisky: *'Males and females suck whisky like milk, and are quarrelsome in proportion: the men fight (round handed), the women fleicht or scold, in the form of a tea-pot—the handle fixed and the spout sawing the air.'* [69] This comment by Charles Reade, appears in his novel about Newhaven, (see below p.25), but a concern for this problem was expressed also by the Kirk Session which set up a committee on intemperance in the 1840s.

The strenuous life of the fishermen and women meant that they would have acquired a formal education only with difficulty. The village did support two schools, but there was some illiteracy amongst the fishermen and even amongst applicants for the pilot's licence—in 1847 the fisheries board refused for the first time to accept fishermen as pilots who could not read, because they would not be able to understand posted regulations. The literacy of the fishwives in the calotypes showing them reading a letter is still, therefore, remarkable (plate 48).

The village was culturally independent, as it was socially. Their culture expressed itself particularly in song. The men's dredging song was *'sung in a peculiar way: the sound is, as it were, expelled from the chest in a sort of musical ejaculations; and the like, we know, was done by the ancient gymnasts; and is done by French bakers, in lifting their enormous dough, and by our paviours. The song, in itself, does not contain above seventy stock verses, but these perennial lines are a nucleus, round which the men improvise the topics of the day, giving, I know not for what reason, the preference to such as verge upon indelicacy.*

The men and women are musical and narrative; three out of four can sing a song or tell a story, and they omit few opportunities.' [70]

The women's singing was a source of greater admiration. George Croal, whose memories included the great musicians of the day, such as Jenny Lind and Liszt, wrote: *'Above all, the cry of "caller ou" was the most conspicuous, and sweet it was. In many cases the notes were emitted by so brilliant a soprano voice that, under proper cultivation, they might have made the fortune of a prima donna.'* [71] This opinion was endorsed by the fiddler Nathaniel Gow and 'In a course of lectures on Scottish music, Mr [George] Wilson, the celebrated vocalist, took occasion to introduce the song … of "Caller Herrin'," and stated that he had preserved the tones of the fisherwomen, with the music of whose cries, as they hawked their wares, he was so struck, that he had often followed them for hours together on the streets of Edinburgh.' (fig. 11) [72]

The most extraordinary, lyrical, account of the fishwives singing was written by Professor John Wilson in the 1820s: *'Saw ye them ever marchin hamewards at nicht, in a baun of some fifty or threescore, down Leith Walk, wi' the grand gas-lamps illuminating their scaly creels, all shining like silver? And heard ye them ever singing their strange sea-sangs—first half-a-dizzen o' the bit young anes, wi' as saft vices and sweet as you could hear in St George's Kirk on Sabbath, half singin and half shoutin a leadin verse, and then a' the mithers and granmithers, and ablins great-granmithers, some o' them wi' vices like verra men, gran tenors and awfu' basses, joining in the chorus, that gaed echoing roun' Arthur's Seat, and awa ower the tap o' the Martello Tower, out at sea ayont the end o' Leith Pier? Wad ye believe me, that the music micht be ca'd a hymn—at times sae wild and sae mournfu'—and then takin a sudden turn into a sort o' queer and outlandish glee? It gars me think o' the saut sea-faem—and white mew-wings wavering in the blast—and boaties dancin up and down the billow vales, wi' oar or sail, and waes me—waes me—o' the puir fishing smack, gaun down headforemost into the deep, and the sighin and the sabbin o' widows, and the wailin o' fatherless weans!'* [73]

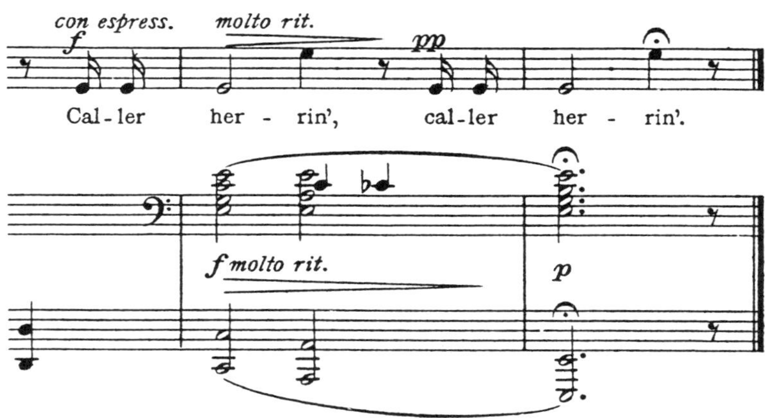

fig. 11
The refrain from Nathaniel Gow's song "Caller Herrin'"

The Problem of the Old Town of Edinburgh and the Village Model

Standing at the top of Calton Hill, just above the Rock House studio, it is possible to see the Old Town of Edinburgh to the south, the New Town to the west, and, further north down by the shores of the Forth, the village of Newhaven (see map, p.8). This panoramic view in the 1840s showed these three worlds, in poignant and dramatic distinction.

In the 1840s, life in Britain had become enmeshed in the consequences of the Industrial Revolution. From a basically stable society, dependent on the land, the population had shifted and, indeed, been shifted into one increasingly on the move. Industrial and agricultural changes—in Scotland, most notably the Highland Clearances, which were designed to change the land from the economy based on the small-holdings of crofting life into large acres swept clear for sheep and game—forced more people into the cities. Industrial success led to industrial squalour; a rising standard of living led to sudden and vicious falls. The failure of the potato crop in the 1840s added another turn to the spiral of confusion and distress.

The cities were in an endemic state of poverty and disease. Dr William Pulteney Alison's report in 1840, *Observations on the Management of the Poor in Scotland*, began with the statement: '... *in the two greatest cities of Scotland, where the science and civilization of the country may be supposed to have attained their highest development, and where medical schools exist, claiming as high a rank in point of practical usefulness as any in Europe, the annual proportion of deaths to the population is not only much beyond the average of Britain, but very considerably greater than that of London.*'[74] Ironically, the situation was complicated by the medical charities in Edinburgh, which attracted the sick from areas where there was no provision for them, and by the erratic, and sometimes non-existent, relief for the poor in other districts and parishes of Scotland.

This was not just matter for personal compassion, but a political breakdown. There were too many people gathered in the cities who were either permanently or sporadically poor, with no real attachment to the social structure. Lord Cockburn expressed this anxiety in 1843: '*Of all the new features of modern society in Britain, none is so peculiar or frightful as the hordes of strong poor, always liable to be thrown out of employment by stagnation of trade. There have been above 10,000 of them in Paisley for more than a year; and a similar cloud darkens every considerable town in Scotland. In Edinburgh, besides its fullest complement of ordinary distress, we have a battalion of what are now known by the almost technical term of "Unemployed Poor" ... being congregated in numbers, and distinguished by a title, they form a separate class, a new state ... can we or any highly manufacturing community expect to be ever free of the risk of the constant recurrence of such scenes?... are not millions of starving people the necessary occasional sloughs of a very manufacturing nation? Whatever political economy may predict for distant futurity, I see no visible prospect of this country being unafflicted by this scourge.*'[75] In the event, Britain did not have a revolution in 1848 in line with other European countries, but it was by no means certain that it would not.

Despite political reform, society was still substantially set in a mould of personal or patronising organisation. The idea of personal charity was of great importance in the Christian ethic, and, to many people, the legal enforcement of aid to the poor undermined that Christian virtue and removed the natural bond between rich and poor.

Poverty was, like morality, the business of the Church. Poor relief depended on charitable collections made by the Church and administered by the parishes. Moreover, Calvinism held that a man was responsible for his own actions and for his own moral welfare; to remove that responsibility, by making charity a political right, removed his moral freedom and reduced him to childish dependence. The onset of disease and famine as well as slumps in trade were sent by God for a purpose, as a scourge and a corrective to man. Suffering followed as a moral necessity. An additional argument, which divided the poor into the 'deserving' and the 'undeserving,' was based on the idea that idleness or sloth was a deadly sin and work was the key to wisdom: '*Go to the ant, thou sluggard, consider her ways and be wise.*'[76]

The concept of a society in which events were moving so rapidly that men could lose control quite innocently—that the invention of mechanical looms could leave weavers without a means of making a living, that a war on the other side of the world could bankrupt a business in Glasgow—did not fit into this system of morality. The rapid rise in population and the movement of thousands of people from Ireland to Scotland, from the Highlands to the south, undermined the effectiveness of parish relief which was not designed to deal with a transient population. The Church had lost control, and in some parishes the officials took the argument that giving money to the poor was morally undesirable to its brutal conclusion: '*The grand object kept in view by almost every parish is the possibility of evading, as far as their power admits of, the duty of relieving the poor.*'[77]

The Church's position was maintained in the 1840s by the Free Church leader, the Rev Thomas Chalmers (fig. 12). He believed that the natural moral balance could be restored on the pattern of the small parish and he had been involved in an experiment to prove this idea earlier in the century. His influence in Glasgow was such that in 1819 the city established a new parish of St John—one of the largest and poorest in the city—especially for him. He demanded that it be severed from the city's public funds and he undertook both to stabilise the situation and eradicate pauperism—excepting only the problem of a sudden failure in manufactures.

Chalmers achieved the personal village scale, which would make his experiment workable, by breaking the parish into 25 districts with from 60 to 100 families. Each was put under the care of an elder and provided with a deacon to handle money to separate moral welfare from cash. Schools and teachers were introduced and the ideal of daily worship within the family was encouraged.

Chalmers found people work and encouraged mutual help and self-denial. He succeeded in demonstrating in the parish of St John that he could restore what he described as 'nature's own simple mechanism'[78] and there was sufficient practical sense in his experiment to make it attractive. His controls, however, were artificial and his 'nature' involved a withdrawal from society as a whole—his crucial exception of responsibilty in the case of a manufacturing slump put the experiment outside current economic reality even before it started. Arguably, it would have formed an effective model for the advance of society or its return to a stable 'village' basis. In the event, it did not. The idea, however, was there, and was attractive.

Chalmers' opinions were supported by political-economic argument. The influential views of the Rev Thomas Malthus on the growth of the population held that a legal enforcement of poor relief would aggravate the problem. In proposing the axiom that population increases in a geometrical ratio while subsistence only increases in an arithmetical ratio, he demonstrated the necessity of poverty and argued that population had to be limited by the 'natural' checks of vice and misery. In his view, providing a legal entitlement to money would destroy the moral restraint which helped to keep the population down; given money, the population would rise more rapidly, making the whole problem worse.

In 1840, Dr Alison succeeded in swinging public opinion away from Chalmers' and Malthus' viewpoint. The Scottish Poor Law Amendment Act was passed in 1845, making provision for the poor a legal requirement. Regrettably, the Act was not as effective as Alison had hoped. The limitations on the relief of poverty continued to strangle the poor. The law, sadly, proved inadequate and merely served to underline the Malthusian contention that poor relief would increase the numbers of the poor.

By 1849, Dr George Bell, the District Inspector of Registers employed to examine the effectiveness of the new law (fig. 13), was so appalled by the conditions in the Old Town that he advocated tearing down whole streets: *'In a word, and to borrow a phrase from Dickens, no "dodge" will effect what is essential in order to the relief of the city of Edinburgh. Something substantial must be done; something evidencing enlightenment and commonsense, instead of rancid, mite-eaten economy. Little corporation arrangements, small parochial schemes, slight sanatary arrangements, crumbs of education, morsels of religion, nothing detached and of the pigmy kind, will tell upon the social and moral condition of the people . . .'* [79] Bell believed that the agricultural workers drawn into the towns should be returned to the land and waste ground brought into cultivation. He approved the model of a Union Farm set up in 1848 in Sheffield and reported to be a success. He proposed the recreating of small-scale communities, with mutual responsibility and shared work, to re-establish self-esteem and eradicate the deadly apathy of destitution.

The natural model of the kind of society Chalmers and Bell were seeking—a stable society, small-scale, independent, self-sufficient, morally alive, culturally sophisticated and with its feet in the national history which had bred John Knox—stood on the shores of the Forth a mile and a half away from the city. The ironic descent from the crest of the Old Town crowned with slums to the moral example of Newhaven, a practical working community, was in a sense too obvious to miss.

The Newhaven photographs can be looked at as D. O. Hill's response and contribution to the debate. The Rock House studio faced the Old Town which was constantly in his view, and the contrast between the desolation of the slums and the lively health of the village was naturally dramatic. Hill's admiration for Newhaven is undoubted and the photographs may be read as an analysis of praise as effective as the reports condemning the slums. Hill was a man who liked to know how things worked—he was, for example, sufficiently interested in practical mechanism to understand the working of a railway train.[80] It seems reasonable that his intention in photographing Newhaven was not merely to celebrate its surface attractions and success but to make an analysis through visual art of the way Newhaven had survived and coped through the social confusion and distress of the Industrial Revolution and its aftermath; a way which maintained social dignity and remained both morally truthful and visually beautiful.

In modern, journalistic terms, we would expect a photographic response to this situation to be an attack on the conditions in the Old Town. George Bell's essay, *Day and Night in the Wynds*, follows a description of a single room in a slum tenement with the impassioned argument: *'The black hole at Calcutta, in which men were stifled, has been described, and the hold of a slaver has been described; but no description has, because none can, be given of the interior of a low Edinburgh lodging-house. It defies the graver of Hogarth, the pencil of David Scott, so familiar with nightmare horrors, the pen of Dickens, and the tongue of Guthrie. How would the artist manage the background and middle distance of the picture, so varied, so full of national history, so pregnant with dark biography? What could an uninstructed gazer make of the little sparks of light upon the black canvass, marking the morning beams of a mortal's day, which became dark as night before his sun had got a footing in the sky? Such lights would seem to him like falling stars—they would not light the gloom.'*[81]

This passage may relate to a conversation with Hill (fig. 13). As a painter, Hill had a passion for light and the physical breadth and freedom behind the idea of aerial perspective. The horrors of city confinement and darkness would have struck him forcibly. The metaphor and the literal lack of light could explain in some measure Hill's own feelings of the impossibility of expressing the situation through art. As an artist who had worked with the sun, how could he work with darkness?

The technical impossibility could have been circumvented by bribing the destitute to come out and pose in the daylight. The reason Hill did not photograph the paupers was that he clearly did not consider it right to do so. In David Octavius Hill's terms, art was designed to show the ideal, the heroic, the poetic; it was intended to be morally educational and uplifting. The Newhaven photographs are his response to the tragedy of pauperism because they present to the eye and the mind an ideal model of a working society, a solution to a terrible problem.

There is an interesting parallel to the calotype study of Newhaven in Charles Reade's novel, *Christie Johnstone*, which used the village as a true moral example. Reade's apology for the work declared that its only merit was 'that of containing genuine contemporaneous verdicts upon a cant that was flourishing like a peony, and a truth that was struggling for bare life, in the year of truth 1850.'[82] The 'cant' in question was the kind of hero-worship proposed by Thomas Carlyle of great public figures—Reade was himself more impressed by the commoner and modest heroism of ordinary life. The plot of the book centres on the young Viscount Ipsden, who is wealthy, idle and unhappy. When the woman he loves, refuses his proposal on the grounds that he has neither virtues nor vices, saying, 'you do nothing and never will do anything but sketch and hum tunes, and dance and dangle ...,' he 'relapsed into greater listlessness ...'[83] The doctor's prescription for his mental state is, 'Make acquaintance with all the people of low estate, who have time to be bothered with you; learn their ways, their minds, and, above all, their troubles ... Fish the herring! (that beats deer stalking). Run your nose into adventures at sea; live on ten-pence, and earn it.'[84]

The novel is fictional in a way the photographs are not; later commentators complained of its inaccuracy, (they also complained that the Viscount did not marry the fishwife). But we are left with the fact that Reade came up from England in 1848 to spend a season in Newhaven and that he wrote a complete novel around the distinctive life of the village as the antithesis of the Viscount's self-destructive indolence. The village acts not merely as a model but as a source of practical inspiration and knowledge—by listening to and by joining in the activities of the fishermen and women, he acquires the understanding which makes him a man. Reade described the village, and especially the fishwife, Christie Johnstone, as a model of vigorous life, morality and culture in contrast to the emasculating dependency of the rich.

Reade may well have known Hill's calotypes. The choice of Newhaven life as the basis of the novel is, at the least, a significant coincidence; the key dramatic event in the book, when the Viscount's English yachtsmen join in the herring fishing, could have been directly inspired by one particular photograph (plate 24). The basis of both the photographs and the book is a substantial and calculated analysis, through art, of the village's life. Hill, like Reade, was moved by the heroism, the social morality and the distinctive culture of the village.

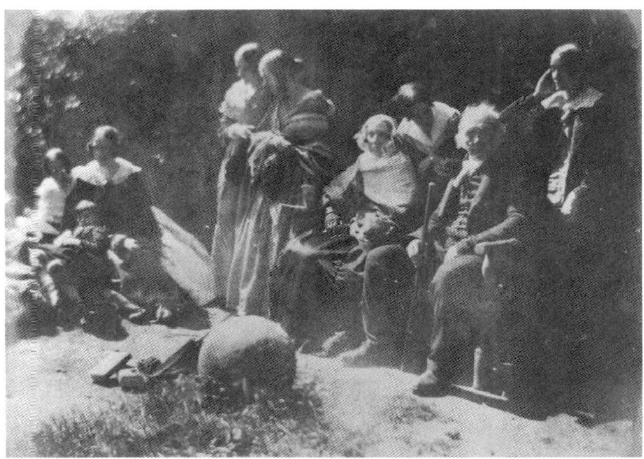

fig. 12
D. O. Hill and Robert Adamson
Rev Thomas Chalmers and his family, 1844
calotype
Scottish National Portrait Gallery

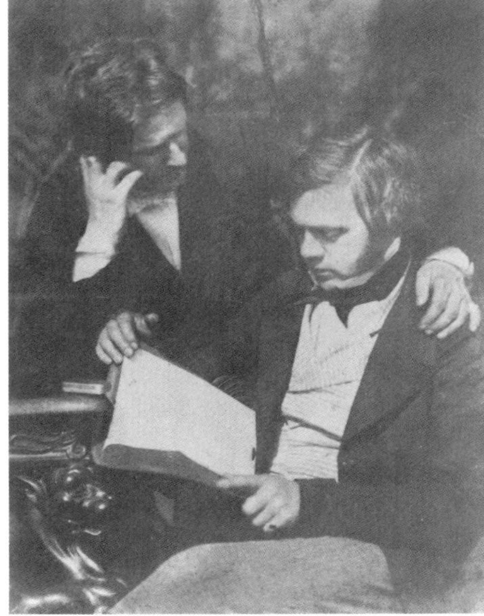

fig. 13
D. O. Hill and Robert Adamson
D. O. Hill and Dr George Bell, 1846
calotype
Scottish National Portrait Gallery

Song and the Advance of Nationalism

When Hill and Adamson advertised their volume on *The Fishermen and Women of the Firth of Forth,* they announced five other subjects. One of these was *Highland Character and Costume.* The fishermen and women may well have been intended as a counterpart to the Highlanders—the Lowland version of the primitive national and natural character, fishing the terrible seas as against hunting for deer in the hills. The Highlander in his tartan and the fishwife in her kilted petticoats were good visual symbols of this national character—the male and the female, the north and the south. This idea could well have prompted Hill to paint in the group of fishwives which appear with Highland soldiers in his painting of *Edinburgh, Old and New* (fig. 34).

One of the characters Hill and Adamson intended for the Highland album was Alexander Campbell of Monzie, who was described by John Stuart Blackie in 1867: *'Passing directly before Campbell of Monzie's door, I determined to call upon the tiger in his den, and in his den I actually found him. He received me with great frankness of old Highland hospitality, gave me a splendid dinner of venison-tripe and full-bosomed grouse, with a magnum of most excellent claret, capped with a tumbler of brandy-and-water ... we had all sorts of laughing and talking and explosive outbursts. He took me through all his various and strange museums, introduced me to his magnificent deer-hounds, and mingled deer-stalking and good fellowship with pious scraps of Gospel and Revival hymns in a manner quite original and refreshing ... he is full of natural vigour and nobleness, but like a wild horse has never been accustomed to the rein, and is not quite understood by the quiet jogging people of whom the respectability of this world is mainly made up. He and I got on like gunpowder, and came down the glen in the dark, singing song for song...'*[85] This eminently romantic description is strikingly similar to the descriptions of the Newhaven fishwives—the hospitality, the independence, the religion, the vigour and the forceful character all find echoes. Blackie and Campbell come singing down the glen in the dark and the fishwives come singing down Leith Walk in the light of the gas lamps.

John Wilson's romantic, nearly operatic, account of the Newhaven fishwives' singing makes their culture a significant part of a nationalist tradition. At the time of the political Union of Scotland with England in 1707, the Earl of Seafield is reputed to have commented, 'Now there's ane end of ane old sang.'[86] The identification of song and poetry with the national culture of Scotland grew in force in the eighteenth century, until it achieved its greatest impact in the work of Robert Burns.

Song was thought of as natural to the people and the land. *'When Fletcher of Saltoun [patriot and contemporary of Seafield] wished to have the making of his country's songs...he meant veritable songs, expressing in appropriate terms his countrymen's sentiments and feelings, amorous, patriotic, pathetic, courageous. He knew that only such would take hold of the public mind ... Our songs, to become part of the country's existence, must be sung, not on the opera stage, with instrumental accompaniments, but lilted in the gloaming, and at the milking hour, warbled with the song of the lark behind the plough, or on the hill-side with the sheep, and they shall live, though it may be a matter of no concern to many whether their author's existence is secured or not.'*[87]

This idea explains the phenomenal success of the eighteenth-century poems of Ossian, written by the Rev James MacPherson as a translation from the ancient Gaelic—mystical tales of giants and heroes in the distant valleys and lonely islands, which proved a source of inspiration not just in Scotland but throughout Europe. In theory, these, like Homer's verse, were the survival of a strong, heroic, verbal tradition, opposed to the decadence of classicism, which in Scotland was expressed in terms of the battles between the Romans and the Caledonians. The tradition of song presented a powerful, native tradition opposed to the morally and culturally decadent Roman decline. *Christie Johnstone* has a passage underlining the modern parallel with this idea, when the rich friends of the Viscount and a group from the village sail out separately to picnic on an island on the Forth—the rich group have brought no written music or entertainment with them and are bored and dumb, the villagers sing and tell stories from a rich flow of invention.

Song was, therefore, not simply a mild source of entertainment but a key to national identity and strength. The emphasis on the fishwives' remarkable singing makes them part of a great historical tradition and the heirs of Ossian. The anxiety for song, which followed the upheavals of the Industrial Revolution, resulted in the serious collection of songs by Walter Scott and others and the writing of songs within the older Scottish tradition, by people like Robert Burns and James Hogg. In the early 1830s, Hogg was asked what changes he had seen in the country in the last fifty years. His sense of the change begins: *'shepherds and farm servants ... are better fed, better clothed, and better educated than the old shepherds and hinds of my first acquaintance; but they are less devout, and decidedly less cheerful and happy.*

On looking back, the first great falling off is in Song. *This, to me, is not only astonishing, but unaccountable. They have ten times more opportunities of learning songs, yet song-singing is at an end... In my young days, we had singing matches almost every night, and, if no other chance or opportunity offered, the young men attended at the ewe-bucht or the cows milking, and listened and joined the girls in their melting lays...I never heard any music that thrilled my heart half so much as when these nymphs joined their voices, all in one key, and sung a slow Scottish melody. Many a hundred times has it made the hairs of my head creep, and the tears start into my eyes, to hear such as the Flowers of the Forest, and the Broom of Cowdyknowes. Where are those melting strains now? Gone, and for ever! ... By dint of hard pressing, a blooming nymph will sometimes venture on a song of Moore's or Dibdin's (curse them!), and gaping, and half-choking, with a voice like a cracked kirk-bell, finish her song in notes resembling the agonies of a dying sow.'* [88]

This passage is, of course, part of a recognisable historical process—old men never like the songs of the young—but Hogg links the particular deterioration of song to a more serious social disintegration. During the Napoleonic wars, prices rose and 'made every farmer for the time a fine gentleman ... Before that time, every farmer was first up in the morning conversed with all his servants familiarly, and consulted what was best to be done for the day. Now the foreman, or chief shepherd, waits on his master, and, receiving his instructions, goes forth and gives the orders as his own, generally in a peremptory and offensive manner. The menial of course feels that he is no more a member of a community, but a slave; a servant of servants, a mere tool of labour in the hand of a man whom he knows or deems inferior to himself, and the joy of his spirit is mildewed. He is a moping, sullen, melancholy man ...' [89] The practical brutality of industrialisation, which we would associate with factory work, applied equally to the Agricultural Revolution. Hogg makes one other point, which is also relevant to the situation in Newhaven. The sociability of the earlier system, where the farmers and servants ate and danced together as well as worked together, linked men and women: *'since the extermination of the penny-weddings, kirns and family-dances, the peasantry have not an amusement in which the sexes join; and this sort of abstraction is the first thing that tends to demoralize society, and to stamp the character of man with a more rude and repulsive tint.'* [90] Seen this way, Newhaven was not just a quaint historical survival, but a remaining model for a healthy—and undemoralised—society.

D. O. Hill's taste for music and for poetry, and especially the Scottish songs, is therefore a clue both to his nationalism and to his own art. Direct reference between the photographs and song emerges in the album of calotypes he put together in the 1850s for the politician, James Wilson. [91] The Newhaven photographs in this album have extracts from fishing songs as captions. The photograph of Jeanie Wilson (plate 49), for example, is presented as:

'A Love Reverie, Newhaven.
Mrs Wilson sings
"When Jamie vowed he would be mine
And won frae me my heart
Oh meikle lichter grew my creel
We said we'd never part"
The Boatie Rows'

The photograph of the women in the lane (plate 43) has the words,

'The Dredging Song, Newhaven
"The herring loves the merry moonlicht,
The mackerel loves the wind;
But the oyster loves the dredging song
For it comes o' the gentle kind."'

The photographs were not designed as illustrations of particular songs any more than they show the fishwives with their mouths open singing. The songs and the photographs would, however, interact—one art interlocking with the other, giving extension and additional dimension. People looking at the photographs would recall the songs; and listening to the songs they would visualise the calotypes. The calotypes were impressionistic or suggestive and 'to a man with a shaping spirit, are the very stuff from which to body forth his own thoughts.' [92]

After his death, it was said of Hill: *'His manner in society was blythe and genial, and he sang a capital song, not unfrequently entertaining his companions with ballads of his own composition.'* [93] As an enthusiast for Scottish song and as the illustrator of the works of Burns and Hogg, Hill thought naturally in terms of poetry and music. What he photographed in Newhaven was partly what he was hearing in the language and the song—the distinctive voice and character of the fishermen and wives. In writing a critical review of Hill's painting and calotypes in 1846, John Brown said, *'His works always exhibit something of the highest beauty,—often a sort of tenderness as unexpected and as plaintive as the "owercome" of an old border ditty sung by himself.'* [94]

This impressionistic idea relates the photographs to music and poetry in an emotional way which cannot be expressed clearly or specifically—the associations like the calotypes were blurred and the more effective for being so. Hill had a reputation as a 'poetic' painter, and he himself voiced his admiration for Turner, in terms of 'the greatness of the mind and the giant power of the poet-painter of the sea.' [95] An idea of what this meant, may be read in Brown's review of John Ruskin's *Modern Painters* in 1847. He analysed three pictures in Ruskin's terms, including a sketch by Hill taken from a window in Inverleith Row: *'done in a fine frenzy of an hour; it has exquisite colour, and is as sweet and deep in its tones as his own voice; but what is it? Look and you will see, wait and you will feel. There is nothing of earth to be seen but the tops of some great trees, among them an old fir with its cones of last year. Lying across them, and giving them power, and getting for itself distance and freedom, is a long line of evening sky: under it and above it clouds of unimaginable colours. The broad sun is sinking, all but sunk down "in his tranquility" and in that line of light, added by the painter (for though the sea was not visible to his eye, he wanted it to be there) you see the sea! and on it the gentleness of the upper heavens. There we have a scene in itself imaginative to all minds of ordinary sensibility, made more so by a mind of higher sensibility, which works under an exalted condition of its whole nature. And fixes for ever upon that mere sketch, the strong and delicate but evanescent feeling as well as sensations of that hour.'*[96]

This is obviously based on a Romantic idea—such expressions as 'a fine frenzy of an hour' and 'an exalted condition of its whole nature' belong within that tradition. Scottish nationalism was substantially 'Romantic' in its ideas of nature—not searching just for simplicity but for wildness and strangeness. That ideas of this kind should prove compatible with the invention of the 'practical,' the 'truth-telling,' camera seems at first sight unlikely.

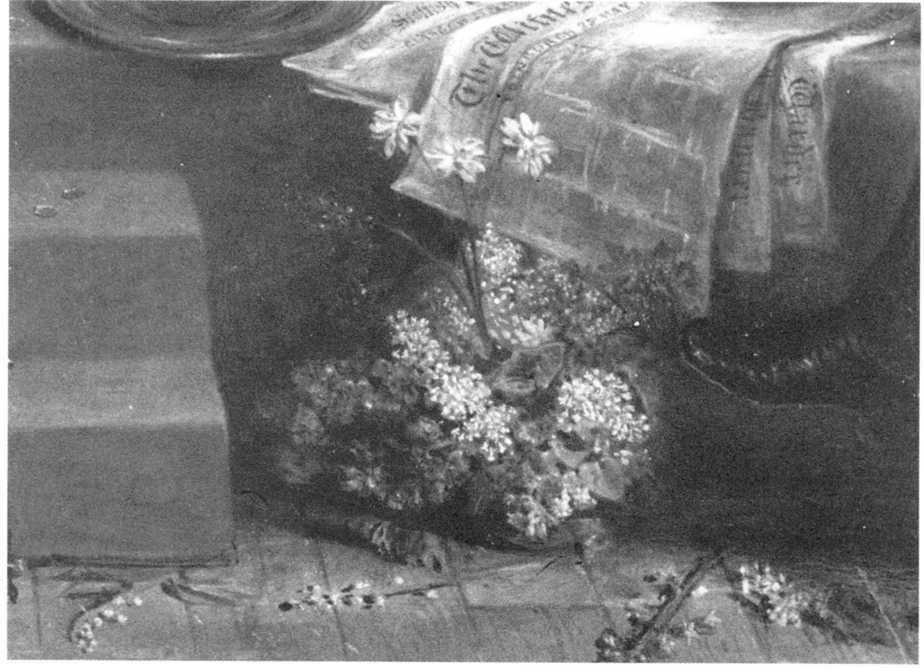

fig. 14
D. O. Hill
The Signing of the Deed of Demission..., detail showing May flowers
Free Church of Scotland

The Pursuit of Nature and Fact

Progress, or movement, in the arts and sciences may be based on intention but requires the more general drive of attention. From the later eighteenth century, the collection and analysis of facts fuelled the arts and philosophy. Sir John Sinclair's great work on Scotland, *The Statistical Account*, was a remarkable example of this; it was an analysis of all the parishes in Scotland, written by the ministers, and in idea the origin of the census. This, for the first time, would give the Scots a clear view of the life of their country.

With fuel of this practical kind, the arts and the sciences were provided with exceptional inspiration. In their writing, both Robert Burns and Walter Scott referred directly to people, places and even apparently minute and trivial details of stray weeds. Scott, challenged for noting 'even the peculiar little wild flowers and herbs that accidentally grew round and on the side of a bold crag near his intended cave of Guy Denzil ...' replied, *'that in nature herself no two scenes were exactly alike, and that whoever copied truly what was before his eyes, would possess the same variety in his descriptions, and exhibit apparently an imagination as boundless as the range of nature in the scenes he recorded; whereas whoever trusted to imagination, would soon find his own mind circumscribed, and contracted to a few favourite images, and the repetition of these would sooner or later produce that very monotony and barrenness which had always haunted descriptive poetry in the hands of any but the patient worshippers of truth.'*[97]

Reality was the counter to sterile mannerism. Nature was a direct source of inspiration; an idea that belonged to the arts, sciences and religion. John Galt's fictional minister, the Rev Cowal Kilmun, came away from the books in his study to consider his sermon: *'One day... as I was taking a stray by myself, meditating on my sermon, and the nothingness of all things in a world of sin and misery, I sat down on a stone on the loch shore, and ruminated of the sun and the seasons, the mysteries of Providence, and the presumption of the narrow discernment of man; marking the gentle flowing in of the tide, as if there was a spirit of love and fondness in nature, willing to embrace all things.'*[98]

A combination of the two ideas, suggested here by Scott and Galt, was used by Hill in his Free Church painting. In the foreground of the picture and occasionally scattered further back on ledges are flowers (fig. 14). The prospectus for the painting ends with a description of them:

'The flowers were a feature in the first Assembly, being the everyday gifts of ladies of the Church, and have since continued to be so; Scotch in their associations, they also mark the eventful month of May, and call up many beautiful thoughts and sayings dear to the heart of Scotland, and applicable to the situation, from that of the greatest of her poets—"The hyacinth's for constancy, wi' its unchanging blue"—to that of Him *who spoke to the multitudes on the Mount, and now, here, to the hundreds of homeless men who had that day given their all for Him, and in doing so emphatically found their promised great reward.*

"Consider the lilies of the field; they toil not,
Neither do they spin; yet I say unto you,
That Solomon, in all his glory, was not arrayed like one of these.
If then God so clothe the grass,
How much more can he clothe you?"'[99]

The real flowers, arguably a mere decoration to the meetings and an excuse to introduce a little colour into a sombre painting, were used by Hill as a mark of nationalism and of time, seen through Burns' love song, 'The Posie,' and as the visual metaphor to relate the ministers' sacrifice to the Sermon on the Mount. By making the 'unimportant' flowers true to life, he made the parable true.

Hill's photographic practice showed an unusual respect for the truth which relates to ideas of this kind. Even in its early years, it was clear that photography's truth gave a limited and distorted view of the world, tempting the photographers to alter and 'improve.' The monochrome of photography was in itelf regarded as a defect. Professional photographers like Antoine Claudet, who held Talbot's patent for portrait photography in London, 'improved' photography by disguising it: *'Likenesses are now produced upon paper, which are then placed before a competent artist, who "touches them up," and makes of them* Portraits ... *No human hand has ever obtained such brilliant effects as these, which result from the combined labours of Nature and Art.'*[100]

Given that Hill was a professional painter, it is a mark of his enthusiasm for the truth of photography that he was not standing at Adamson's elbow with a loaded paint brush. The calotype was physically a temptation—both the negative and positive were made on drawing paper and there was no technical difficulty, as there was with the daguerreotype, in drawing or painting on top. The studio did touch up the negatives in pencil or wash to remove chemical spots or failures and sometimes strengthened the lines of hair or drapery. Only on four or five occasions did Hill add a small detail to a negative—a little star over Elizabeth Rigby's head, a bird in a cage.

This respect was extended to the subject matter. In taking the Newhaven photographs, Hill showed a concern for actuality which may be understood by comparing them with the later commercial photographs of fishwives and with the more sophisticated genre photography of Henry Peach Robinson. Hill and Adamson took their equipment down to Newhaven and may have set up a working studio there. The later photographers invited fishwives into their existing studios and provided them with elaborately painted backdrops of Newhaven

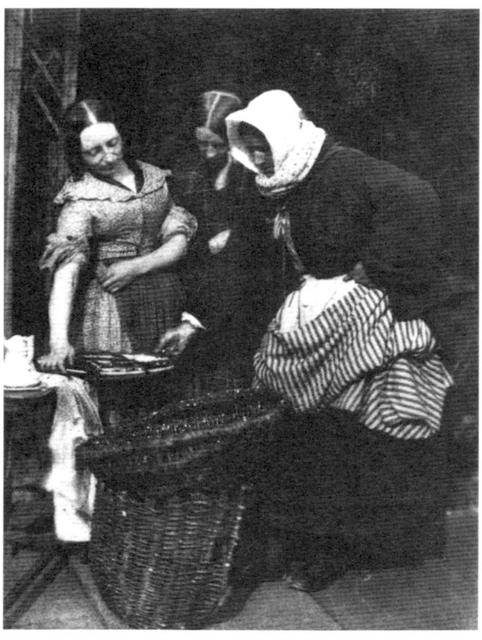

fig. 15
D. O. Hill and Robert Adamson
Mrs Flucker selling fish to a housewife
carbon print
Scottish National Portrait Gallery

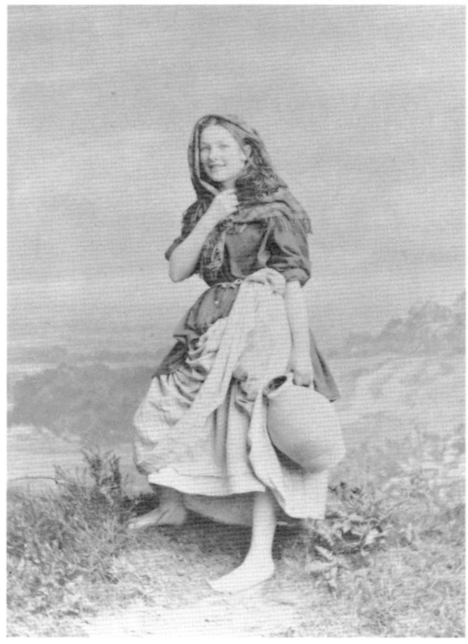

fig. 16
Henry Peach Robinson
On the Hill-Top, 1860 (studio photograph, with real plants arranged on a moveable platform and a painted backdrop)
illustration to *Pictorial Effect in Photography*, 1869

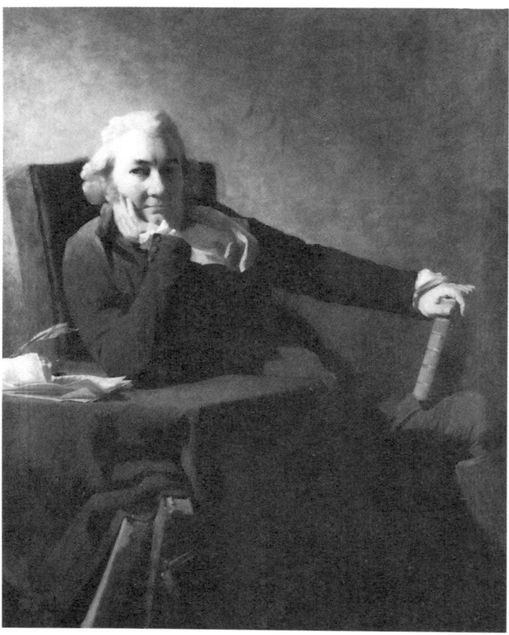

fig. 17
Henry Raeburn
Robert Cunninghame Graham, about 1794
oil painting
Scottish National Portrait Gallery

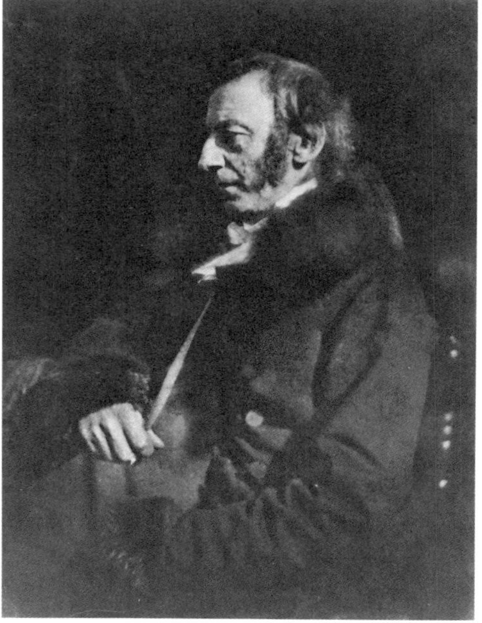

fig. 18
D. O. Hill and Robert Adamson
The 2nd Marquis of Northampton, 28 September 1844
calotype
Scottish National Portrait Gallery

or the city streets (figs. 9 & 10). Most of the backgrounds to Hill and Adamson's Newhaven photographs are so generalised in character that it is not obvious that they were taken in the village, and it has been wrongly assumed that many of the calotypes were taken at Rock House—an appropriate few probably were, like the photograph of Mrs Flucker selling fish to a housewife (fig. 15). As a landscape painter who painted from nature (to the point of catching rheumatic fever) Hill had a respect for the truth of place. He had shown this a decade earlier, specifically in relation to Newhaven, when he exhibited three pictures in the 1835 Academy exhibition: *The Peacock Inn—sketch at Newhaven; Evening: scene on the beach at Newhaven—painted on the spot;* and *Sketch of an oyster boat painted on Newhaven beach.* The idea was both mystical or poetic, and practical because the fishermen and wives would be more natural and would relate with confidence to their own background. In the proper setting, Hill could see groupings and behaviour he would wish to photograph and could call more readily on the co-operation of his subjects.

Hill's pursuit of truth, in this context, is most impressive in the idea of photographing a complete view of fishing life. A simplistic idea of Newhaven as 'picturesque' would have focussed on the beautiful young fishwives or 'characteristic' gnarled old age—paintings and photographs of handsome fishwives or peasant girls found a ready market and girls were commonly more amenable as models. The preference for this definition of 'picturesque' may be seen more than a decade later, in the work of Henry Peach Robinson (fig. 16). Robinson's practice differed also in that he had difficulty photographing people—he was unable to persuade strangers to be natural in front of the camera: *'As regards models, I seldom find the "real thing" to quite answer my purpose. The aboriginal is seldom sufficiently intelligent to be of use, especially if you have intention in your work.'* [101] Robinson's solution was to buy clothes from country people and dress up experienced models who could hold a 'natural' pose and expression. Robinson's was a dressed-up, theatrical reality—real clothes with the wrong people inside. Hill's photographs treated the people, their dress and their setting as a matter of unity. He was interested not just in what he could make, but in what was there which could in itself be persuaded to make more than imaginative construction might re-make falsely. In working out of a studio context and in working without professional models, Hill had less precise control but more inherent truth.

The generalised ideals and conceptions which had held the floor in the eighteenth century had to rely on educated classical knowledge rather than a practical sense of the world. The camera, used with skill, belonged to the later stages of art and science in which a powerful curiosity and interest in reality—in what was there—had been awakened.

The interest that followed from this, in human individuality and character, was in direct opposition to the eighteenth-century pursuit of the ideal, articulated in Sir Joshua Reynolds' influential *Discourses Delivered to the Students of the Royal Academy: 'My notion of nature comprehends not only the forms which nature produces, but also the nature and internal fabric and organization, as I may call it, of the human mind and imagination. The terms beauty, or nature, which are general ideas, are but different modes of expressing the same thing, whether we apply these terms to statues, poetry or pictures. Deformity is not nature but an accidental deviation from her accustomed practice. This general idea therefore ought to be called Nature; and nothing else, correctly speaking, has a right to that name. But we are so far from speaking, in common conversation, with any such accuracy, that, on the contrary, when we criticize Rembrandt and other Dutch painters, who introduced into their historical pictures exact representations of individual objects with all their imperfections, we say,—though it is not in good taste, yet it is nature.*

This misapplication of terms must be very often perplexing to the young student. Is not art, he may say, an imitation of nature? Must he not therefore who imitates her with the greatest fidelity be the best artist? By this mode of reasoning, Rembrandt has a higher place than Raffaele. But a very little reflection will serve to show us that these peculiarities cannot be nature; for how can that be the nature of man, in which no two individuals are the same?' [102]

By contrast, this idea had already been rejected in Scotland by the portrait painter, Allan Ramsay (and it is significant that his father was a poet), who saw the human race as individuals and could not accept a generalised, classical ideal of beauty. It is arguable that the Scottish school, with its preference for truth and character over an abstract sense of beauty, was readier than the English to adopt the camera as a tool of art and welcome the invention of photography. The visual difference between the portraiture of Reynolds and that of Sir Henry Raeburn (fig. 17) has much to do with this Scottish interest in character. It is presumably not a coincidence that the English landscape painter, Joseph Farington, who visited Raeburn's Edinburgh studio in 1801, remarked: *'Some of Mr. Raeburn's portraits have an uncommonly true appearance of Nature and are painted with much firmness,—but there is great inequality in his works.—That which strikes the eye is a kind of Camera Obscura effect, and from those pictures which seem to be his best, I shd. conclude He has looked very much at Nature, reflected in the Camera.'* [103]

The direct interest in nature as the true model for art, combined with this sense of the importance of individuality, was learnt by Hill most certainly from the landscape painter, Alexander Nasmyth. This combined with, and was reinforced by, the Romantic interest in imperfection, which was important in Hill's approach to his art. His admiration for the calotype was expressed in these words: *'The rough surface & unequal texture throughout of the paper is the main cause of the Calotype failing in details before the process of Daguerreotypes—& this is the very life of it. They look like the imperfect work of a man, not the much diminished perfect work of God ...'* [104] Imperfection was a part of the character of the whole; polished perfection was suspect and repellent, with no depth and nothing to catch and hold the mind. This idea applies both to the manner and the subject matter of art.

The calotypes were often compared to the work of Rembrandt. When Sir David Brewster reviewed the work of Major Playfair, John and Robert Adamson and his own son, Captain Henry Brewster, in the Edinburgh Review in January 1843, he claimed largely, 'Several of these have all the force and beauty of the Sketches of Rembrandt.' [105] The early photographs taken by this St Andrews group are experimental and have little claim to force or beauty, so presumably Brewster (whose understanding of art was minimal) was reminded of Rembrandt by the physical appearance of the calotypes—their strength of light and shade and rich brown colouring. Later critics and artists talking about Hill and Adamson's work may be taken more seriously. William Etty saw in the calotypes 'revivals of Rembrandt, Titian and Spagnoletto.' [106] Clarkson Stanfield, to whom Hill sent a particularly fine group of calotypes, including exceptional prints of the fishing photographs, went so far as to say that he 'would rather have a set of them than the finest Rembrandts I ever saw.' [107] The water-colourist, John Harden, said they were 'as Rembrandts but improved.' [108]

Hill certainly thought about Rembrandt in relation to the calotypes. He talked of a portrait he took of the Marquis of Northampton (fig. 18) as 'a singularly Rembrantish & very fine study.' [109] Working with small-scale photographs while looking for a grand effect he would have been interested in the idea, expressed by Reynolds: *'Rembrandt's manner is absolute unity'* a *'fulness of effect ... produced by melting and losing the shadows in a ground still darker than those shadows.'* [110] He can be seen to use Rembrandt's manner of bouncing light from one surface to another. His affection for the surface confusion of the calotype and indeed his own manner of painting thickly (referred to offensively by a friend as 'plastering *alla scozzese'* [111]) may be related to, and at least reinforced by, Rembrandt's manner of etching, arbitrarily cross-hatched, and painting—'his Lights he loaded with a Thickness of paint so considerable, that he seemed rather to model than to paint.' [112] This last quotation comes from a book Hill owned, Charles Rogers' *A Collection Of Prints In Imitation of Drawings*, and adds a further comment 'The manner of Rembrandt's working is a kind of Magic.' Part of the fascination of calotype photography lay in that sense of magic, the strange capturing of reality in a little paper space.

In Charles Rogers' opinion, Rembrandt's greatest strength lay in his portraits: *'they had a striking Likeness, and seized the Character of every countenance. Nature is not embellished; but so truly, so simply, so faithfully, and with such life imitated, that his Heads appeared animated, and coming out of the canvass.'* [113] It was both this principle of truth and liveliness that Hill looked for and found in the calotype.

Artists like Reynolds qualified their admiration of Rembrandt because of his interest in 'peculiarity' or 'deformity.' This was more readily accepted by those who took a Romantic view of nature and humanity. The concept of imperfection as a necessary part of character appeared constantly in descriptions of the leading figures of the day, men Hill admired and photographed, serving to point up their heroic status, rather than to undermine it. A description of John Wilson by John Gibson Lockhart may be used as an example: *'His declamation is often loose and irregular to an extent that is not quite worthy of a man of his fine education and masculine powers; but all is redeemed, and more than redeemed, by his rich abundance of quick, generous and expansive feeling ... Inaccuracies of language are small matters when the ear is fed with the wild and mysterious cadences of the most natural of all melodies, and the mind filled to overflowing with the bright suggestion of an imagination, whose only fault lies in the uncontrollable profusion with which its scatters forth its fruits.'* [114] That Hill himself was a man of this kind may be read into the more critical remarks made by John Brown in 1846: *'He has a rich, versatile, rapid, facile mind, crowded with thick coming fancies: but he wants concentration to turn all these to account.'* [115]

That this romantic idea that surface faults (if not actual moral sins) are excusable and even desirable should appear in the Church is unexpected. But the sermons of Thomas Guthrie contain just such an idea. In a passage which begins by discussing the picturesque beauty of nature, he concluded, *'Christians have individual peculiarities which, as much as their faces, distinguish them from each other; and this is rather a beauty than a blemish—a charm rather than a fault ... Nor is this variety, as among the flowers of moor and meadow, an element merely of beauty. It is a power, an element of the highest utility in the Church. Hence the mistake of those who would have all Christians modelled on their own pattern, as, for example, of some modest, retiring, gentle spirits, who cannot appreciate the worth and usefulness of those whom God has cast in a rough mould and made of stern stuff.'* [116]

Models and Precedents for Newhaven

Within the general context of nationalism and Romanticism, with its interest in individuality, there are three important examples in the Scottish arts of the approach to humanity and the admiration of nature, which lead to the study of Newhaven. These are Robert Burns' poem, 'The Jolly Beggars', David Wilkie's painting, *Distraining for Rent*, and Walter Scott's novel, *The Antiquary*.

In Hill's vignette of Lincluden Abbey (fig. 19)—the frontispiece of his book, *The Land of Burns*—one of the figures appearing in Burns' dream is the old Scottish soldier from 'The Jolly Beggars', who boasted:

'... I lastly was with Curtis among the floating batt'ries
And there I left for witness an arm and a limb;
Yet let my country need me, with Elliot to lead me,
I'd clatter on my stumps at the sound of the drum...'

Hill has placed him beside great military figures of Scotland's past, Wallace, Bruce, Douglas and Randolph: *'The tattered and mutilated warrior beside them is the son of Mars of the Jolly Beggars, keeping watch over the kettle of the kirk and state, illustrating the patriotic resolves which animated even the lowest of the people at the time of the threatened French invasion; so felicitously brought out by Burns in the song of his old hero.'* [117]

John Gibson Lockhart analysed the attraction of 'The Jolly Beggars' in comparison with the work of the contemporary poet, George Crabbe, who *'would have described the Beggars like a firm though humane Justice of the Peace—poor Robert Burns did not think himself entitled to assume any such airs of superiority. The consequence is, that we would have understood and pitied the one groupe, but that we sympathize even with the joys of the other. We would have thrown a few shillings to Mr Crabbe's Mendicants, but we are more than half inclined to sit down and drink ourselves along with the "orra duds" of those of Burns ...'* [118]

There are two strands here which relate to Hill's approach to Newhaven. The more startling may have been the concept of a beggar as a significant individual and as a hero, a disregarded cripple but part of the national bulwark of defence. The concept of heroism belonging not just to the great military names but to the individual soldiers is important. Several of the calotypes treat the fishermen especially as heroic figures—appropriate to their status as volunteers in time of war, and as the pilots who saved lives in storms at sea (plates 17 & 23).

The psychological approach to the subject is equally important—the idea that the greater art is created not just from the distant fact-finding view of society, or the kind of superior sympathy which offers pity or advice, but from the direct making of a social relationship.

John Brown said of D. O. Hill: *'Though little known as a delineator of human character, he has many of the mental qualities proper to this department: he can throw himself out of himself, and be another; he has humour, which implies, we have always thought, not merely character in its owner, but a power of seeing into the character of others; and he has that thorough human-heartedness and love of his kind, that makes him lay out his affections on them wherever he sees them.'* [119] The photographs themselves are evidence of a generous social friendliness; the Newhaven calotypes are true because Hill was looking at the people themselves, not at himself reflected in them. This generates that strong sense of direct contact, regardless of time, between us and the fishermen and women in the photographs.

Although the Newhaven fishwives were noted for their beauty and confidence, they could not make the photographs themselves. The dismal calotype taken by one of the lawyer members of the Edinburgh Calotype Club proves this with no further comment (fig. 20). Calotypes by the watercolour painter, William Collie, working with market women in Jersey, were compared to the Newhaven pictures in 1847 and are arguably based on a similar idea (fig. 21). But they may be distinguished in several ways: the tonal range is smoother, the colour more uniform and the compositional groups smaller in relation to the paper. *The Art Union* revealingly remarks that 'a degree of refinement has been obtained of which the art has seemed incapable.' [120] In an adverse sense, this is true. Collie's groups have a ladylike weakness and a distance, which is opposite in character to the Newhaven calotypes. The difference is not a real one between the fishwives and the market women; it is a radical difference in approach—most importantly, there is no meeting of minds between the photographer and his subjects.

The general critical opinion of Sir David Wilkie's early paintings, which were Scottish genre scenes, linked them with the seventeenth-century Dutch pictures of 'low life,' by artists like Teniers or Ostade. Wilkie's patron, Sir George Beaumont, complained that he did not attempt 'deep pathos.' [121] John Gibson Lockhart dismissed his work: 'I think Wilkie's species of painting may be said to bear the same relation to the highest species which sentimental comedies and farces bear to regular tragedies.' [122] Lockhart was looking for paintings of religious allegory and scenes from the Bible. Wilkie's own religion would incline him naturally to the more sympathetic example of the Calvinist Dutch genre.

With the picture he painted in 1815, he developed the principle of genre to address ideas of pathos and moral elevation. The painting, *Distraining for Rent*, is an illustration of the despair of financial ruin (fig. 22). It shows a bankrupt farmer, unable to pay his rent, whose house has been taken over by the bailiff. His two assistants are listing the family's

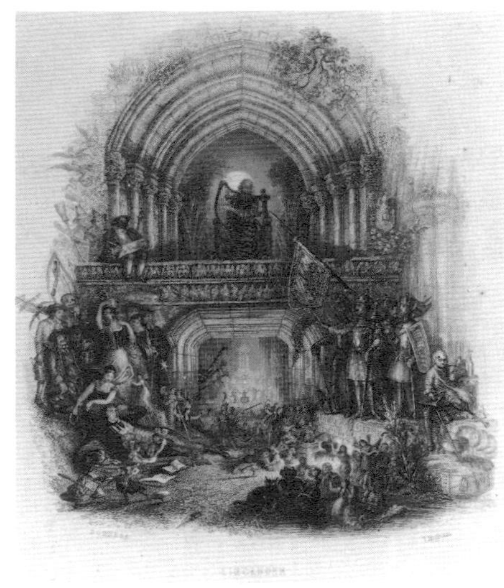

fig. 19
David Octavius Hill
Lincluden, The Poet's Dream
engraving for *The Land of Burns*, 1840

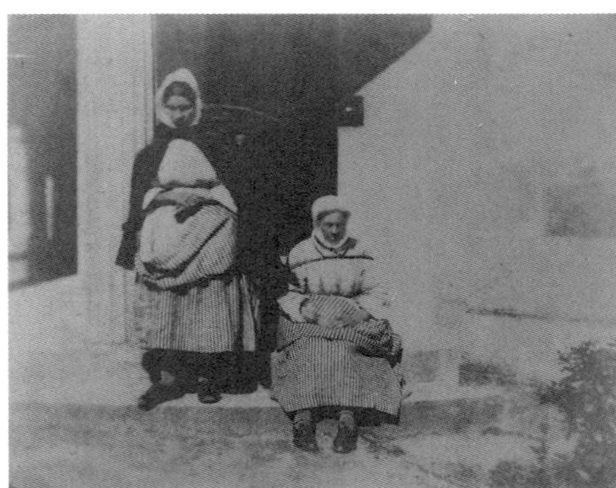

fig. 20
A member of the Edinburgh Calotype Club
Newhaven fishwives, about 1845
calotype
Scottish National Portrait Gallery

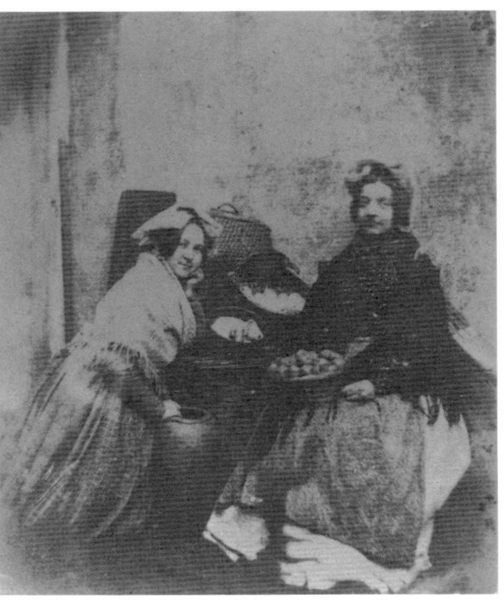

fig. 21
William Collie *Jersey market women, about 1847*
calotype
Scottish National Portrait Gallery

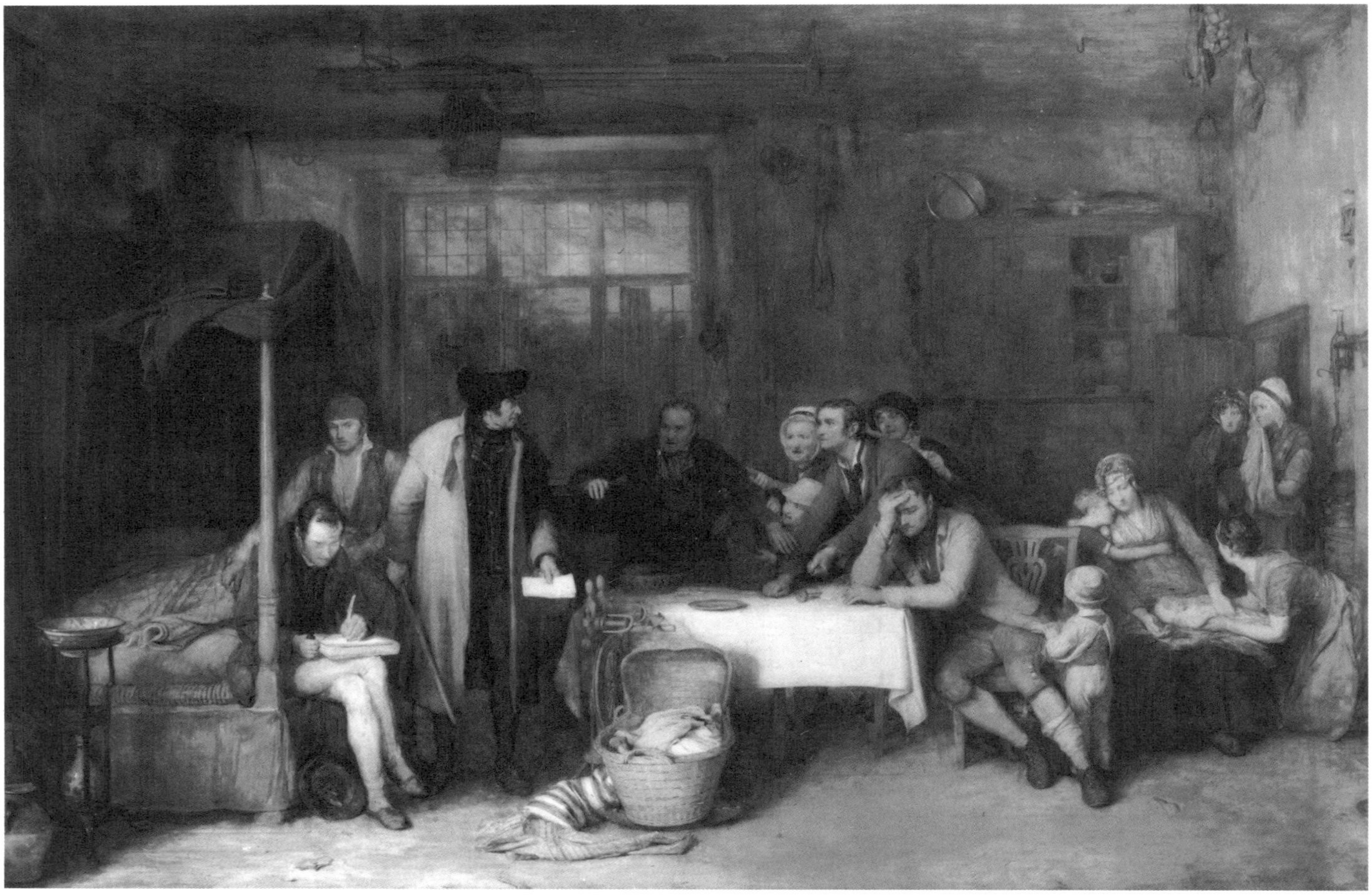

fig. 22
David Wilkie *Distraining for Rent*
oil painting
National Gallery of Scotland

few possessions, from the wife's spinning wheel, her own source of income in supporting the family, to the child's rattle. The farmer and his wife are in a state of helpless despair—too far sunk in misery to protest. Their neighbours, actively horrified by the situation, are protesting angrily on their behalf.

Wilkie exhibited the picture in the Royal Academy and was taken aback to find it spoken of as a subversive attack on landlords. The British Institution, which bought the picture, was unnerved by the public reaction and hid it for seven years. The subject was altogether too powerful and politically sensitive because the ending of the Napoleonic Wars, which led to a drop in the high price of corn, had caused an agricultural failure. The scene was not simply painful but over-familiar.

Wilkie had, moreover, broken the conventional rule of this kind of moral painting, found in the work of Hogarth or George Morland, by which it is clear that the victim suffers for good reason. Sir George Beaumont protested that he 'should have shown why his landlord had distrained; he might be a dissipated tenant.'[123]

Whether or not Wilkie intended *Distraining For Rent* to be a politically radical picture, it presented another revolutionary idea that was confused by the political reaction. He had, in fact, removed himself from the comic—regarded as natural in expressive scenes of 'low life'—and changed the elementary morality regarded as appropriate in such pictures. The despair in his central figures is truthful and overwhelming; they call not for judgement but for sympathy. We are looking, not at a page from a moralising chapbook, but at a tragedy; the farmer and his family have been overtaken by disaster and it is irrelevant whose fault it may be. This is to do with the 'facts' of real life and, more importantly, it is the shifting of genre from a 'low life' viewpoint to one where a tenant farmer may be taken seriously as a subject for tragedy in art. Painting had been used for so long to the idea of a hierarchy of subjects in which the elevated themes belonged to the idealising 'history' painting, that taking tragedy, so to speak, downstairs was a startling idea, and, for a time, hard for Wilkie's audience to 'see'.

By the 1840s, the radical edge of*Distraining For Rent* was blunted. In 1846, D. O. Hill borrowed the picture for the Royal Scottish Academy's annual exhibition. Cheap evening openings enabled large numbers of factory and office workers to see the picture and to read the accompanying leaflet, which was mostly devoted to quoting Dr John Brown's critical opinion of the painting. This read, in part: 'It is to our liking Wilkie's most perfect picture ... there is more of human nature, more of the human heart, in this than in any of the others. It is full of "the still, sad music of humanity,"—still and sad, but yet musical, by reason of its true ideality, the painter acting his part as reconciler of men to their circumstances. This is one great end of poetry and painting.'[124] The introduction to this leaflet urges the visitors to study and 'read' the other works on the walls in the same spirit as John Brown's remarks. Amongst those other works were a group of Hill and Adamson's calotypes. The parallel between the satisfactory ideal of Newhaven and the tragic ideal of *Distraining For Rent* could be made directly.

The third of the influential models for the Newhaven calotypes remains the most obvious. Walter Scott's novel, *The Antiquary*, has as its heroic and tragic focus a family of fishermen and women, the Mucklebackits. The main plot of the book is melodramatic and satirical and the force of reality lies in the passages with the fishing village. Scott's introduction explained this as a specific intention:

'I have ... sought my principal personages in the class of society who are the last to feel the influence of that general polish which assimilates to each other the manners of different nations. Among the same class I have placed some of the scenes, in which I have endeavoured to illustrate the operation of the higher and more violent passions; both because the lower orders are less restrained by the habit of suppressing their feeling, and because I agree with Mr. Wordsworth, that they seldom fail to express them in the strongest and most powerful language. This is, I think, peculiarly the case with the peasantry of my own country, a class with whom I have long been familiar. The antique force and simplicity of their language often tinctured with the oriental eloquence of Scripture, in the mouths of those of an elevated understanding, give pathos to their grief, and dignity to their resentment.'[125] (fig. 23)

Scott followed Wilkie's example[126] in presenting his central tragic scene, the funeral of the young fisherman who has drowned for no clear reason on a fine night, as a complicated and subtle insight into the psychology of grief through the reactions of the whole family. The description has the confusion and ambiguity of real life and is powerfully sad. The Mucklebackits became real in the public mind, in a way the other characters in the book did not.

A number of the calotypes relate to the novels of Walter Scott and photographs taken at Lord Cockburn's neo-baronial house, Bonaly Tower, are illustrations to *The Antiquary*. The sculptor, John Henning, dressed up as 'Edie Ochiltree', the 'blue-gown beggar' of the story, and Cockburn's daughter—without dressing up—posed as the Antiquary's daughter (fig. 24). In a larger group, which included Lord Cockburn, Henning was the only costumed figure, but there is a strong possibility that Hill meant Lord Cockburn, who was passionately interested in the relics of Scotland's history, to stand for the Antiquary as well as himself. The Newhaven photographs are not staged to tell Scott's story but they relate naturally to *The Antiquary* because they were similarly truthful. Hill, like his contemporaries , was so far influenced by Scott as to see reality partly through his eyes, so that Elizabeth Johnstone Hall could be Mrs Mucklebackit as much as she was herself. In the album given to James Wilson, the photograph of her is annotated with a quotation from the novel, 'It's no' fish ye're buying, it's men's lives' (plate 52) and the calotype of James Linton and his boys (cover) is identified as 'Sanders Mucklebackit of Musselcrag.'

The seed and inspiration for the Newhaven calotypes lies in the three key works by three of Scotland's greatest and most influential artists. They express an interest in nationalism and a respect for the poorer classes as the remaining source of true Scottish culture; the idea of a moral ideal that may come from an actual model rather than an elevated abstraction; and a preference for individuality and independence. That they were all three tied to a conscious study of the natural truth makes the Newhaven calotypes a natural and proper corollary to the work of Robert Burns, David Wilkie and Walter Scott.

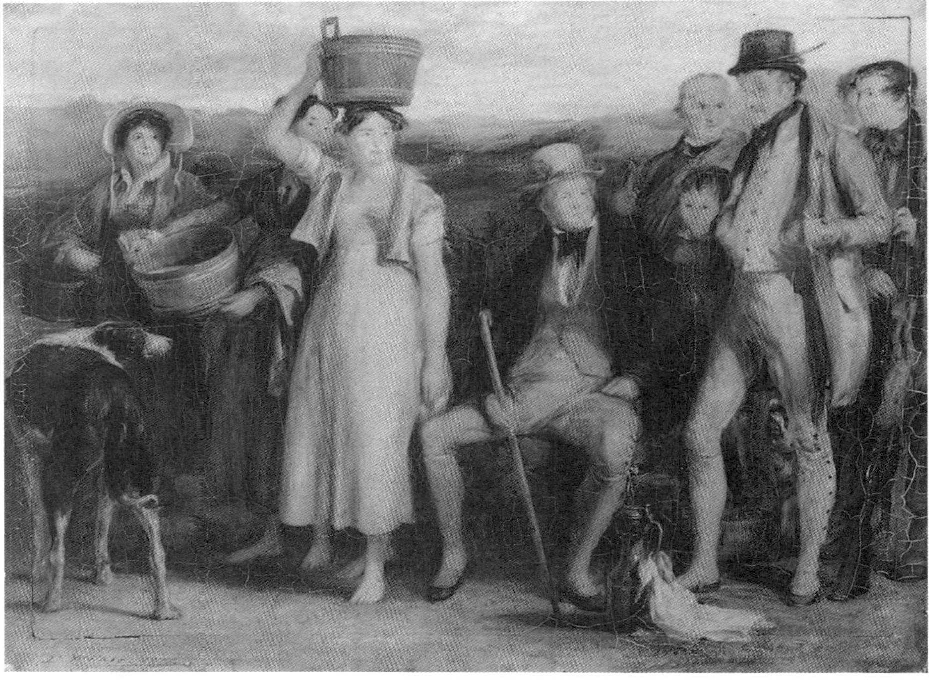

fig. 23
David Wilkie
The Abbotsford Family, Walter Scott and his family painted as tenant farmers
oil painting
Scottish National Portrait Gallery

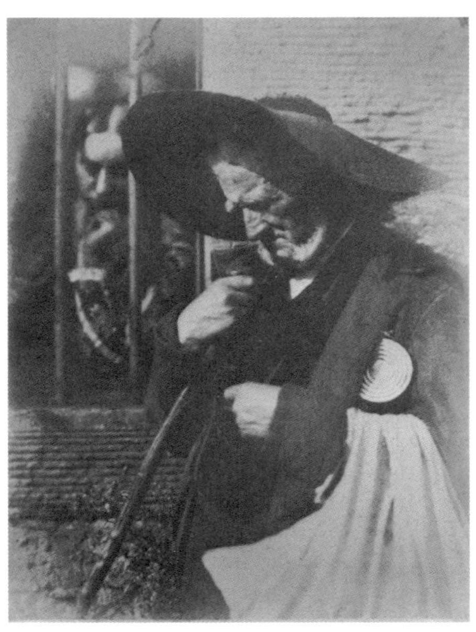

fig. 24
D. O. Hill and Robert Adamson
John Henning and Miss Cockburn as Edie Ochiltree and Miss Wardour, from The Antiquary
calotype
Scottish National Portrait Gallery

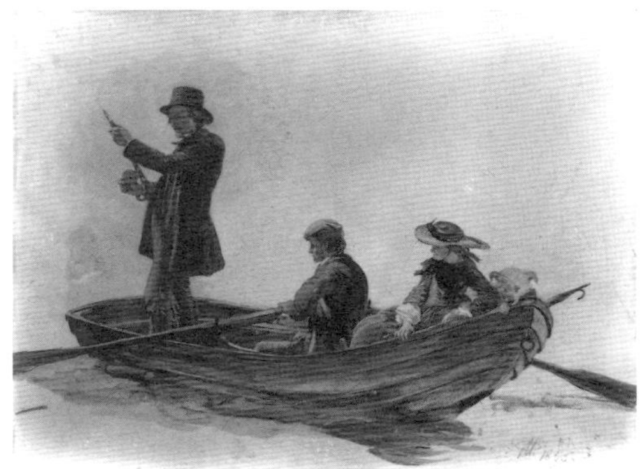

fig. 25
George Harvey
Rev Thomas Guthrie and his children, fishing on Lochlee, 1855
oil sketch
Scottish National Portrait Gallery

The Origins of the Narrative Structure in the Newhaven Series

The idea of a documentary series of pictures showing a full account of the life of a community had its general origins in an interest in ethnology—the drawings of natives discovered on distant voyages, 'captured' and brought back home to satisfy scientific or simple curiosity. But these drawings tended to be casual in character, lacking any particular sense of understanding or structure. Effectively, there was no graphic tradition for Hill to draw on when he was considering the construction of *The Fishermen and Women of the Firth of Forth.*

It seems possible that Hill's idea of the structure of this series came rather from a literary or even verbal tradition. Oratory was a crucial element of Scottish culture and the sermon was a focus of intense interest. It was customary in Edinburgh to attend at different churches and to discuss and criticise the character and quality of the preachers. *'There is, or at least at that period was, nothing which stimulated and raised the mind of Scotland like a sermon; it has been, from the time of Knox at least, the chief intellectual enjoyment of a keenly critical community, which has found in that weekly occurrence not only the exhibition of power and skill which all men love to watch, but the additional and still warmer interest of a personal share in the event, an awakening of all the critical faculties, an extended and universal discussion in which iron sharpeneth iron throughout a whole population.'* [127]

The sermon was designed to inspire its hearers, and to reach them, not just through passion but in an educational manner, moving from simple and comprehensible ideas and analogies to a more profound understanding. It was crucially important in the context of individual free will and a man's responsibility for his own salvation that all the people listening, ill and well-educated, should understand. In the words of the Rev Thomas Guthrie (fig. 25): *'With matter divine and matter human, our Lord descended to the level of the humblest of the crowd, lowering himself to their understandings, and winning his way into their hearts by borrowing his topics from familiar circumstances and the scenes around him. Be it a boat, a plank, a rope, a beggar's rags, an imperial robe, we would seize on anything to save a drowning man; and in his anxiety to save poor sinners, to rouse their fears, their love, their interest, to make them understand and feel the truth, our Lord pressed everything—art and nature, earth and heaven—into his service ... it were well, perhaps,that we sometimes ventured to follow his example.'* [128]

There is a relationship between this kind of writing or speaking and the Newhaven photographs. In the first instance, they depend on an attractive, natural approach to their subject; the calotypes may be examined for such information as the manner of baiting a line or the way to carry the creels. Behind this surface, the viewer may, with a little thought, see the deeper, social and moral basis—the self-reliance, the importance of the family, the working of religion and the inherent virtue in hard work. The relationship is also interestingly strong in its method. The documentary series, as we are familiar with it in the twentieth century, has this narrative character. It starts with the place, the harbour, the village street and moves in physically to the individual houses, then to the people who live there and to a sequential account of their lives. In our day, this habit of building up a report on specific facts has become one of the reflexes of the press; then it came from the need for a strong structure and a way of fixing ideas in the mind by human touches, by reference to the ordinary and to simple facts. It is an obvious device to start at the front door, to open the door, to meet the people inside; and it is surprising how much writing in Scotland, of a formal and sophisticated kind, depended on this device for its strength.

Lord Cockburn's expression of the sacrifice made by the Disruption ministers when they walked out of the Church in 1843, is written in this way—building up from the small details to the more profound idea: *'The dismantling of the manse, the breaking up of all the objects to which the hearts and habits of the family were attached; the shutting of the gate for the last time of the little garden, the termination of all their interest in the humble but respectable kirk—even all these desolations, though they may excite the most immediate pangs, are not the calamities which the head of the house finds it hardest to sustain. It is the loss of station that is the deep and lasting sacrifice, the ceasing to be the most important man in the parish, the closing of the doors of the gentry against him and his family, the altered prospects of his children ...'* [129] George Harvey's Disruption painting, *Quitting the Manse* , picked up Cockburn's idea and expresses the sacrifice as the leaving of the house—the physical removal symbolising the spiritual withdrawal.

It would seem particularly appropriate to Hill to use the simple structure of the sermon, with its close reference to nature, in treating the lives of the fishermen and women. It was a structure which was understood by the people in the photographs and was, in effect, an important part of their own culture. The content was in a like manner comprehensible to the people in the photographs—their own deeper social structure and morality presented truly to the camera. The generous and active co-operation between the fishermen and women and the photographers is based on their understanding as well as Hill's. The effectiveness of the photographs is related to the same idea of the effectiveness of the sermon—to be a good sermon its truth needed to be 'comprehended and felt by the poor woman on the steps of the pulpit as thoroughly as by the intelligent strangers who are attracted solely by his eloquence.' [130]

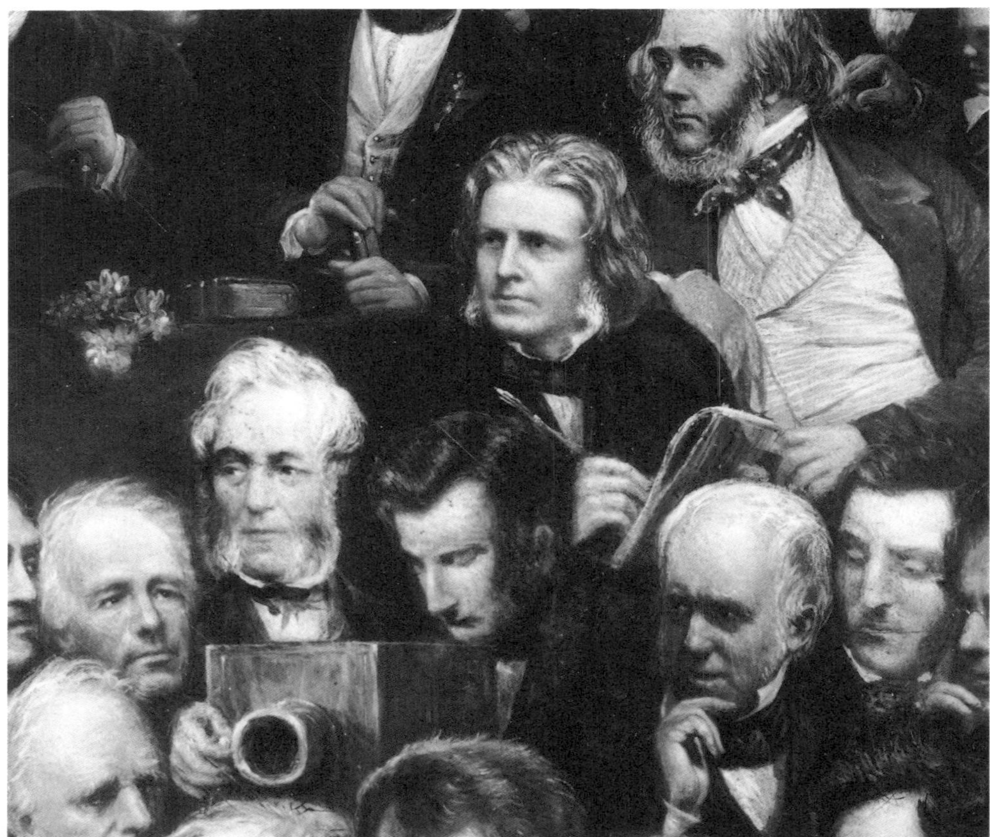

fig. 26
David Octavius Hill
Signing the Deed of Demission…, detail showing Hill, Adamson and Bell.
Note that Hill and Bell have 'aged' in the picture
Free Church of Scotland

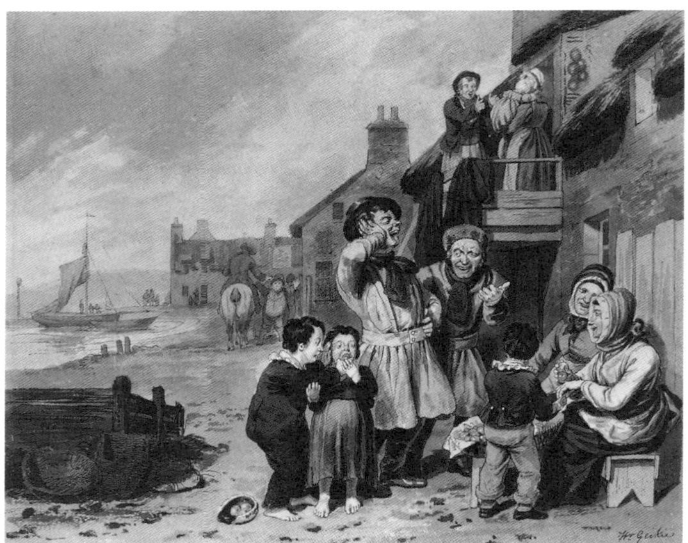

fig. 27
Walter Geikie
Shore scene with fishing families
watercolour
National Gallery of Scotland

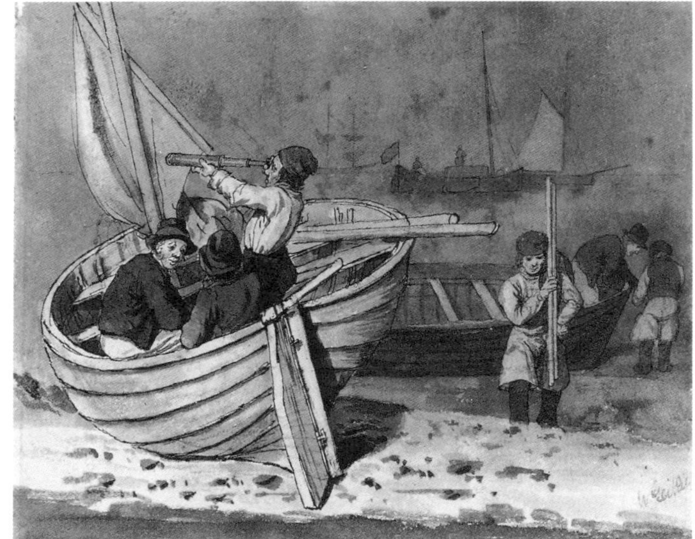

fig. 28
Walter Geikie
Sketch of fishing boat
watercolour
National Gallery of Scotland

The Handling of Time in the Calotypes

There is a problem in George Bell's essay on the conditions in the Old Town, which is tackled in the Newhaven photographs: *'The describing of such a scene involves very much more than the telling of what one has beheld. It involves a reference to the past and future of the people as well as to the present. It involves the transfer of our perception of their moral condition, which is the spirit, or rather the demon of the scene.'* [131] This problem, of encompassing time within art and expressing a whole truth, rather than a momentary impression, is one which Hill grappled with at great length in his Disruption picture, a painting which is based on the truth of photography to an extraordinary degree, using hundreds of photographs in its making. When it was finished, twenty years later, one of the reviews said: *'The picture is not chronological. It does not present events in succession as they occur in time, but simultaneously as they occur in a dream. Several incidents are thus indicated which were yet undreamt of in 1843, but without which the story of the Church would be so far incomplete ... He has given us a twenty years' history.'* [132] The picture represents the signing of the deed of demission from the Church of Scotland—the major act of sacrifice which cast the ministers adrift from the establishment. But it also encompasses, within that specific idea of an event which took place on two consecutive days in May 1843, the grander idea of the later progress and success of the Free Church. This was done by including, for example, references to successful missions and the building of new churches and colleges in the following decades, by grouping people with particular interests and showing them with the plans and documents from the future. The whole idea of the church was achieved by including people who had been elsewhere in the world at the time but who sympathised or joined the Free Church later. A certain visual confusion arises from a decision Hill made to allow some people (including himself) to age in the picture (fig. 26), marking the passage of twenty years.

Since abandoning the mediaeval idea that it is proper to show several phases or moments in time within one picture—as for instance in showing travellers at different points on a journey—western art worked within a convention that the frame should contain a unity of time and place. The intention of the Renaissance and later artists was to present a general or ideal expression of this unity, which educated and concentrated examination would discover. That is to say, that the eye should lead the mind from the surface of the picture to an understanding of the general philosophical basis behind it. It was, for example, commonly considered that a portrait should give an idea of the whole person, both in terms of character and in terms of time, and not as the sitter was in one transient mood or aspect.

Particular attention to the details of nature and its working within science and art at the turn of the century had put this idea under stress. David Wilkie's close study of nature, the practical reality of his subjects and the accuracy which with he painted fleeting expression, all conspired to make the sense of time in his pictures more specific. He talked of the difficulty generated by 'that one instant to which our elaborate art is limited,' [133] which made the expression of a sophisticated or general idea harder to achieve. It is worth briefly exploring this difficulty because it belongs also to photography, which is, by its nature, liable to be of this very specific character.

In the 1840s, photography was not capable of the kind of incidental genre that the graphic artists had mastered—the capacity to see and recall, whilst committing to paper, action and interaction in society, which was mastered by Rembrandt and which emerges in the work of David Wilkie and Walter Geikie in early nineteenth-century Scotland. Cameras fast enough to capture such action were not in common use until the twentieth century—but, it is worth emphasising, the camera is only capable of such a rapid and sophisticated response to social activity in the limited way that a pencil is capable; in the wrong hands, it simply spoils a piece of paper.

In his sense of time and speed of observation, Wilkie had mastered a skill we might consider photographic. This idea of the 'instant' is an idea that reaches a peak in the work of Henri Cartier-Bresson, the master of 'the decisive moment'. He has said, 'We are passive workers in a world that moves perpetually. Our only moment of creation is that 1/125th of a second when the shutter clicks, the signal is given, and motion is stopped.' [134] This 'taking' of a reality, which is all the more poignant for being fleeting, is no part of an 'accident' of photography. It is a particular and interesting skill based on the ability to see and calculate at speed: *'An event is so rich in possibilities that you hover around while it develops. You hunt for the solution. Sometimes you find it in the fraction of a second; sometimes is takes hours, or even days. There is no standard solution, no recipe; you must be alert, as in a game of tennis'.* [135] The distinction between Cartier-Bresson's work and the similar visual acuity in, for example, the work of Rembrandt or Wilkie, is that the graphic artists could not draw at 1/125th of a second. In their case, they needed to recollect detail from memory.

Hill's idea of the 'instant' would not relate to the work of contemporary photographers, so much as to that of a graphic artist like Walter Geikie, whose drawings of street life in Edinburgh in the 1820s and 1830s include a number of studies of Newhaven (figs 7 & 27). The drawings show people moving or talking, in mid-gesture, with their passing expressions recognisable as cynicism, doubt, even the drunken anxiety of a man about to be sick. Each drawing is an individual moment, highly engaging, appealing to our fascination for immediacy and that vivid sense of humanity and reality that may come from split seconds of sensation. Geikie's drawings have the sense of capture that we would associate with the modern photographic paparazzi, and it is doubtless not a coincidence that stories are told of angry subjects who pursued him with threats.

There is an interesting link between Cartier-Bresson and Geikie, which is in contrast to D. O. Hill. The twentieth-century photographer has cultivated invisibility. Yves Bonnefoy described him taking a photograph: '*Years ago ... I saw Cartier-Bresson whip out his Leica and shoot—without interrupting a conversation and with a rapid, apparently absent-minded glance which did not even take in the camera, as if it were one with his eyes and his whole being.*'[136] Cartier-Bresson does not impose himself on the situation he is photographing, he observes from a distance. In the majority of his photographs, the subjects have not observed him or are not particularly concerned by him. Geikie's capacity to see in a precise way, freezing time, could well be related to the distance that is inherent in Cartier-Bresson's work. Although he was to an extent a sociable man, he was deaf and dumb which inevitably made him separate from society.

D. O. Hill's working method was sociable and involved the active co-operation of his sitters. 'Coldness on the part of those to be photographed,' he remarked ruefully, 'unmans me quite.'[137] His documentary photography is 'social' documentary in the active sense that his sitters were fully conscious of him and responding to him. He was conversing with them, not with another bystander. Cartier-Bresson works as an outsider, Hill as an insider.

Hill and Adamson did tackle movement in the Newhaven photographs. They produced an acceptable 'action' picture in the calotype of oyster dredging (plate 19) by lodging the boat on shore and propping the sail outwards with a pole—a study which has an interesting parallel in a drawing by Geikie (fig. 28). But Hill preferred the nature of a more 'general' response, which he could achieve convincingly in a sociable reconstruction. He was looking for the general and he was looking for the ideal, and he achieved it by leaving out most of the episodic details. His view came from the standpoint of the portrait painters' sympathy rather than the reporters' objectivity.

This was achieved in the Newhaven calotypes partly by exploiting the physical character of the process. The feeling of liveliness in the pictures—as opposed to frozen movement or expression—is based on the subtly shifting image which has sunk slightly into the paper. He often exaggerated the coarse focus to lose distractingly specific detail, and strengthened the contrast in tone to make the light 'shift' more effective.

The calotypes, as he said, would always be giving out new lights.[138] In that thought, the time is given by the viewer, in considering the photographs at length. Hill deliberately set up the Newhaven photographs with this idea in mind, as in the photograph of the two fishwives walking to market, one with her hand on the other's shoulder, the other with her face turned back to her friend (plate 39). It is a decorative picture, it prompts thoughts about their picturesque dress, about the remarkable load they carry with such grace. It is also, more profoundly, a picture about the success of Newhaven society—which is shown to have a basis in close friendship. The photograph of the boy, known as *King Fisher* or *His Faither's Breeks* (plate 60), is at first sight a mildly entertaining picture of a lad in his father's cast-off trousers. But this is the only photograph of a child alone in the Newhaven series, which implies that his father has died at sea and he has taken on not just his father's clothes but adult responsibility—as unsuited to his size as are the breeks. This same idea was used by the French Realist painter, Jules Bastien-Lepage, forty years later in his picture, *Pas-Meche* [Bad luck] (fig. 29), of the boy working with the canal barges, whose big boots are also a signal that he is an orphan. The photographs were not, like our newspaper or magazine illustrations, designed to have their full impact in one viewing. The correct manner of viewing the photographs is like becoming properly acquainted with people—visit them once and see what they look like, take the time to visit them again and you may discover what they are. It is necessary to travel beyond the surface of a photograph expressing one minute in their lives to the general idea expressing their whole lives.

In one way, Hill can be seen to have enjoyed an advantage appreciated by painters looking for the timeless picturesque. It was considered a useful device in portrait painting to dress a sitter in unreal generalised clothes or classical costume. A sitter in fashionable clothes was fixed to a historical date. The fishwives' distinctive costume took them out of the exact sense of time inherent in more fashionable dress. Women's costume in the 1840s was occasionally ugly and the enthusiasm for ringlets, which obscured the line of the face, made successful portraiture tricky. The stripes and folds of the Newhaven costume and the simpler lines of the women's hair and white caps must have added to the pleasure and success of the photographs. But Hill's interest was not exclusively in the easily-seen 'picturesque'. A notable example of the reverse is his pleasure in the top hats worn by the fishermen. The stove-pipe hat was fashionable and was considered by Elizabeth Rigby to be, 'a mysterious combination of the inconvenient and the unpicturesque, which, except in the light of a retribution, it is puzzling to account for.'[139] Hill treats the hats with relish; plate 30 is substantially composed around them.

The treatment of hats may seem unimportant, but it is evidence that Hill's admiration for Newhaven was for its contemporary reality. He was not presenting the village as a pastoral ideal divorced from real life. A clearer sense of this may be had by reading the views of Peter Henry Emerson, who photographed the English Fens in the 1880s and 1890s. *'All nature near towns'* he wrote, *'is tinged with artificiality … Among fisher-folk this may be seen in the sealskin cap, in the rustic it shows itself in the hard, billycock hat, in landscape pure it may be seen in some artificial forms of the river-banks, or in artificial undergrowths; the work of the beast, the stamp of vulgarity, that hydra-headed monster which always appears whenever a few men are gathered together, is sure to be found somewhere.'* [140] In Hill's landscape painting, as well as in his photography, he was happy to incorporate such artificiality or, rather, modernity and to treat the facts of his own time as part of an ideal.

Hill was not looking for a simplistic way of dealing with time by leaving its natural clues out of his pictures altogether. But his breadth of treatment in subject and in the physical character of the photographs, blurs and enlivens the subject. That this should work metaphorically as well as literally, may be understood in the difference between the figure of the fishwife drawn by Geikie reading a sensational broadsheet about the murderer and 'bodysnatcher' William Burke (fig. 30), and the calotypes of the fishwives reading a letter (plate 47). For the Geikie drawing we have the information we need to understand what the fishwife is doing and what her feelings are likely to be. For the calotype, we do not. As a result, the calotype can hold the attention for a longer time, while we speculate who the letter is from and what it might say. The letter itself becomes a generalised letter, representative of the many that have come in the past and the many that will come in the future.

The effect of the Newhaven series was designed from a flexible view of time, referring to the past and future as well as a broad present. Movement within the pictures and their general drawing combine with the sense of nature to make the subjects more real to us: *'They have all the modesty and all the infinite variety of nature, and, to a man with a shaping spirit are the very stuff from which to body forth his own thoughts.'* [141] This unspecific reality succesfully transcends time.

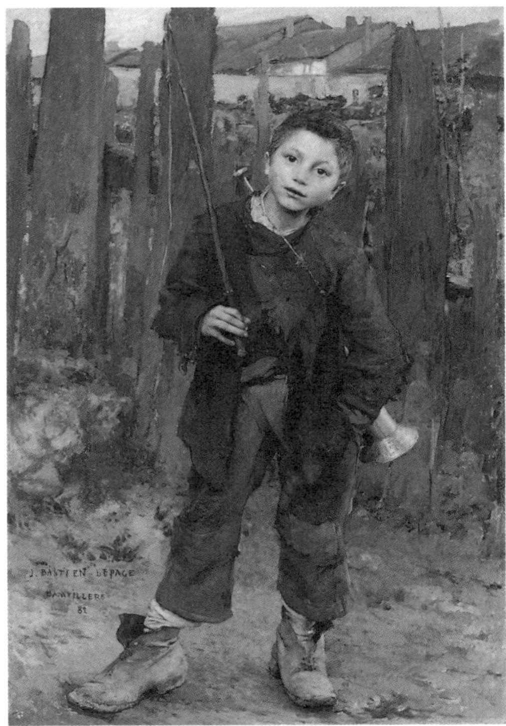

fig. 29
Jules Bastien-Lepage
Pas Mèche (Bad Luck)
oil painting
National Gallery of Scotland

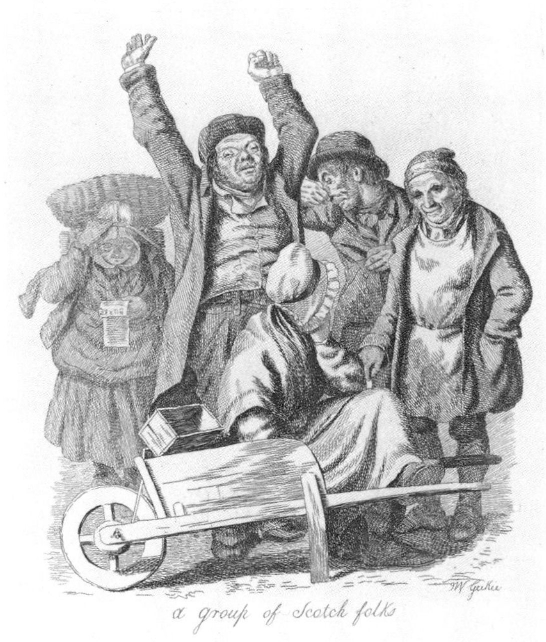

fig. 30
Walter Geikie
Edinburgh street scene
etching
National Gallery of Scotland

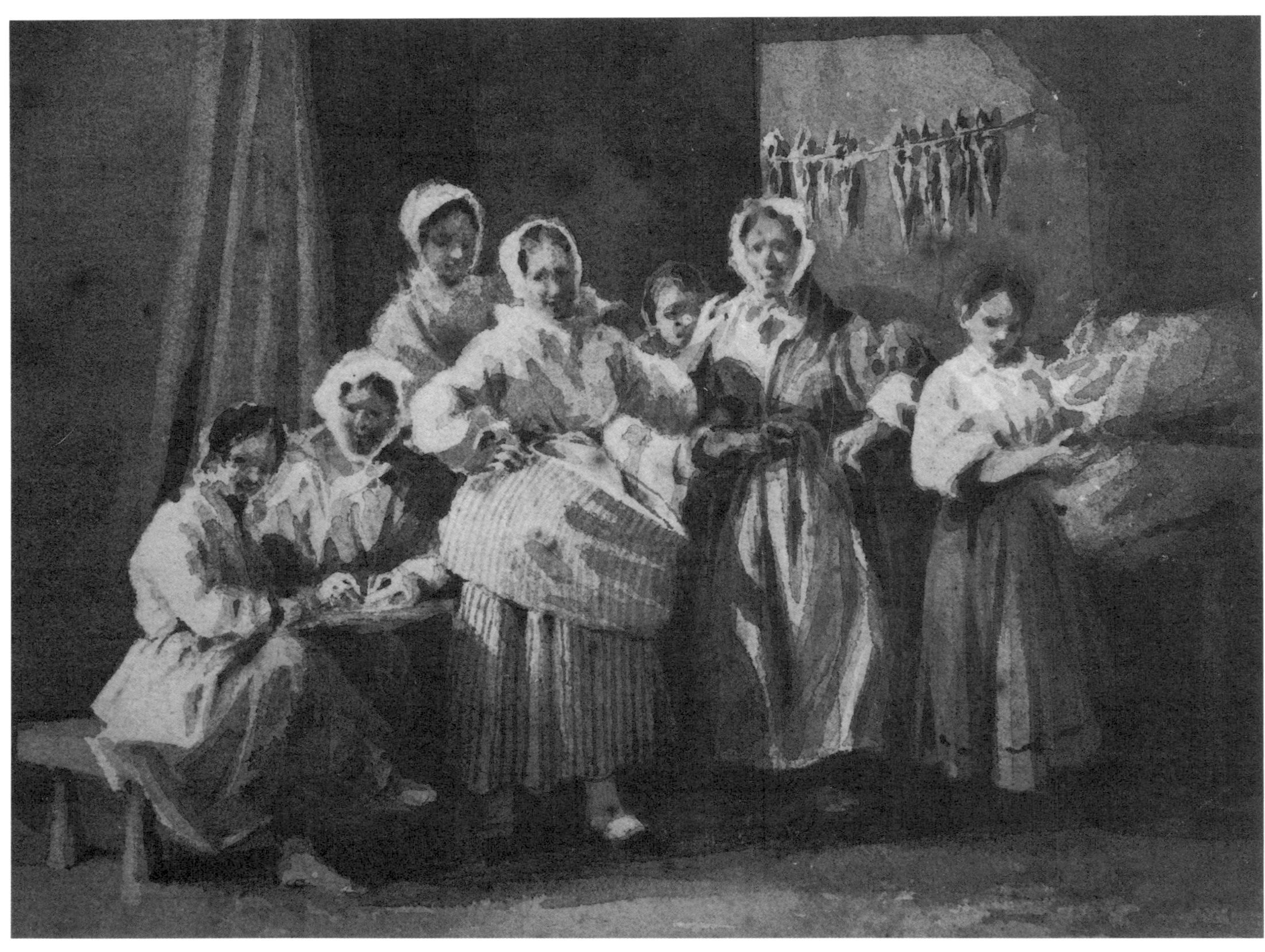

fig. 31
John Harden
Newhaven, November 1843
copy in watercolour of the Hill and Adamson calotype
National Library of Scotland

The Art of the Calotype

The distinctive art of the calotype, in the hands of D. O. Hill and Robert Adamson, was developed from its own technical character, considered in relation to earlier art forms and as a new and revolutionary art. Their interest in this character and truth was in striking contrast to the view of many of the contemporary photographers, including Talbot himself, who were seduced by the polish of the daguerreotype into thinking of the calotype as faulty and unrefined. Sir David Brewster rejected the calotype altogether as a medium for portraits in 1847, having failed to see the beauty of Hill and Adamson's work: *'The defect arises, to a certain extent, from the rough grain, so to speak, of the paper, and also from its imperfect transparency—for in the positive picture every imperfection of the paper is copied , and every luminous point reappears as a black one—so that the positive picture has the appearance of being stippled, as it were, with grains of sand, which give a painful coarseness to the human face.'* [142] There was no meeting of minds between Hill and Brewster—indeed from the uncharacteristic hesitance of this passage, it may be the result of a mutually uncomprehending conversation between them. Hill's expressed enthusiasm for the process has an echo of Brewster's criticism which makes it his side of the argument: *'The rough surface & unequal texture throughout of the paper is the main cause of the Calotype failing in details before the process of Daguerreotypes—& this is the very life of it. They look like the imperfect work of a man—and not the much diminished perfect work of God ...'* [143]

The calotype image is a variable chemical image—its colour is dependent on the mixture of the chemicals and on the heat and light of the sun. It is apparently monochrome but in fact the chemical reaction could give a richness and depth of colour which enlivened the print—in contrast to the most accomplished daguerreotypes, which were 'as flat and as blae as a slate.' [144] The daguerreotype sat on the surface of its little silvered mirror; the calotype sank physically into the fibres of the Whatman Turkey Mill paper, a high quality paper made for watercolour painting, which was used both for the negative and the positive. Deflected light bounced from the mirror; the paper showed a natural white between the areas of dark chemical print, a paper light that could be looked at, which shifted slightly where the image was caught and distorted by the paper fibres. In effect, its warmth and slight visual confusion gave the calotype photograph an unfixed life.

Hill's first interest in the medium and technology of the calotype sprang from an almost immediate recognition of its possibilities, based on his own education and interest in art. The 'resemblance' Hill identified lay between watercolour, aquatint, mezzotint and the lithograph, in important work ranging from Rembrandt, Claude's *Liber Veritatis*, the late eighteenth-century portrait mezzotints and the engravings of Turner's *Liber Studiorum*.

The practice of the contemporary Sketching Society, which included Clarkson Stanfield[145] among its members, is of particular interest in this connection. The Society met in the evenings and spent two hours drawing, using sepia ink, umber, burnt sienna, India ink and lamp black on white paper. Monochrome, in this fairly loose sense of variations of a colour combined with black, resembles the chemically reactive monochrome of the calotype. This manner of sketching is well-illustrated by the work of the skilful amateur, John Harden, who encountered Hill and Adamson's calotypes in November 1843. His interest in the photographs led him to transcribe them in terms of watercolour paint and the surprisingly successful results are a good illustration of the resemblance between the two media (fig. 31).[146]

Monochrome could be used for abstraction and generalisation. The remarkable character of Hill and Adamson's calotypes is due to the recognition of the potential strength in monochrome expressed in massed and concentrated light and shade, which could give even a small picture great force. It should not be supposed that Hill and Adamson simply discovered this effect. Adamson's control of a notably fickle process was extraordinary—according to Hill, he was *'the most successful manipulator the art has yet seen ... Adamson says the manipulation is very liable to go wrong in the hands of most people—that tho' several have now and then produced a good specimen—they find it difficult to succeed often.'* [147] The photographs he produced with Hill are distinct in character from those printed, for example, by Nicolaas Henneman for William Henry Fox Talbot. They are normally richer in colour and coarser in focus and tonal range, which all enhance the sense of movement and light.

Hill's compositions favoured the coarser focus because the camera lenses they were using were still comparatively imperfect. The circle of the lens cast its focussed image within the paper rectangle as an oval shape, so that there was a sharp falling-off of focus between the centre and corners of the photograph. Technical logic persuaded most of the early photographers to stay in the centre of the paper, to ignore, or even to cut off, the unfocussed areas. Hill took his compositions up to the edge and even into the corners of the paper and regularly ignored the centre. This achieved a generality (avoiding the obvious contrast between focussed and unfocussed) and a sense of breadth and largeness which makes contemporary comparisons between Hill and Adamson's calotypes and full-scale oil paintings intelligible.

Less obviously, Hill achieved such effects through technological sophistication. Generalisation of the effect conceals its calculated accuracy and control. The cameras made by Thomas Davidson were highly regarded by the amateur photographer, the Rev Calvert Jones, and the professional, Antoine Claudet.[148] The camera they used most commonly is likely to have had at least three different lenses, whose variability is identifiable in the Newhaven calotypes. From the few dated Newhaven images, it seems likely that between 1843 and 1845 Hill and Adamson acquired a lens with a clearer focus for groups (compare plates 44 & 56). The speed of Davidson's lenses can be judged not just by the comparative liveliness of the portraits but also by the shadows. In a low raking light, shadows will move almost visibly. The portrait of the fishwife (fig. 32) is remarkable for its speed and accuracy in catching the shadow of her lace-edged cap falling on her cheek. A photograph such as the St Andrews Fishergate group (plate 15) is a *tour de force* considered only in the capturing of the central shadow. To this must be added the calculation of the setting, the camera angle, the organisation of the women and children so that each figure made its impact, and the exact relation of dark and light shapes. In organisation alone, the picture fore-shadows the film industry. It may be that the east wind dropped and the sun shone steadily on the day chosen and at the very time for the shadow. It is more likely not. Such a picture could easily have taken weeks to prepare and take, and stands as a marker for many other pictorial ideas which must have been frustrated.

In closer photographs, they were able to manipulate light, bouncing it from a painter's canvas, an open book or a mirror. Here also they broke the technical rules and sometimes faced the sun to put a silhouette of light around a group—as in the uncharacteristic pale magic of the fishwives in the lane (plate 43).

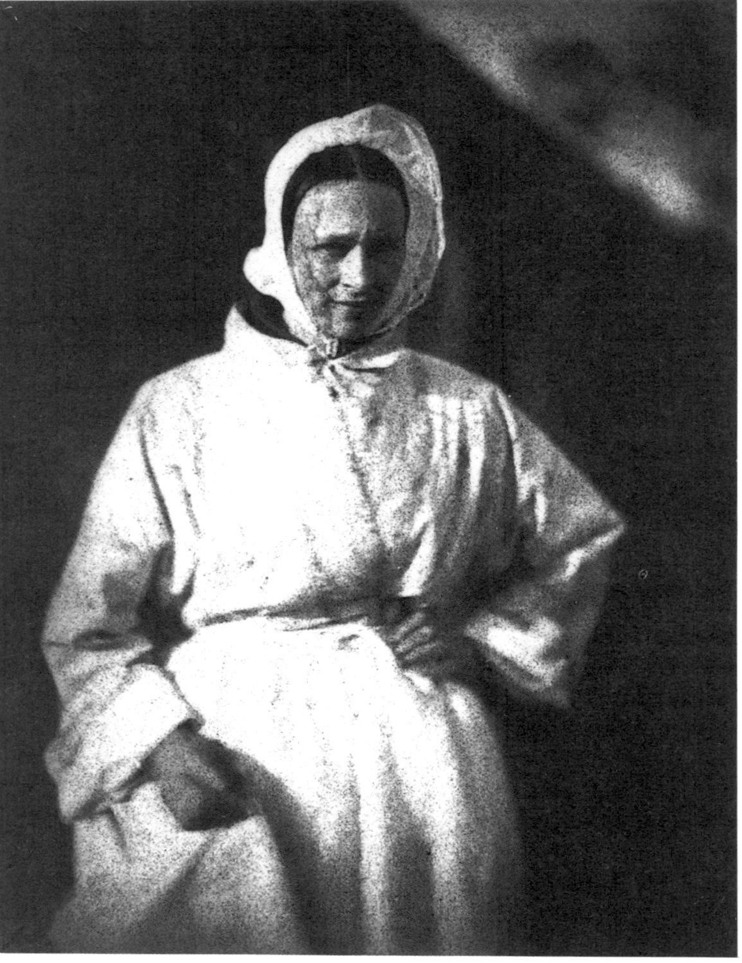

fig. 32
D. O. Hill and
Robert Adamson
Unknown fishwife with light casting a shadow of her lace cap across her face
modern print from original negative

The Purpose of the Calotypes

References to the commercial sale of the calotypes make evident that they were expensive. A special portrait session cost the sitter a guinea, individual prints were 7s 6d, or, if they were produced in quantity as part of the studio's commercial stock, 5s. The albums of 100 calotypes were to sell at 40 to 50 guineas. All this suggests that the photographs were designed for an élitist, wealthy market. This impression is reinforced by Hill's plan for selling albums in England, when he wrote to David Roberts: *'my ambition is to leave my name on a great and noble work worthy of England and of this* English *invention—and it has often appeared possible nay probable and most seemly that the Queen of England—and the leading nobles would patronise a work of this nature—a noble and worthy launch in the eyes of the Arts of Europe of a great English discovery* [this emphasis on the Englishness of the calotype is likely to be part of Hill's argument in attempting to persuade Talbot to allow them to market the calotypes south of the Border, where the patent ran]*—But the very excellence of the art exhibited in the Calotype is a bar to its popularity with the unlearned public—it is absolutely necessary to success, that means may be taken by those who have the power to get the scheme backed by the names of those entitled to lead in taste and in patronage.'* [149] Evidence of this kind may be taken to mean that Hill took the Newhaven calotypes to satisfy an upper class voyeurism. In actual practice, what it means is that Hill needed the patronage and support from people who were educated to understand originality in art and who could, in their turn, influence the taste of others (or, in a more cynical view, had the wealth and power to influence others). All the painters of the day, whatever their philosophy and however successful, were in the same position. Hill specifically refused to undertake the kind of photography which would make money alone: *'I think the art may be nobly applied—much money could be made of it as a means of cheap likeness making—but this my soul loathes, and if I do not succeed in doing something by it worthy of being mentioned by artists with honor—I will very likely soon have done with it.'* [150]

The calotypes were on public view on a number of occasions. They were on show in the Royal Scottish Academy exhibitions in 1844, 1845 and 1846; in 1844, they were to be seen in the town of Cupar in Fife, in Paris, at the Academie des Sciences, in York at the British Association meeting and at Mr Grundy's Repository of the Arts in Liverpool; in 1845, they were available for viewing with John Murray and at Colnaghi's gallery in London and were examined by the Graphic Society; early in 1848, they were the first objects for discussion at the first of a series of public conversaziones held by the Society of Antiquaries for Scotland; in 1850, they were again shown to the British Association; and in 1851, they were a part of the Great Exhibition in London. [151] From these examples alone, it follows that the calotypes were seen by a wide public audience and their potential influence was considerable.

Hill's ambitions had involved him in several proposals for broadening the base of support of art and for extending the education, both of the general public and of the artists themselves. He *'was all his life of a speculative turn, and was animated at the same time by a warm desire for the improvement of public taste... It is understood to have been through his influence that his brother, the late Alexander Hill, was induced to enter upon the print publishing business, through which so many fine and costly engravings have been placed at the disposal of the public.'* [152] Alexander Hill's activities as a publisher and seller of prints were crucial in the development and success of fine art engraving in Edinburgh; he also sold the calotypes in his gallery.

Hill was, at the time of the partnership with Robert Adamson, the Secretary of the Royal Scottish Academy, which meant, among other things, that he was heavily involved in the fight to secure the independence of the Academy from the interference of the Royal Institution and the Board of Manufactures, 'the self-appointed dispensers of other people's patronage.' [153] After that fight succeeded, he was himself appointed to the Board of Manufactures and was one of the people who fought for the building of the National Gallery of Scotland.

As Secretary, he was responsible for securing the loan of important pictures like Wilkie's *Distraining For Rent* and Turner's *Wreck of a Transport Ship* for the annual exhibitions so that they might be seen and studied in Scotland. His wholehearted enthusiasm for the idea of education is further shown by the cheap evening openings, mentioned above, which were his responsibilty. The serious intention of these openings was expressed by the anonymous introduction to the leaflet: *'already the galleries are nightly crowded ... by those pent up all day in the office, the warehouse, the shop, and the manufactory—these in many cases being accompanied by their wives, sisters, and young people, and being for the most part of those to whom a visit to a Pictorial Exhibition is evidently a delightful novelty... We are desirous, as much as in us lies, to further this movement towards promoting an understanding and a love of art among the people. It is not more to the honour and fame of Scotland, that she produced a Burns from the bosom of the people, than that they—the masses—know intimately, understand thoroughly, and feel and love intensely, the writings of their own poet. We would also have them know, feel, and love in an equal degree, the immortal works of one who may be truly said to be their own Painter—as great (shall we say greater?) in his art as Burns was in his ... In order to assist in the study of this and other works, those of our readers who might be liable to fall into the mistake that pictures are meant to gratify the eye without interest-*

ing the mind or the affections, we extract from a contemporary (the "Witness") a lengthened essay on the work above alluded to ... There are many other works on the walls of kindred and varied excellence—we say to the visitors, study them—read them—in a spirit akin to that exhibited in the following remarks...' [154]

These activities are forceful evidence that Hill did not regard the production of art as a simple transaction between the artist and the patron. A picture was not painted just to decorate a nobleman's wall; a photograph was not taken for the idle curiosity or passing pleasure of a few individuals. The idea was moral: *'The contemplation of that which is beautiful and harmonious begets a disposition of mind harmonious and congenially alive to excellency,—a disposition which may be so cultivated as to grow into a habit. By a more positive re-action, the continued familiarity with the aspect of dignity and grace tends to produce, through outward imitation, similar qualities. And those two processes set a third in motion: the mind, which is familiarized with excellence and harmony, acquires a keener perception of what is discordant and base, and revolts the more from it.'* [155] Contemplation, living with and 'learning' a picture made it an active object which would, if sufficiently profound in character, influence people's lives for good. D. O. Hill wrote, *'I think you will find that the calotypes like* [...] *pictures, will be always giving out new lights of themselves, and thus by showing themselves* [?gentlemen] *of varied qualifications and requirements* [continuing] *to be agreeable companions in a house.'* [156]

When Hill first entered into partnership with Adamson, he was interested in the idea of using photography for book illustration. He may have prompted Hugh Miller's review of the calotype work in July 1843, which proposed it as, *'a new mode of design for the purposes of the engraver, especially for all the illustrations of books. For a large class of works the labours of the artist bid fair to be restricted to the composition of tableaux vivants.'* [157] The proposal for the set of six albums on particular subjects, which included the fishermen and women is, of course, part of this intention. This was a design to bring the photographs, or engravings after the photographs, into a more general public view.

Hill also initiated what may have been the first photographic library, in the Royal Scottish Academy. In 1852, he wrote to David Roberts of *'a project of mine to form a Calotype department of the Library of which I have formed the basis with 500 of my own. I think I have influence enough with not a few of the Calotypists to get copies of their best.'* [158] By 1853, the Academy reported that they had received *'a variety of interesting and valuable accessions ... The Council are desirous to assure Photographers, that by making the Academy Library a central depot of copies of their more esteemed productions in Sun-Painting, they will thereby render an acceptable service to Art—the principles of which, in return, if understood and applied by adepts in their Photographic processes, may be made to communicate a high pictorial value to their productions.'* [159] This was part of a more distinctly professional purpose—the practical use and education of the artists themselves.

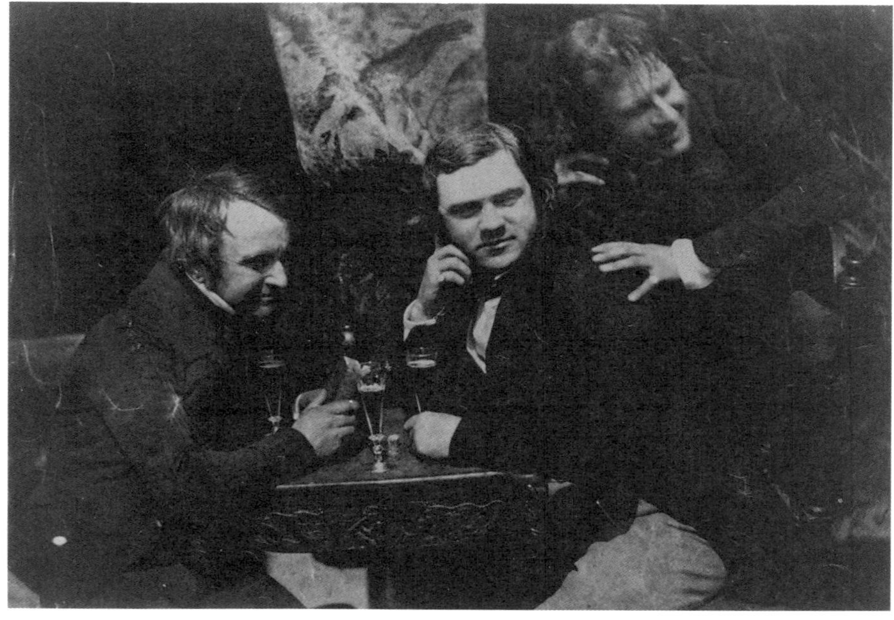

fig. 33
D. O. Hill and Robert Adamson
James Ballantine, George Bell and Hill
calotype
Scottish National Portrait Gallery

The Calotypes and the Artists' Study of Nature

When D. O. Hill first came to Edinburgh in the 1820s, one of the most startling sights of the city was to be found in the graveyards where the new graves were locked and barred. This bizarre precaution arose from the scientific study of nature. The city's surgeons, learning and teaching from anatomical dissection of the human body, found that the common abhorrence to the idea made it difficult to acquire suitable bodies, and some turned to paying for the 'resurrection' of recent burials. The scandal that followed when the criminals, Burke and Hare, committed murder to sell the bodies of their victims is a black illustration of the driving interest in actuality.

The study of the human body was crucial to the arts, where the 'history picture'—a picture of human life at a high pitch of heroism or ideality—was the peak of ambition. The development of art education in Britain depended substantially upon the gathering of models—in Edinburgh, for example, the collection of plaster casts of classical antiquities, stored in the Royal Institution, which also housed the Royal Scottish Academy in the 1840s. That these had a powerful effect and lay in the foreground rather than in the back of people's minds, may be seen in John Brown's reference to the calotypes of the fishwives: *'and these clean, sonsy, caller, comely, substantial fishwives,—what a refreshing sight! As easy, as unconfined, as deep-bosomed and ample, as any Grecian matron. Indeed, we have often been struck, when seeing them sitting together round their oyster creels, with their likeness to those awful and majestic women, the Fates of the Elgin Marbles, the casts of which are in the Gallery of the Royal Institution.'* [160]

The direct study of the human figure was of equal concern, but more difficult to achieve. D. O. Hill applied for permission to re-enter the Trustees Academy in the evenings during the 1830s in order to practise figure drawing under the genre painter, Sir William Allan, but it was not until 1839 that a life class was set up in Edinburgh. The consequence of this must have been that the Scottish painters of Hill's generation were effectively thrown back on nature if they wished to draw the human figure from the life. The 'nature' they used was often themselves. David Wilkie used to dress up as different characters and assume expressions so as to examine them in a mirror. The number of self-portraits among the calotypes is a guide, not to Hill's vanity, but to his interest in experiment—the calotype acting as an extension into art of the mirror. There is here, as elsewhere, a parallel with Rembrandt's practice.

This habit encouraged a theatrical tendency among the genre painters, who were all the more ready to dress up and assume different characters. The strangest extension of this idea, much enjoyed by Wilkie, was the 'tableau'—usually the re-creating of a famous picture by people dressed up and posed who were able to stand in stillness for a matter of seconds. Tableaux were surprisingly elaborate in their construction for so short an effect—the first that Wilkie ever saw, in a theatre in Dresden, was an interior after Teniers, which he described as 'the most beautiful reality I ever saw ... but so evanescent is the group, that the curtain drops in twenty seconds, the people being unable to remain for any longer period in one precise position.' [160]

It is understandable that Wilkie himself, whose natural, expressive groups were the end result of considerable and laborious work, should find this frozen acting particularly fascinating—even the possibility of studying a large group in costume, posed and properly lit for twenty seconds was a remarkable luxury. It is equally reasonable that any of the artists interested in the construction and study of groups were happy to design and pose for such tableaux. As a result, the Scottish artists and a few of Hill's other friends and family had the experience to hold a broad range of poses—even holding expression (fig. 33)—which enabled Hill to take apparently spontaneous pictures. Even in these groups, the figures were supported by stands and clamps or by tables, chairs, piles of books. With the inexperienced sitters, Hill was presented with a greater problem—to keep a group looking natural while it was being constructed and to make the supports hold the individuals comfortably in position. That he succeeded in doing this with the fishermen and women is a considerable tribute to his skill as a kind of human architect. Whilst the individual portraits may have more power and a more consistent success, the group photographs may be considered as a more extraordinary experiment, which has no parallel in contemporary photography.

It is probable that Hill also felt that photography offered a solution to anxieties about the effects of formal teaching on art. In 1835, James Nasmyth had written Hill a letter responding to a pamphlet Hill had sent him which proposed a national academy. In Nasmyth's opinion, academies tended to *'cultivate potatoes under hot beds and so produce a mob of mediocrity. I do think that there is such a native elasticity in true genius that it will by its own efforts leap over all stumbling blocks and by making nature and not art its model for the most part ... Nature is the real Academy.'* [162] Hill himself had more respect for formal education but he would have shared the anxiety about the students' confinement to studying earlier masters by copying engravings or plaster casts, which could lead solely to facile competence or to mannerism. Nasmyth's dislike of mannerism focussed on *'Fewseli, Courbould, M'Angelo, or Stothard ... the disgusting pedantry of showing forth the mean knowledge of the position of a few muscles and by mistaking the means for the end and giving us skinned men placed in attitudes to show off the artist's knowledge of anatomy in place of telling the story of the picture ... give me your Rembrandt ... and they may walk off with all the skinned men as have such muscles as shine through the dress be it ever so thick. I am really not up to that mark of the sublime yet.'* [163]

This was an attack on mannerism, but also related to the academic emphasis on life study from the nude. By analysing the structure of muscles rather than surface appearance and by working towards a classical idea of perfection, artists painting in the academic tradition deliberately lost the sense of nature that comes from casual detail. An 'ideal' concept of a figure carrying a load is obviously distinct from a particular fishwife carrying a heavy creel. The way people wear clothes may come from the way they live or the way they work. Hill entered into partnership with Robert Adamson to use the calotype 'especially to the execution of large pictures representing diff[eren]t bodies & classes of individuals.' [164] An interest in such individuality would see such details as working costume or the actual stance adopted by Mrs Flucker when opening oysters (plate 37) as important in nature. The 'complete' idea of the fishing series carried with it a whole picture of the life in general terms, made artistically truthful and, indeed, educational in every detail from the play of light and shade to the intriguing way the stripes of the fishwives' petticoats folded and bent.

Hill's interest in the practical usefulness of photography was echoed by other artists. William Allan spent some time at Rock House in 1843 and arranged portraits of himself and John Harden. He may have asked Hill to take the calotypes of Mohun Lal for his own painting and the exotic costume groups could relate to his paintings of Circassians. George Harvey persuaded Hill and Adamson to take photographs in Greyfriars' Churchyard for a big moral painting set there. There are a number of paintings by other artists like John Watson Gordon and Charles Lees which used the calotypes as direct studies.

Inevitably it was Hill himself who made the most use of the photographs and his experience was not entirely happy. When he first embarked on the Disruption picture (fig. 3) at least one of his friends thought him 'a little crazy'. [165] He intended to spend three years in its painting and only finished it twenty years later. By 1846, he had doubled the picture in size and was still advertising for sitters to come and be calotyped and his original conception was altered and expanded by photography to the point where the project was in danger of becoming more than a little crazy. By photographing the ministers and supporters of the Free Church as individuals or as groups in which each individual was clearly recognisable, Hill presented himself with a nearly intractable problem—how to paint hundreds of portraits as a coherent composition. The final effect was satirised by the artist, Sam Bough, as 'potatoes all in a row.' [166] The reviews of the painting in 1864 have almost as much admiration of the labour involved—and indeed sympathy for Hill's sufferings—'heroic self-denial and continuous labour of a kind which few could give and which no-one unacquainted with the production of figure pictures of a more subordinate character could possibly imagine' [167]—as admiration of the painting itself. However, photography enabled Hill to paint the Free Church as an ideal of a church composed of equals. The resulting picture is not wholly satisfactory, but it is immensely ambitious and is arguably one of the most deliberately democratic paintings ever made.

Hill's experience in using photography for other paintings in the 1840s was more mixed. He is known to have employed photographs as studies in several paintings, including the posthumous portrait of Thomas Chalmers and his grandson, the paintings of the Ballochmyle railway viaduct and the picture of Edinburgh from the Castle (fig. 34). Others, like his painting of Durham Cathedral, may well have involved photography. Even with less ambitious pictures he did not find it easy to translate the calotypes into paint. In the case of the posthumous portrait of Chalmers, he lost the strength of the face and failed to catch the features of the boy with any conviction. Here the photograph was both very good and generalised in its focus. With unsuccessful photographs, he may have been less inhibited and it is certainly true that the paintings of Edinburgh and Ballochmyle, based on technically unsuccessful photographs, have an assurance lacking in the portrait of Chalmers. [168]

Hill was not alone in finding the photographs difficult to use as sketches. George Harvey declared of the Greyfriars' photographs that he 'had found them quite useless ... He had never yet been able to use photography in any way as an adjunct to his art.' [169] This may be a result of the excellence of the calotypes; they are so complete and satisfactory that translating them into paint merely lessened them.

But there is a more important consideration. Hill was cautious in what he said about photography as an art form because of the general doubt of its ability to express the ideal; he was more than sensitive to 'a few cold bucketings of ignorant criticism which my desire to foster and improve this handmaiden of Fine Art, has exposed me to.' [170] However, his over-riding enthusiasm breaks out visibly—the photographs themselves are not confined by a modest concept of handmaidenly usefulness—and his qualifying vocabulary is equally immodest; 'It is worthy of notice,' he said in the prospectus for the Disruption picture, 'that the Portraits made chiefly for this Picture ... were mainly the means of first raising the process to the rank of a Fine Art, or rather to that of one of its most magical and potent auxiliaries.' [171]

The truth of the calotypes was a truth of art, not a simple transcription of nature. Hill talked of the album he proposed of a hundred calotypes as 'a sort of Liber Studiorum in its way.'[172] The *Liber Studiorum* was J. M. W. Turner's series of engravings after his landscape paintings which were arranged to demonstrate the different kinds of landscape. They were finished art works of particular character—a result in themselves, not just a starting point. The photographs which Hill and Adamson took after the first few weeks of experiment were mostly of this kind—finished art works, not an elementary practical aid for painters but 'something worthy of being mentioned by artists with honor…' [173] This made them more difficult to use as sketches but meant that their general influence on art was liable to be more far-reaching. The number of artists and critics who were enthusiastic about the calotypes is a gauge to their effect: they included William Etty, Clarkson Stanfield, David Roberts, John Gibson, Elizabeth Rigby, William Dyce, James Drummond, Thomas Duncan and Anna Jamesone. The inflence on later photographers is clearly considerable. The line of inherited enthusiasm from Thomas Annan to James Craig Annan to Alfred Stieglitz in America carried their influence into the wider world.

John Harden spoke of the calotypes as having 'a sepia like drawing style of the most perfect truth—lovely & veritable.' [174] He saw them as part of a great advance in science and art. Both Hugh Miller and Elizabeth Rigby were fascinated by the truth of the calotypes in relation to painting. Hugh Miller's review in July 1843 was intrigued by the way they endorsed the painters of the past: *'In glancing over these photographic sketches, one cannot avoid being struck by the silent but impressive eulogium which nature pronounces through their agency, on the works of the more eminent masters.'* [175] In 1846, Elizabeth Rigby planted a discussion of Hill and Adamson's work in her review of books on modern German painting: *'the beautiful and wonderful Calotype drawings—so precious in every real artist's sight, not only for their own matchless truth of Nature, but as the triumphant proof of all to be most revered as truth in art. Every painter, high or low, to whom Nature has ever revealed herself, here finds his justification. Let Mr. Hill apply the Calotype instrument to a simple manly head in a commanding position, it creates a Sir Joshua,—give it an old face wrinkled with age, it returns us a Rembrandt,—summon three or four bare-legged urchins, we see Murillo's beggar boys,—place it before a group of Newhaven fishermen, we have Tenier's Dutch Boors or Ostade's Village Alehouse—or against a crumbling brick wall, and Peter Le Hooghe lies mezzotinted before us. Take it to tangled Sylvan landscapes, it presents us with a Hobbima, a Gainsborough, or even, what we had not sufficiently prized before, a Constable—give it fretted spires and leafy banks, distant towns and glittering streams, playful shadows and struggling lights, sunny storms and watery beams—and give it lastly, the very motes dancing in the air before them all—and the detractors of Turner lick the dust—the loftiest eulogy of Mr. Ruskin is justified. Every truth that art and genius has yet succeeded in seizing here finds its prototype; but what shall we conjure up in heaven or earth that shall produce a Dusseldorf picture? Nature disowns it.'* [176]

This extraordinary passage is specifically based on Hill and Adamson's photographs, so the powerful truth Elizabeth Rigby invokes is not in her mind as an inherent truth of photography. As one of Hill's most interested models, she must have been well aware that it was a constructed truth. While the praise may be seen as excessive it gives an insight into the way the calotypes helped to educate, to open people's eyes. It is of importance that she first 'saw' Constable with true appreciation through the truth of photography.

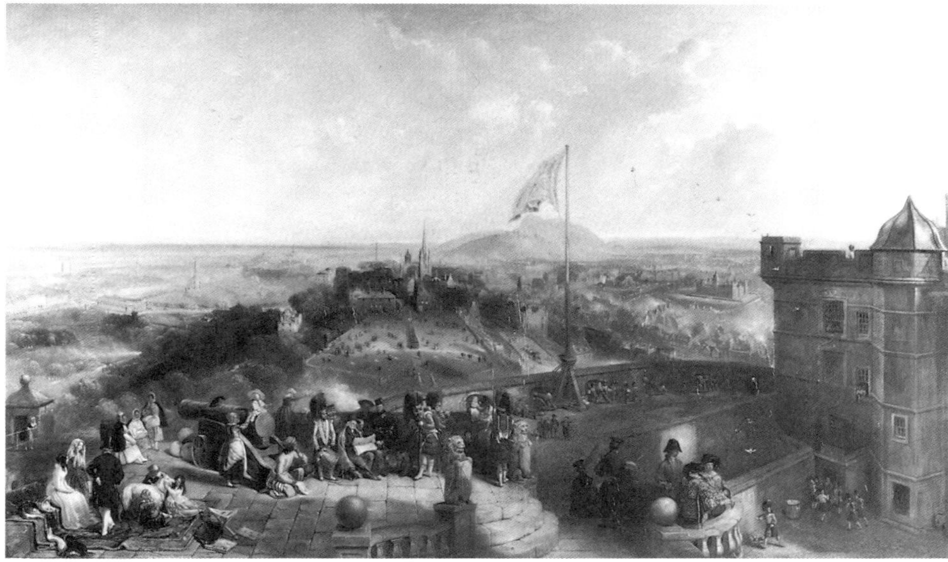

fig. 34
David Octavius Hill
Edinburgh, Old and New
oil painting
National Gallery of Scotland

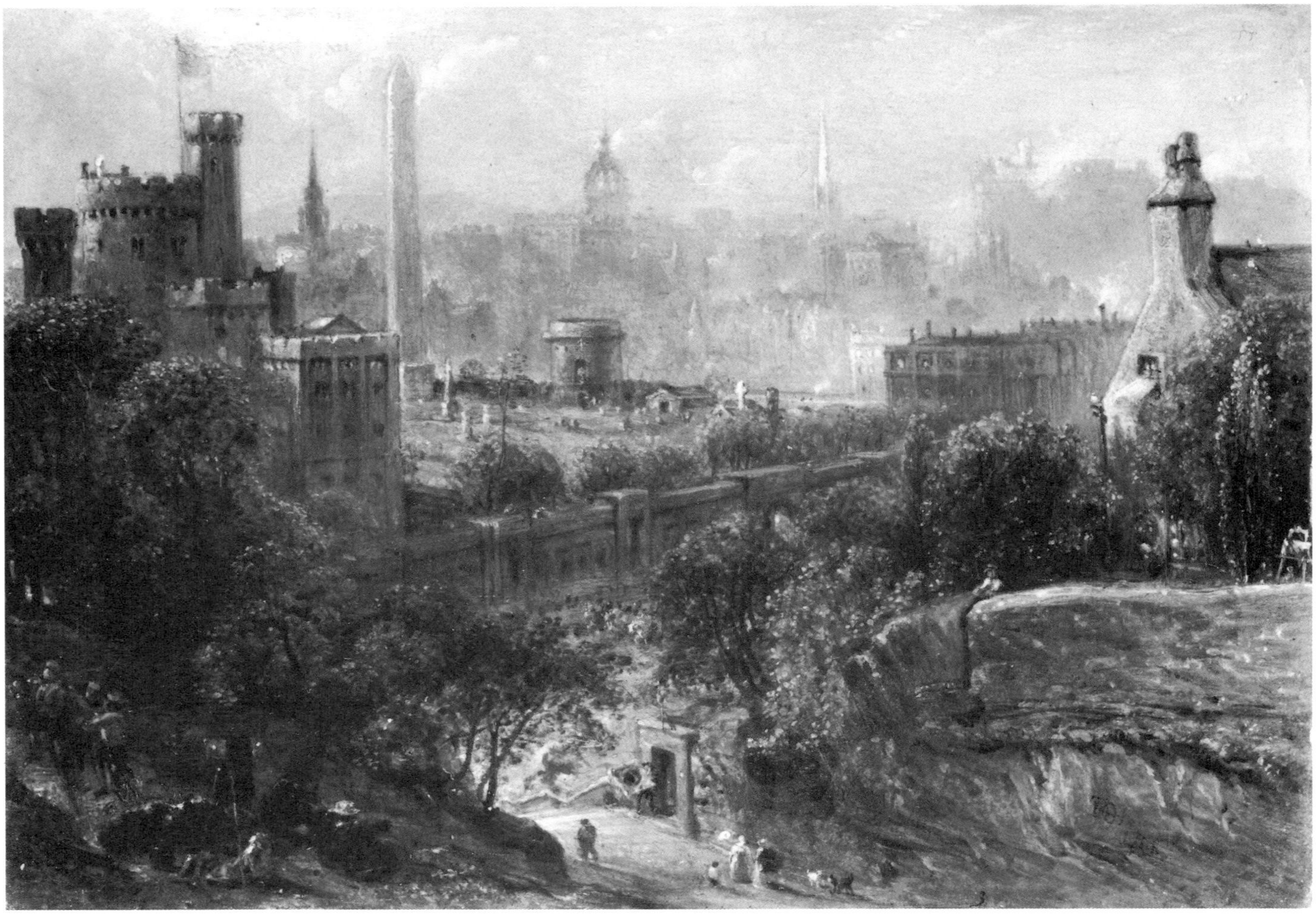

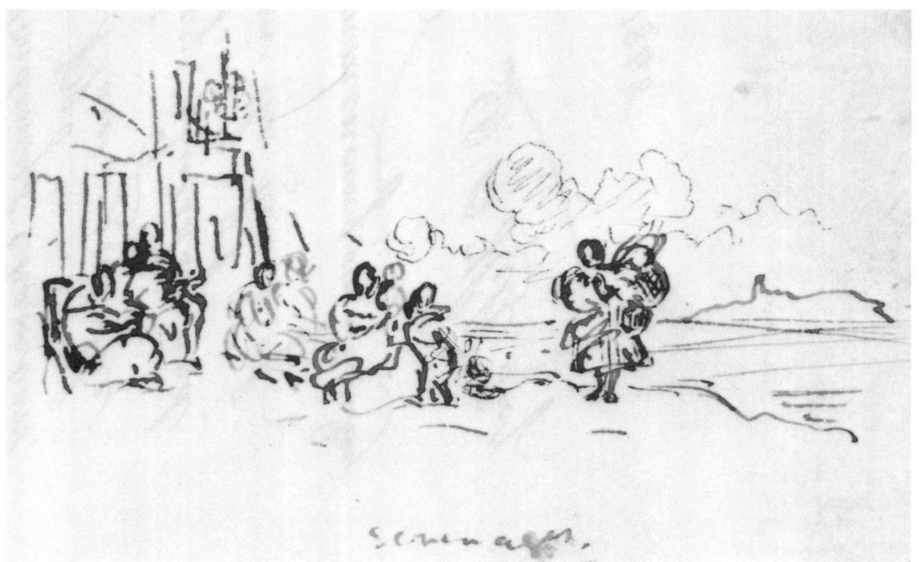

fig. 35
David Octavius Hill
In Memoriam: The Calton, 1862
Edinburgh City Art Centre

fig. 36
David Octavius Hill
Newhaven sketch: Seven Ages
ink drawing
National Gallery of Scotland

Afterthought

When D. O. Hill's only daughter, Charlotte, died at a sadly early age in 1862, he painted two small pictures for her husband. These two paintings were landscapes 'inscribed "In Memoriam" representing severally "The Calton" and "The Grange", successively the scenes of the happiness of a daughter now no more.' Hill was expressing his grief through landscape. The picture of Calton Hill (fig. 35) is painted from just above Rock House—on the right in the sunlit garden is Hill's easel with a painting, on the left on the dark slope of the hill is Robert Adamson's camera. The centre of the picture is occupied by the Calton burial ground where the sunlit monuments make crosses and obelisks of light pointing up to the pale misted line of the Royal Mile where the new spire of the Free Church and the old Tron spire flank the crown of the Cathedral. The painting is allegorical, using the real city to express life, death and the hope of resurrection, and the two pictures were reviewed in 1864 as 'perfect gems, gems of the opal kind with the colour and the fire, as it were, not laid upon the surface but all coming out from within. The "Calton" ... exemplifies the artist's manner at his best, and is peculiarly opalescent. Both pictures are gems into which—not merely as in many at which—we gaze, and could gaze for hours without wearying.'[177]

The prominence of the camera in 'The Calton' makes this a late tribute also to Hill's friend and partner, Robert Adamson. A month after Adamson's death in 1848, Hill exhibited two paintings in the Royal Scottish Academy's exhibition which were presumably based on the Newhaven calotypes. One, a large group called *The Boats in Sight* was not considered good by the critics; 'an over-crowded canvass, raw and inharmonious in colouring, and with a very laboured look.' The second was a single figure and, according to *The Scotsman*: *'a slight but very delightful piece of painting, managed with great skill and much natural truth.'*[178] The subject was 'The sands at sunrise—the accustomed look-out "to hail the bark that never can return."' Hill gave the last part of this title to the calotype of two fishwives (plate 42), in the album he gave to James Wilson, and this may have been the model for the picture. The *Edinburgh Evening Courant* review, published on 28 February, was more interested in the picture: *'Of the works which Mr. Hill has exhibited, we prefer the fisherwoman on the rock, although it may appear of less importance than some of the others. It is replete with sentiment and feeling. It is sketched with a freedom of touch and a delicacy of colouring that gives a fine effect to the dark dress relieved by the brilliancy of the sky. These are subjects well suited to the taste and feelings of this artist. He executes with the finest effect those subjects—such as the border tower or the ruined and lonely fortress—which afford objects for contemplation and sentiment, and appear congenial to the taste and the feeling of his mind.'*[179]

The two pictures were presumably devised with a general idea of contrasted happiness and sorrow, the sociable crowd greeting success and the fishwife's solitary vigil waiting for news of death. They were undoubtedly an expression of Hill's emotional involvement in the lives of the fishermen and women and have the same depth of meaning shown in a sketch of Newhaven entitled *Seven Ages* which Hill made in 1848 (fig. 36). But there is reason to suppose that the picture of the fishwife either was meant to be, or subsequently became, a tribute to Robert Adamson in Hill's mind. The link is not difficult to make. When Adamson returned to St Andrews late in 1847, he crossed the river Forth by the ferry from Newhaven; Hill is likely to have escorted him as a sick man at least so far and his last sight of him may well have been from the shore.

This is purely speculative. But between February and March, something caused the *Courant* reviewer to return to the painting and review it for a second time: *'It is replete with sentiment, and excites the sympathies in a high degree. This artist has a fund of sentiment and pathos, by which he imparts a peculiar character to scenes of loneliness and desolation. The figure of the lonely fisherwoman bidding a last adieu to her kindred embarking on the deep is touching in the extreme ...'*[180]

D. O. Hill's enthusiasm and admiration for Newhaven life can be measured by the number of the calotypes he and Adamson took and by the generous co-operation of their subjects. The additional possibility that his strength of feeling for that life can be measured by this 'slight' painting cannot be discounted; his interest was not a general, impersonal one, but loving, involved and expressing the general through the specific, feeling the particular through the general.

Notes and References

1 Lord Cockburn to William Empson, 22 November 1847, National Library of Scotland, Dep 235

2 See A. D. Morrison-Low, 'Dr John Adamson and Robert Adamson: An Early Partnership in Scottish Photography' *Photographic Collector*, vol 4 no 2, Autumn 1983, 198-214

3 In the Edinburgh Photographic Society's collection, now part of the national collection of photography in the Scottish National Portrait Gallery

4 Quoted in *Disruption Worthies. A Memorial of 1843*, Edinburgh, 1876, xvi

5 Advertisement in the *Witness*, 24 May 1843

6 Sir David Brewster to William Henry Fox Talbot, 3 July 1843, Science Museum MS.

7 Ibid.

8 Advertisement in the *Witness*, 8 July 1843

9 Hugh Miller 'The Calotype' *Witness*, 12 July 1843

10 D. O. Hill to David Roberts, 12 March 1845, private collection MS.. This letter, which is crucial to an understanding of the partnership, is quoted in full in John Ward and Sara Stevenson, *Printed Light. The Scientific Art of William Henry Fox Talbot and David Octavius Hill with Robert Adamson*, Edinburgh, 1986

11 James Good Tunny 'Early Reminiscences of Photography' *British Journal of Photography*, 12 November 1869, 545

12 James Nasmyth to D. O. Hill, 30 April 1845, Royal Scottish Observatory MS.. I am grateful to Larry Schaaf for drawing this correspondence to my attention

13 The Scottish National Portrait Gallery holds about 2,400 images. Additional images have been added to the collection since the publication of the catalogue

14 Nasmyth to Hill, 30 April 1845, Royal Scottish Observatory MS.

15 Brewster to Talbot, 18 November 1843, Science Museum MS.

16 Sir Thomas Dick Lauder (Secretary to the Board) to Hill and Adamson, 22 December 1843, Royal Scottish Academy MS.

17 Advertisement in the *Edinburgh Evening Courant*, 3 August 1844

18 Thomas Davidson, letter to the Editor, *Liverpool Photographic Journal*, October 1859, 264

19 The camera was invented by Alexander S Wolcot and patented in America 8 May 1840. For a diagram, see Robert Taft *Photography and the American Scene*, 1964 edition, New York, 26. Davidson described a mirror camera he had made in a paper to the Royal Scottish Society for the Arts on 11 January 1841, National Library of Scotland MS. Acc 4534/107. The mirror for Hill and Adamson's camera is now in the Royal Photographic Society's collection

20 See note 18

21 Quoted in H. Schwarz 'The Calotypes of D. O. Hill and Robert Adamson: some contemporary judgements' *Apollo*, February 1972, 124

22 Hill to Roberts, 25 February 1845, private collection MS.

23 Roberts to Hill, 9 November 1849, Royal Scottish Academy MS.

24 Hill to Roberts, 12 March 1845, private collection MS.

25 Charles Heath Wilson to Hill, April 1845, Royal Scottish Academy MS.

26 Hill to Roberts, 26 April 1845, private collection MS.

27 Hill to Roberts, 19 December 1845, private collection MS.

28 Elizabeth Rigby (later Lady Eastlake), review of books on modern German painting, *Quarterly Review*, March 1846, 337-8

29 John Murray to Talbot, 19 May 1846, Fox Talbot Museum MS.

30 *The Letters of Dr John Brown*, edited by his son and D. W. Forrest, London, 1907, 64

31 Hill to Roberts, 14 March 1845, private collection MS.

32 *Witness*, 22 April 1846

33 Advertisement in the *Witness*, 28 May 1846

34 See catalogue note 124, by David Harris, *The Photographs of David Octavius Hill and Robert Adamson*, (Saskatoon, exhibition catalogue) 1987 and S. Stevenson, 'David Octavius Hill and the Use of Photography as an Aid to Painting,' *History of Photography*, vol 15 no 1, Spring 1991, 47-59

35 Hill to Roberts, 12 August 1847, MS., current whereabouts unknown

36 Hill to Lady Ruthven, draft letter, Royal Scottish Academy MS.

37 Roberts to Hill, 9 November 1849, Royal Scottish Academy MS.

38 James Craig Annan, 'David Octavius Hill, RSA, 1802–1870,' *Camera Work*, July 1905, 17

39 John Brown, review of the Royal Scottish Academy exhibition, *Witness*, 22 April 1846

40 Frances Ann Kemble, *Record of a Girlhood*, London, vol 1 1878, 242-245

41 Captain John Washington, *Report on the loss of life, and damage caused to fishing boats on the East coast of Scotland, in the gale of 19 August, 1848. Parliamentary Papers: Accounts and Papers, vol 51* 1849, xx

42 Robert and William Chambers, *The Gazetteer of Scotland*, Edinburgh, vol 2, 1832, 812

43 Diary of James Gall, 17 July 1841, MS. National Library of Scotland Acc 5745(i)

44 Edgar March, *Sailing Drifters*, London, 1952, 226

45 Washington, op. cit., xx

46 *Witness*, 8 December 1847

47 Washington, op. cit., xx

48 Ibid.

49 Mrs George Cupples, *Newhaven. Its Origin and History*, Edinburgh, 1888, 20-21

50 See Claudia Kidwell, 'Short Gowns,' *Dress*, vol 4 1978, 30-61

51 *Memoirs and correspondence of Lady Eastlake*, edited by Charles Eastlake Smith, 1895, 92

52 Chambers, op. cit., 812

53 Quotation from *Chambers' Journal* in *Etchings Illustrative of Scottish Character and Scenery by the late Walter Geikie, R.S.A.*, 1841 (various authors), 12

54 Ibid., 48

55 Chambers, op. cit., 813

56 As note 53

57 Sir Walter Scott, *The Antiquary*

58 Cupples, op. cit., 49

59 Papers of the Society of Free Fishermen, regulations of the Society, 1817, Scottish Record Office MS., GD 265

60 Ibid., correspondence, 5 March 1845

61 As note 59

62 Gall, op. cit., 19 September 1840

63 Ibid., 17 July 1840

64 Ibid., 16 July 1845

65 Anon 'Dr. James Fairbairn, Newhaven,' *Calotypes by D. O. Hill and Robert Adamson*, (by Andrew Elliot, J M Gray and other writers), Edinburgh, 1928, 54

66 Ibid., 53

67 Chambers, op. cit., 813

68 *The New Statistical Account of Scotland*, Edinburgh and London, vol 1, 1845, 781

69 Charles Reade, *Christie Johnstone*, (1st published 1853), London, 1889, 57

70 Ibid., 56

71 George Croal, *Living Memories of an Octagenarian... from the years 1816 to 1845*, Edinburgh, 1894, 14

72 Geikie, op. cit., 44

73 'Noctes Ambrosianae' *The Works of Professor John Wilson*, edited by J F Ferrier, vol 1, Edinburgh and London, 1855, 250

74 William Pulteney Alison, *Observations on the Management of the Poor in Scotland*, Edinburgh and London, 1840, preface

75 *Journal of Henry Cockburn 1831-1854*, Edinburgh, 1874, vol II, 2

76 Proverbs, Chapter 6, verse 6

77 Captain Thomson, treasurer of the House of Refuge, quoted in Alison, op. cit., 7

78 Mrs Oliphant, *Thomas Chalmers*, London, 1896, 128

79 Dr George Bell, *Day and Night in the Wynds*, 1849

80 See Jack Simmons' opinion of Hill's lithographs, *Views of the Opening of the Glasgow and Garnkirk Railway*, *The Victorian Railway*, London, 1991, 127-8 and 148

81 Bell, op. cit., 78

82 Reade, op. cit., note, 330

83 Ibid., 202

84 Ibid.

85 *The Letters of John Stuart Blackie to his Wife*, edited by Archibald Stodart Walker, 1910, 169

86 *The Dictionary of National Biography*, London, vol xlii, 1895, 30

87 Rev David Hogg, *The Life of Allan Cunningham*, Dumfries, 1875, 2

88 James Hogg, 'On the changes in the habits, amusements and conditions of the Scottish peasantry,' (1st published in *Quarterly Journal of Agriculture*, vol III, February 1831- September 1832) reprinted in *A Shepherd's Delight. A James Hogg Anthology*, edited by Judy Steel, Edinburgh, 1985, 41

89 Ibid., 43

90 Ibid., 49

91 In the collection of the British Library

92 Brown, op. cit.

93 Obituary, *The Scotsman*, 17 May 1870

94 Brown, op. cit.

95 Hill to Roberts, 10 June 1850, John Paul Getty Museum MS., 84 x 91003

96 John Brown, review of volumes 1 and 2 of *Modern Painters*, *North British Review*, 1847, vol 6, 401

97 Quoted in J. G. Lockhart, *The Life of Sir Walter Scott, Bart*, London, 1893, 226

98 'Tribulations of the Rev. Cowal Kilmun,' (1st published 1835-6) *John Galt. Selected Short Stories*, edited by Ian A Gordon, Edinburgh, 1978, 101

99 D. O. Hill(?) *'The Plan and Argument of the Picture,' The Disruption of the Church of Scotland: An Historical Picture... Representing the Signing of the Deed of Demission... Painted by D. O. Hill, R.S.A., Edinburgh, 1866*, 17

100 *The Art Union*, June 1845, 171

101 H. P. Robinson, *Picture-Making by Photography*, London, 1897, 52

102 Joshua Reynolds, *Discourses Delivered to the Students of the Royal Academy*, (introduction by Roger Fry), London, 1905, 193-4

103 *The Diary of Joseph Farington*, edited by Kenneth Garlick and Angus MacIntyre, New Haven, vol v, 1979, 1631

104 Hill to Henry Bicknell, 17 January 1849 (wrongly dated by Hill, '1848,' but recognisably part of a later correspondence), MS. in the George Eastman House collection

105 David Brewster, 'Photogenic Drawing, or Drawing by the Agency of Light,' *Edinburgh Review*, 76, 1843, 327

106 Hill to Roberts, 25 February 1845, private collection MS.

107 Stanfield took his album of the calotypes to a meeting of the Graphic Society in 1847, reported in *The Athenaeum*, no.1017, 24 April 1847, 440. This is the crucial album in the Harry Ransom Humanities Research Center, University of Texas

108 Quoted in Daphne Foskett, *John Harden of Brathay Hall*, Kendal, 1974, 52

109 Hill to Roberts, 25 February 1845, private collection MS.

110 Reynolds, op. cit., 230

111 Charles Heath Wilson to Hill, April 1845, Royal Scottish Academy MS.

112 Charles Rogers, *A Collection Of Prints In Imitation Of Drawings To Which Are Annexed Lives Of Their Authors*, 1778, vol 2, 217

113 Ibid.

114 J. G. Lockhart, *Peter's Letters to his Kinsfolk*, (1st published in 1819), edited by William Ruddick, Edinburgh, 1977, 118

115 Brown, op. cit. note 37. The word 'facile' has a complimentary sense in this context.

116 Thomas Guthrie, *Speaking to the Heart or Sermons for the People*, London, 1862, 145

117 D. O. Hill, *The Land of Burns*, Glasgow, 1840. The text for these engravings after Hill's landcapes was otherwise written by John Wilson, who was understandably defeated by 'this somewhat bold capriccio.'

118 Lockhart, op. cit., 43

119 Brown, op. cit. note 37

120 *The Art Union*, June 1847, 231

121 Quoted in Lindsay Errington, *Tribute to Wilkie*, (Edinburgh, exhibition catalogue) 1985, 51

122 Lockhart, op. cit., 118

123 Errington, op. cit.

124 Leaflet published by the Royal Scottish Academy, 3 April 1846, in a collection of MS. relating to Hill, Edinburgh Central Library, C52527

125 Sir Walter Scott, *The Antiquary*

126 Lindsay Errington is of the opinion that Scott wrote *The Antiquary* after seeing

Distraining for Rent (unpublished article on 'Walter Scott and the Visual Arts'). I am grateful to Dr Errington for allowing me to quote this opinion.

127 Oliphant, op. cit., 61

128 Guthrie, op. cit., 2

129 Cockburn, op. cit., 31

130 Ibid., 174

131 Bell, op. cit.

132 See note 99, quoted from the *Daily Review*

133 David Wilkie to Clarkson Stanfield, January 1832, copy pasted to the back of the picture, *Distraining for Rent*, in the collection of the National Gallery of Scotland

134 Quoted on the cover, *Henri Cartier-Bresson. Photographer*, London, 1986

135 H. Cartier-Bresson, *The World of Henri Cartier-Bresson, London* ,1968, preface

136 Yves Bonnefoy, foreword, *Henri Cartier-Bresson, Photographer*, London, 1986, 6

137 Hill to Roberts, 14 March 1845, private collection MS.

138 Hill to Bicknell, see note 104

139 Elizabeth (Rigby) Eastlake, 'The Art of Dress,' *Music and The Art of Dress*, (essays reprinted from the *Quarterly Review*), 1852

140 P. H. Emerson, *Naturalistic Photography*, New York, 1899, book 3, 22-23

141 John Brown, review of the Royal Scottish Academy exhibition, *Witness*, 22 April 1846

142 David Brewster, review of the progress of photography, *North British Review*, 1847, vol 7, 479

143 See note 104

144 John Brown, referring to 'Claudet's best... A clever, leaden, flat miniature, with a background as hard and as blae as a slate,' 'Mr. Hill's Calotypes,' *Scotsman*, 10 February 1862

145 See *The Spectacular Career of Clarkson Stanfield 1793-1867*, Sunderland (exhibition catalogue), 1979

146 I am indebted to Joe Rock for drawing these to my attention.

147 Hill to Roberts, 12 March 1845, private collection MS.

148 See the correspondence between Calvert Jones and Talbot, in which he refers to 'two capital lenses by Davidson, which arrange themselves for all sizes of paper,' 29 May 1841 and 1 October 1845, manuscripts in the collection of Lacock Abbey, LA 41-34 and LA 45-133

149 Hill to Roberts, 12 March 1845, private collection MS.

150 Hill to Roberts, 14 March 1845, private collection MS.

151 The Cupar and Liverpool exhibitions were specifically of the Disruption calotypes, the others would all have included examples of the Newhaven pictures

152 D. O. Hill, obituary, *The Scotsman* 17 May 1870

153 R. S. Rintoul, 'Encouragement of Art in Scotland,' offprint from the *Spectator* belonging to Hill, in the collection of MS. relating to Hill in the Edinburgh Central Library C52527

154 As note 124

155 Rintoul, op. cit., 3

156 Hill to Bicknell, see note 104

157 Miller, op. cit.

158 Hill to Roberts, 18 November 1852, National Library of Scotland MS. Acc 7723

159 *26th Annual Report of the Royal Scottish Academy*, 1853

160 Brown, op. cit. note 32

161 Quoted in Allan Cunningham, *The Life of Sir David Wilkie*, 1843, vol 2, 333

162 Nasmyth to Hill, postmarked 'Aug 5 1835,' MS. in the collection of the Royal Observatory of Scotland

163 Ibid.

164 Brewster to Talbot, 3 July 1843, MS. in the collection of the Science Museum

165 See note 111

166 Sam Bough, quoted in Sidney Gilpin, *Sam Bough, R.S.A. Some account of his life and works*, 1905, 124

167 Sir George Harvey quoted in the prospectus, see note 99

168 See Stevenson, note 34

169 George Harvey, *British Journal of Photography*, 1863, 57

170 Hill to Roberts, 12 March 1845, private collection MS.

171 See note 99, 3

172 Hill to Roberts, 14 March 1845, private collection MS.

173 Ibid.

174 Quoted in Foskett, op. cit.,

175 Miller, op. cit.

176 Elizabeth Rigby, op. cit. note 28

177 J. B. Manson ('Euphranor'), *Contemporary Scottish Art. A Series of Pen and Ink Sketches Drawn from the Exhibition of 1864*, Edinburgh, 1864, 38

178 Review, *The Scotsman*, 29 March 1848

179 Review, *Edinburgh Evening Courant*, 28 February 1848

180 Review, *Edinburgh Evening Courant*, 27 March 1848

THE FISHERMEN AND WOMEN OF THE FIRTH OF FORTH

Note on the Plates

Those of the fishing photographs taken in 1843, of which plate 43 is a known example, may have been taken with a different intention to those taken after the announcement of the publication in 1844. This example is generalised in character and shows an interest in grouping, light and shadow, which suggest that Hill was, in the first instance, thinking in practical terms as a painter and using the camera as an instrument for 'sketching'. A photograph which can be dated to 1845, plate 46, is, by contrast, not merely clearer in focus but more specific in its intention—to show the village's religious life—and it is also specifically identified—we know who the people are. Both in its character and idea, it shows a greater involvement between the photographers and their subjects. It is, therefore, not unreasonable to suppose that Hill's idea of photographing the life and culture of the village was developed in 1844, after the first year's experiments.

There is no consistent indication in the placing of the fishing photographs in contemporary albums of the order in which Hill and Adamson would have published them in *The Fishermen and Women of the Firth of Forth.* The arrangement of the photographs made here is a proposal based on a general plan of place, working life, domestic and cultural life, which underlies the more sophisticated character of the individual calotypes. The choice, from about 130 images, is personal and partly dependent on the quality of the original prints (the photograph of Mrs Flucker selling fish to a housewife, fig 15, is clearly important to any 'story line' which runs through the sequence, but we have only a poor carbon print of that image). By printing from negatives Hill and Adamson would have regarded as failures, we have aimed to give a better view of their ambitions for the project—both philosophical and aesthetic.

The plates are reproduced actual size (plate 16 was taken with the smaller camera which was little used after 1843), with the exception of plate 40 which is reduced in size from 300 x 224 mm. The original calotypes copied for this publication come from the Scottish National Portrait Gallery; The Photography Department of the Harry Ransom Humanities Research Center, The University of Texas at Austin (Gernsheim collection); Mrs Eleanor Robertson; and Mrs Peggy Notman. The new calotypes have been made by Michael and Barbara Gray from negatives in the Edinburgh Photographic Society's gift and from additional negatives in the Glasgow University Library, Special Collections (Dougan collection). Additional titles have also been taken from the albums which belonged to John Scott (National Library of Scotland), James Wilson (British Library) and the Royal Academy (National Portrait Gallery, London).

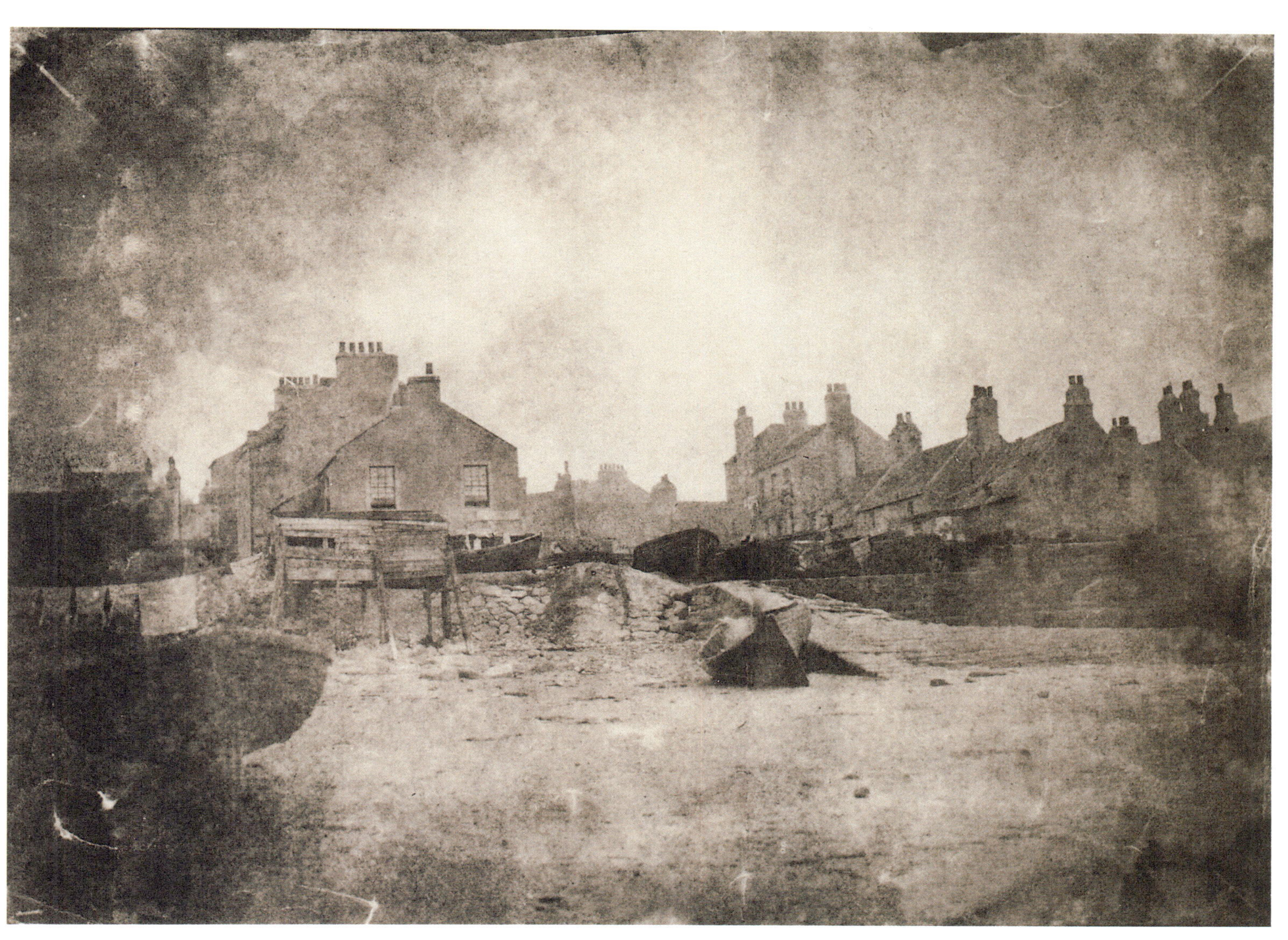

1

Newhaven Seen from the Beach

Modern print from Edinburgh Photographic Society negative inscribed: 'D300 ½ last / 95'

PGPEPS 78

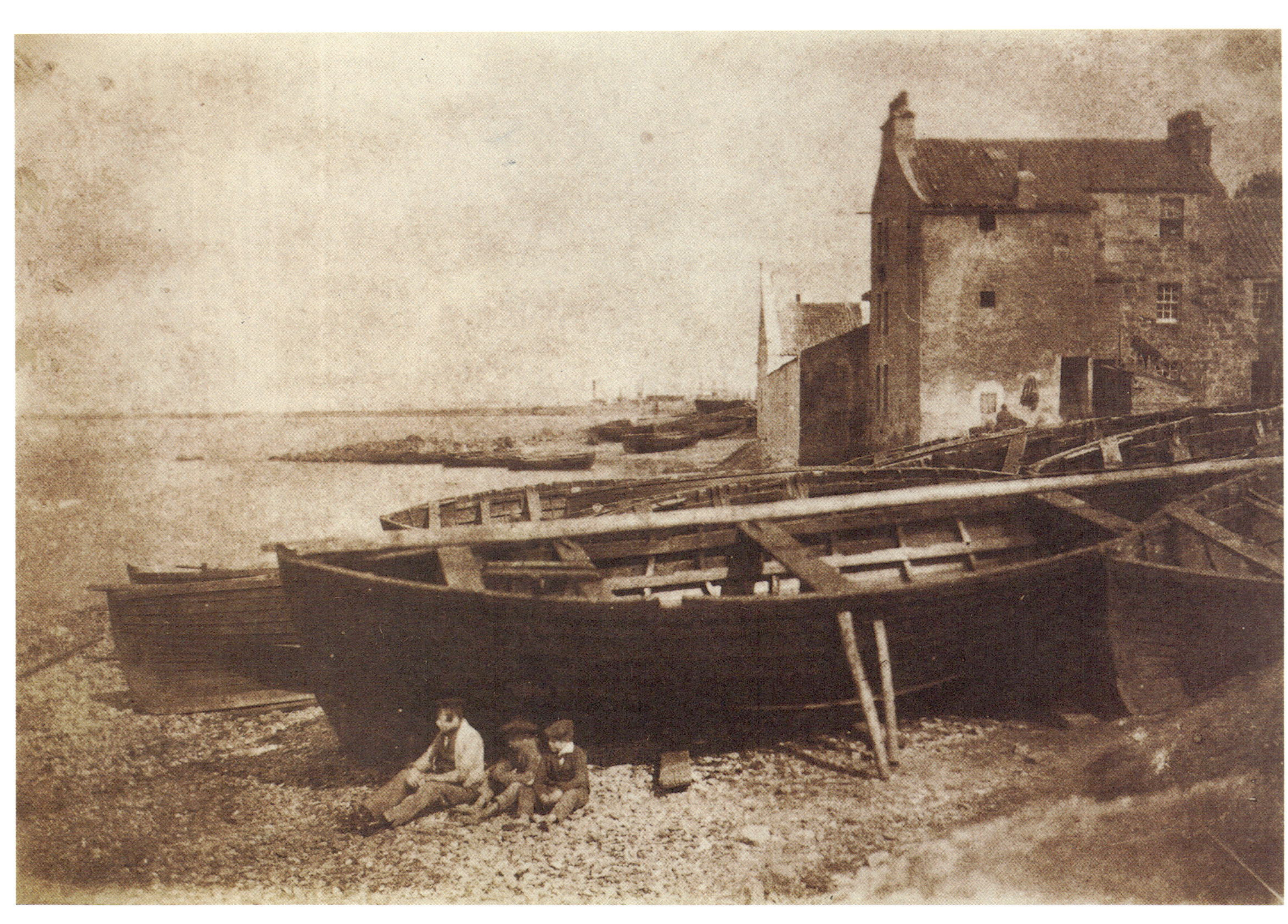

2

View along Newhaven Beach

Scottish National Portrait Gallery, J. Irvine Smith Album

PGPHA 314

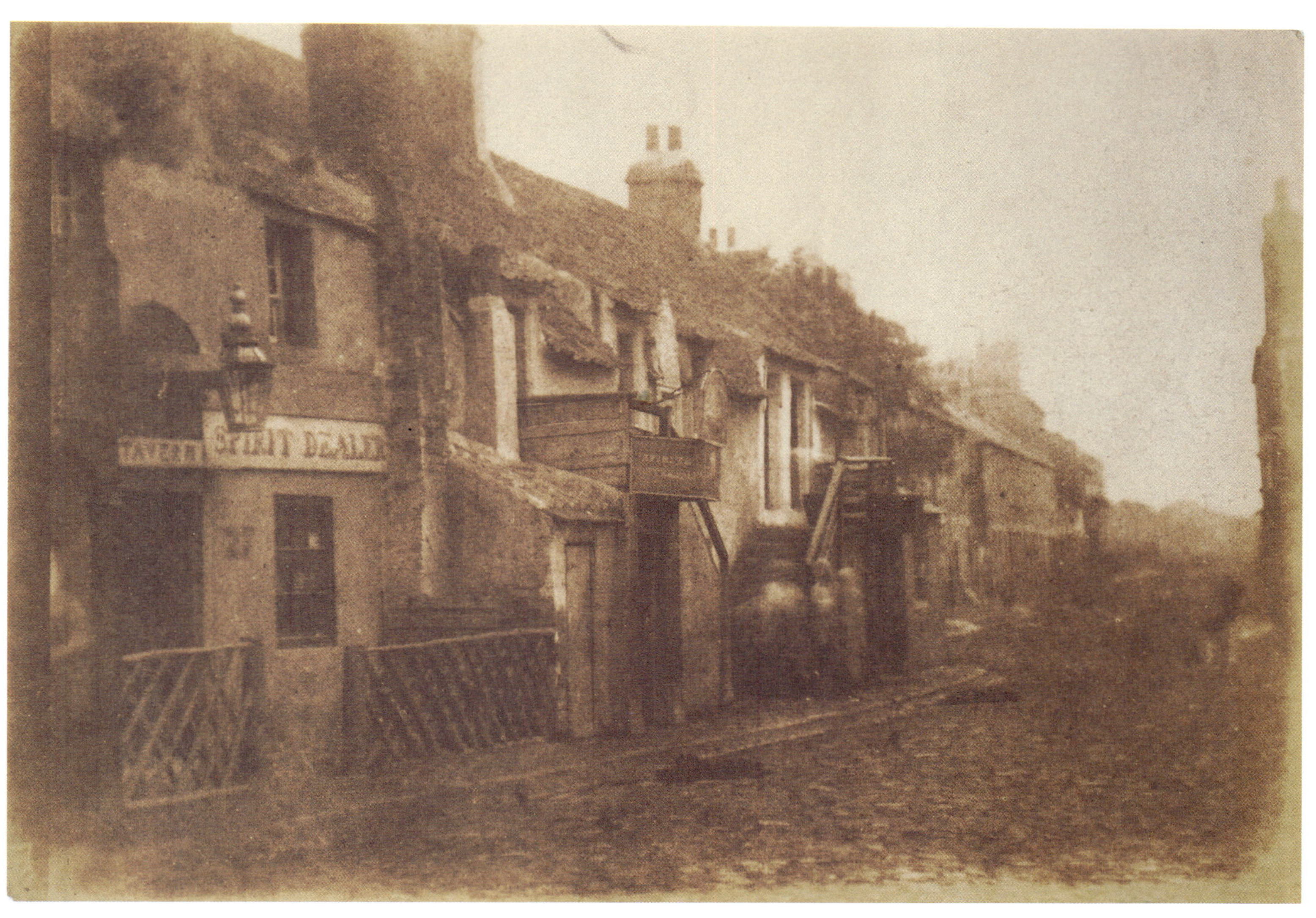

3

Newhaven Street

Scottish National Portrait Gallery
PGPHA 312

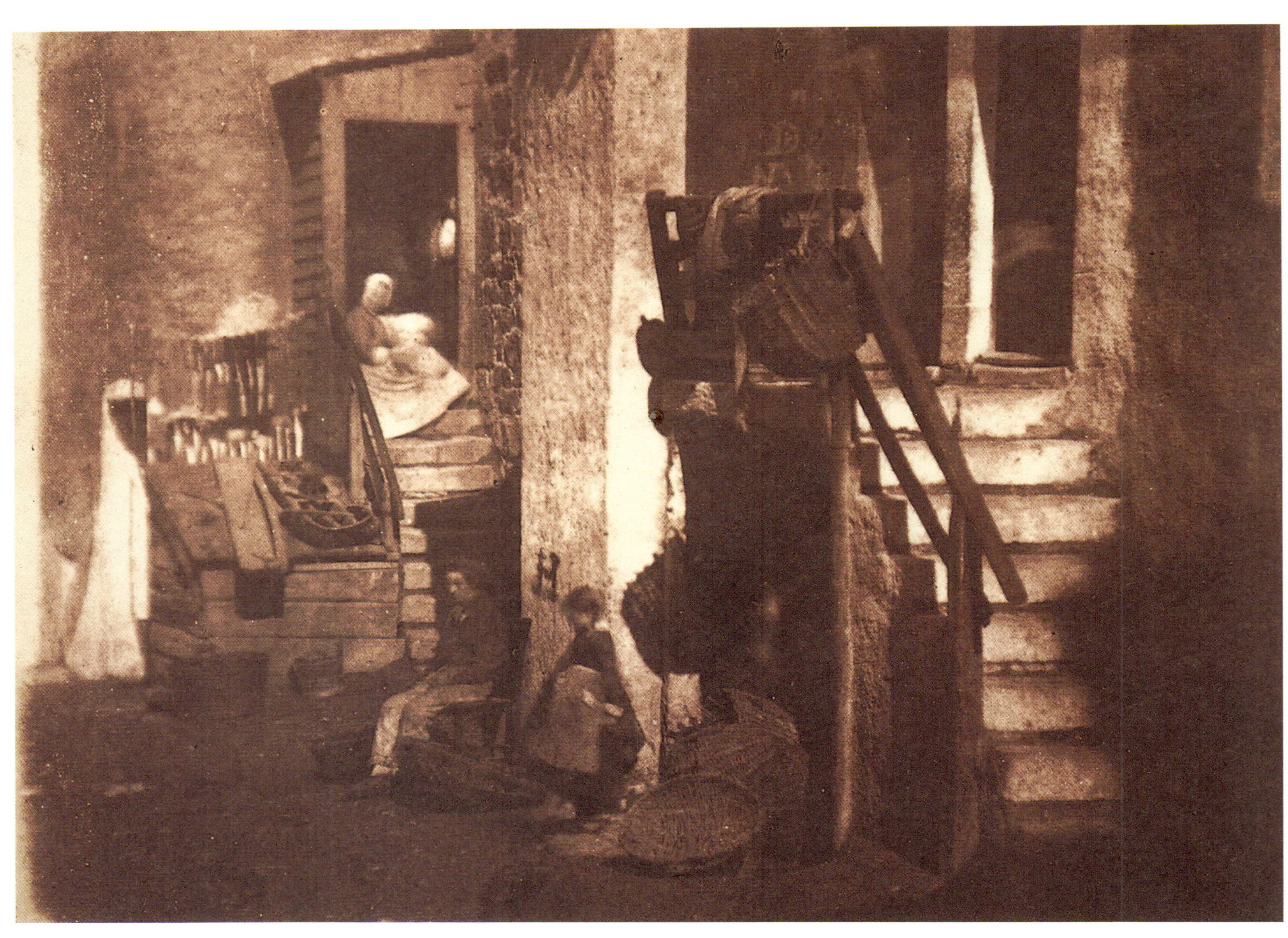

4

'Outside Stairs in the Fishing Village of Newhaven'

Harry Ransom Humanities Research Center, Clarkson Stanfield Album 092

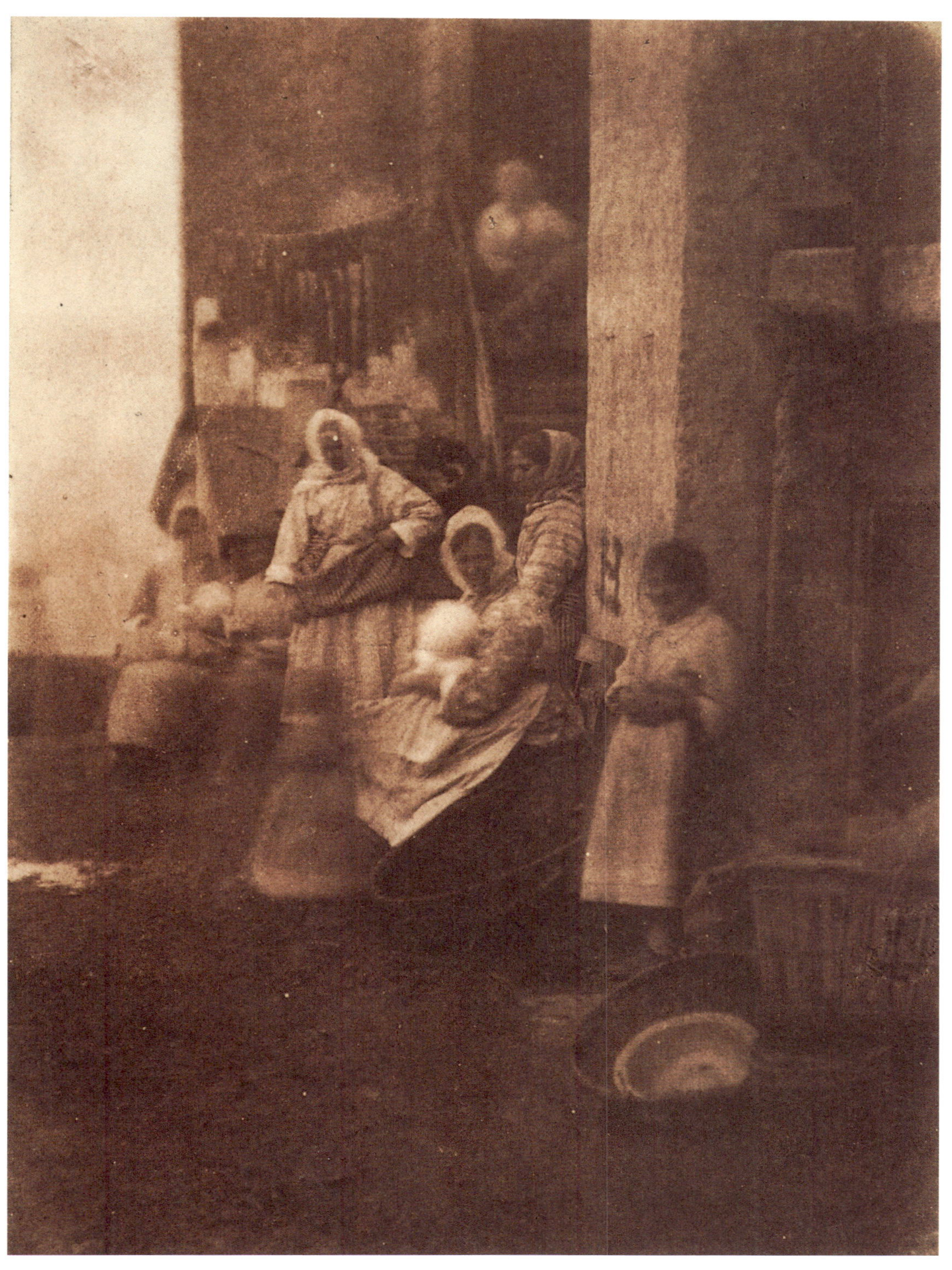

5

Newhaven Houses, 'The Fishing Village'

Harry Ransom Humanities Research Center, Clarkson Stanfield Album 075

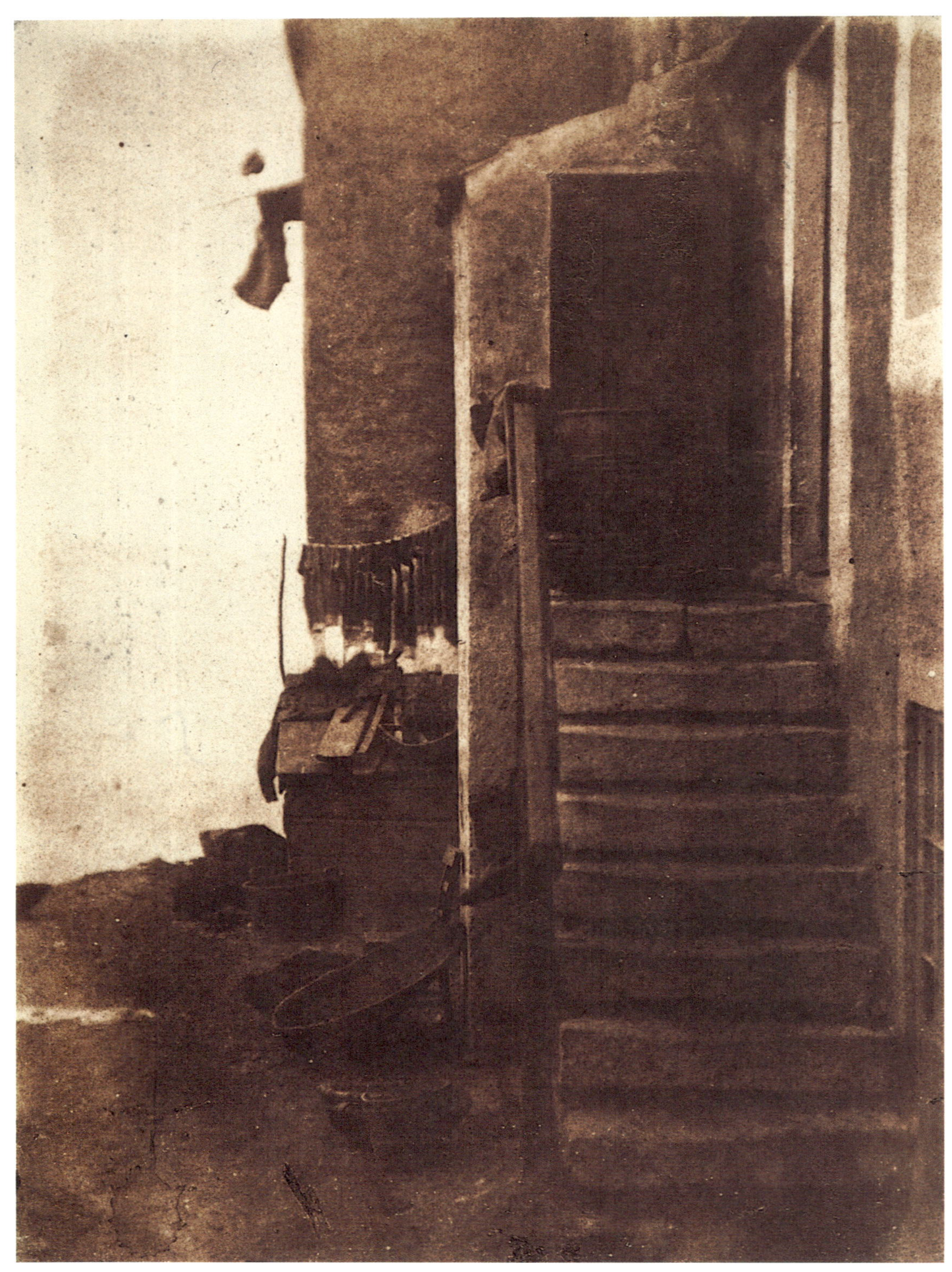

6

'An Outside Stair' Newhaven

Harry Ransom Humanities Research Center, Clarkson Stanfield Album 082

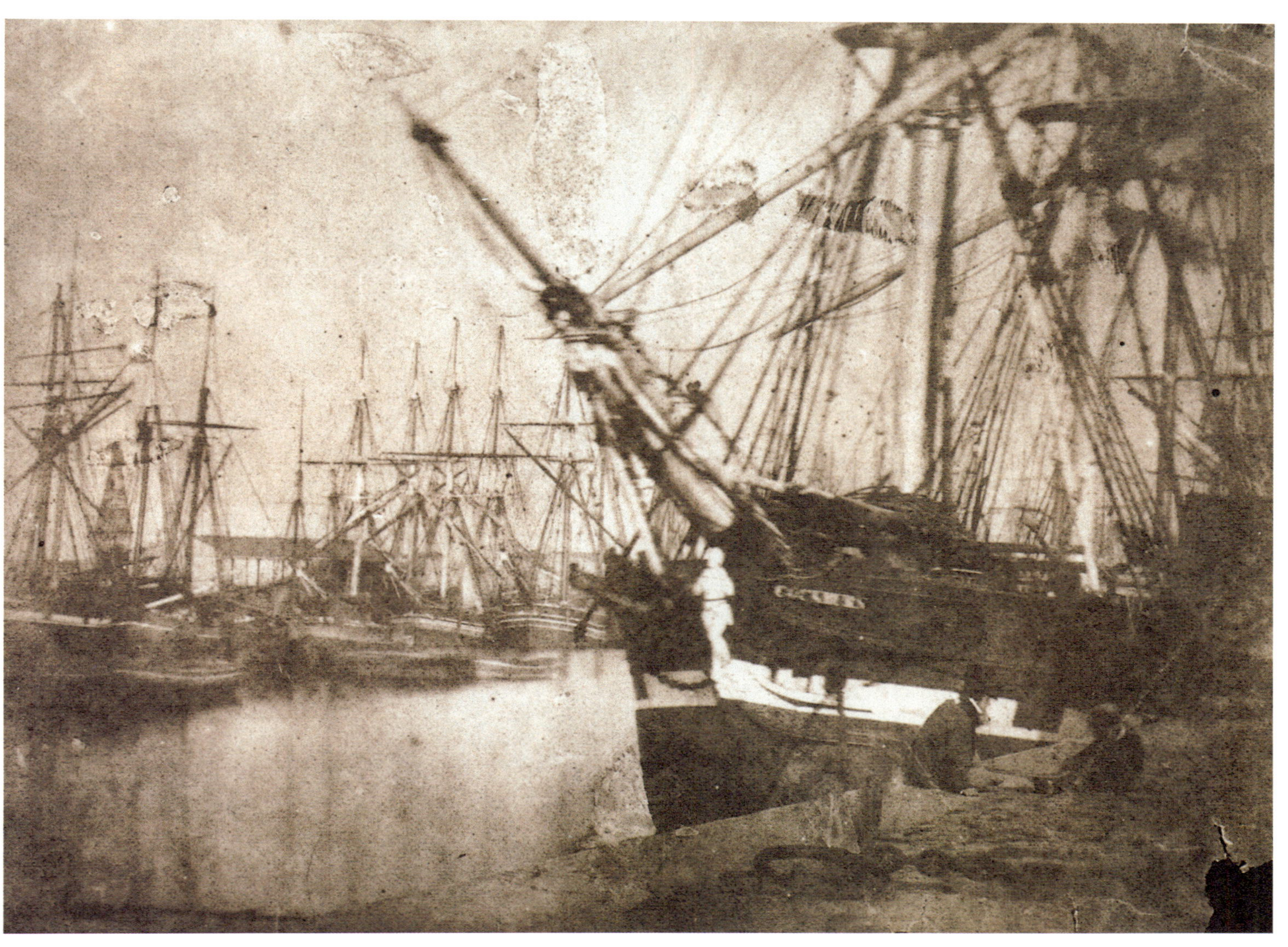

7

Ships in Leith Docks

Modern print from Glasgow University negative, Dougan Collection

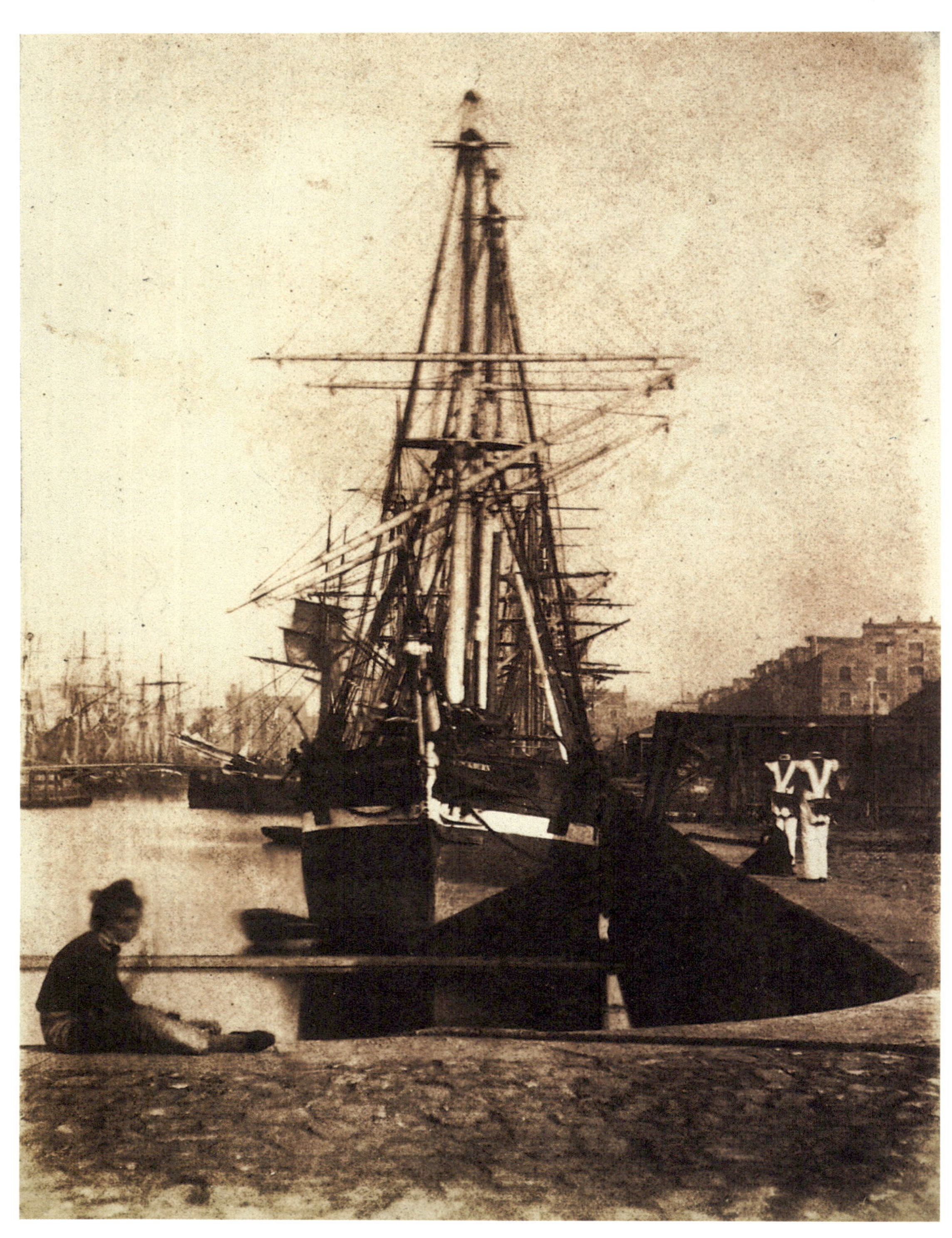

8

'Leith Docks'

Harry Ransom Humanities Research Center, Clarkson Stanfield Album 059

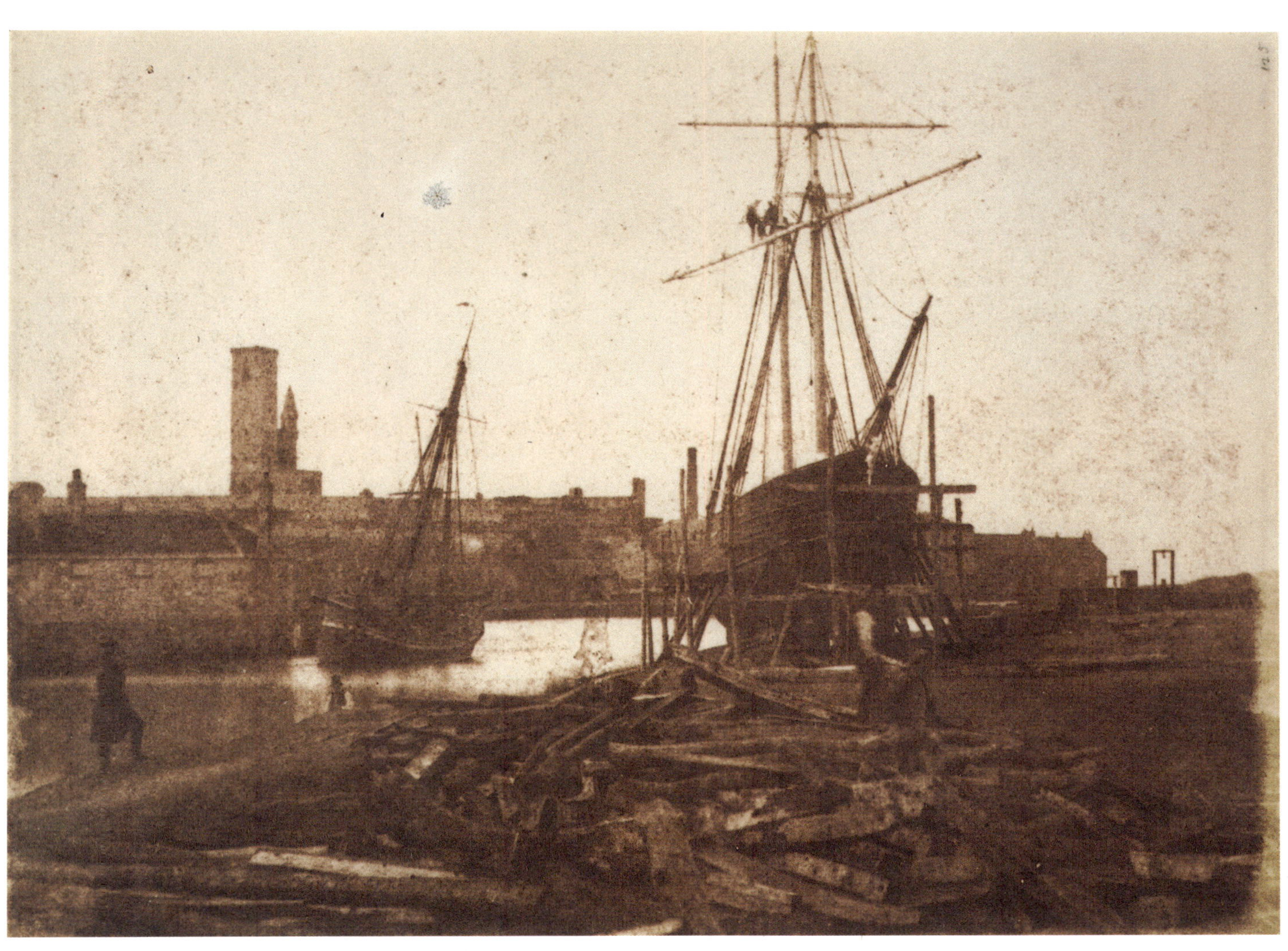

9
St Andrews Harbour
Scottish National Portrait Gallery
PGPHA 294

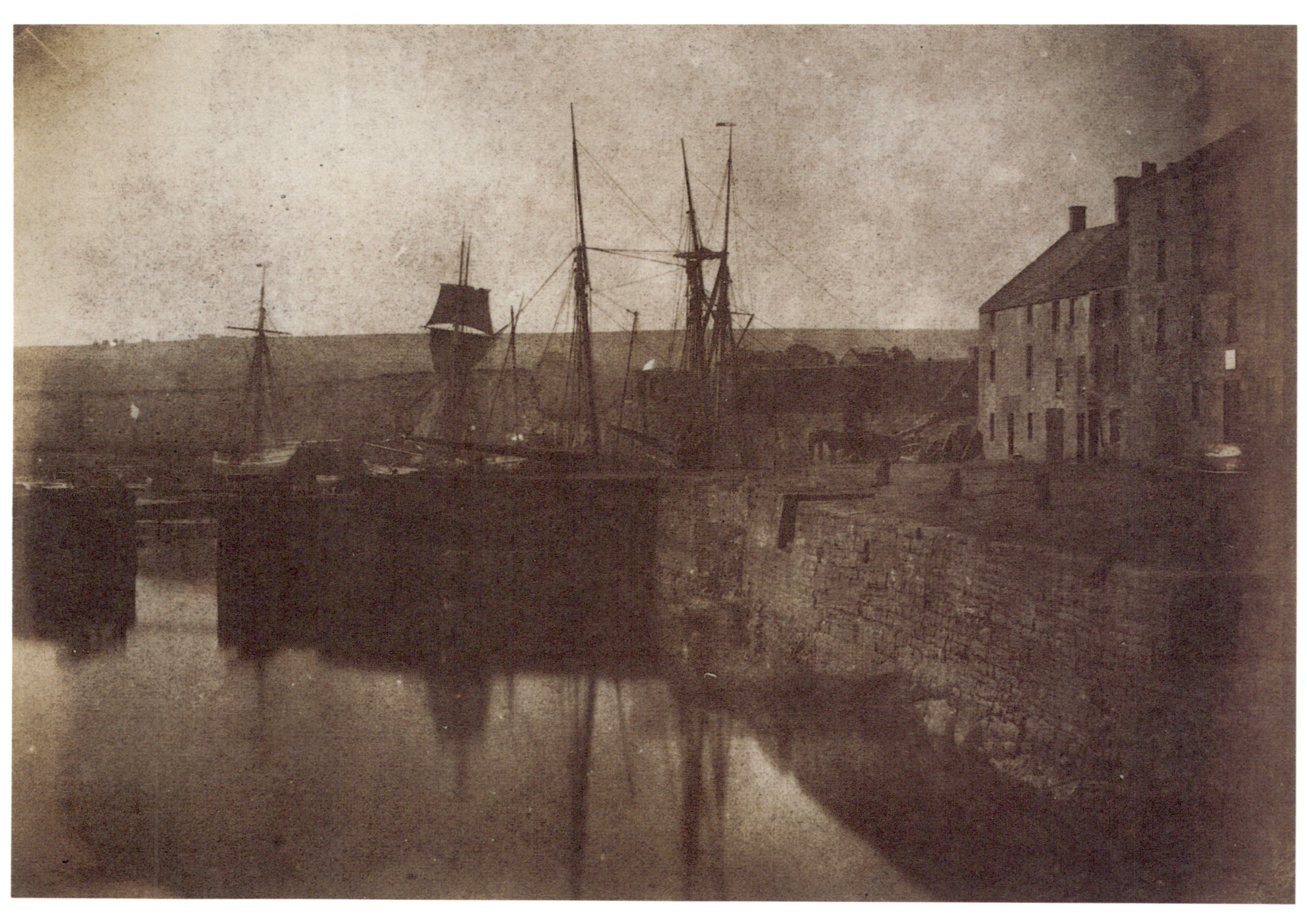

10

St Andrews Harbour

Scottish National Portrait Gallery
PGPHA 296

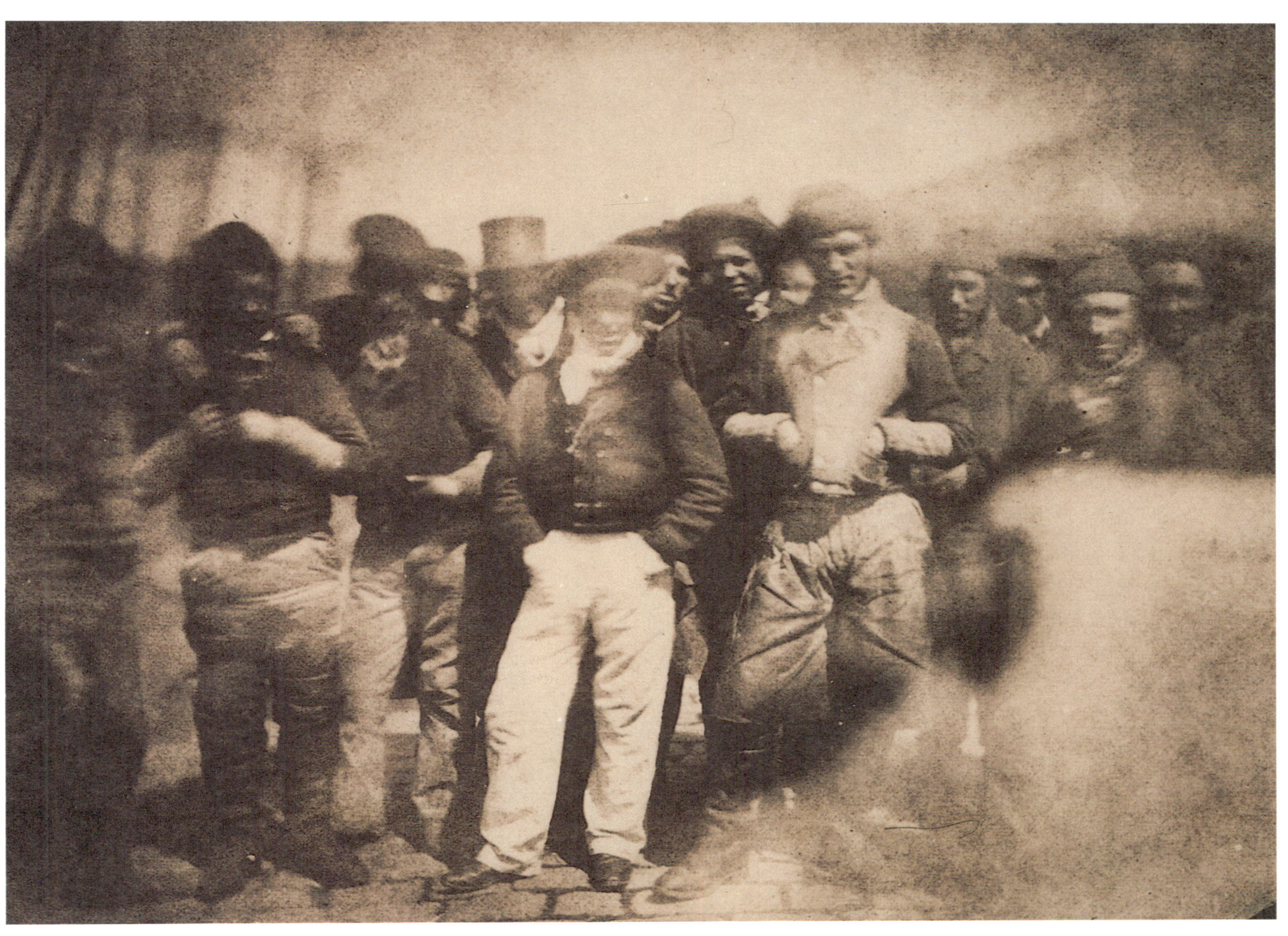

11

A Group of Fishermen on a Quayside or Pier

A double negative, inscribed: 'June 21 / 45 Group of fishermen two pictures on one paper / 56 / Gun (?) / 27 / ½ last'

Modern print from Edinburgh Photographic Society negative

PGPEPS 43

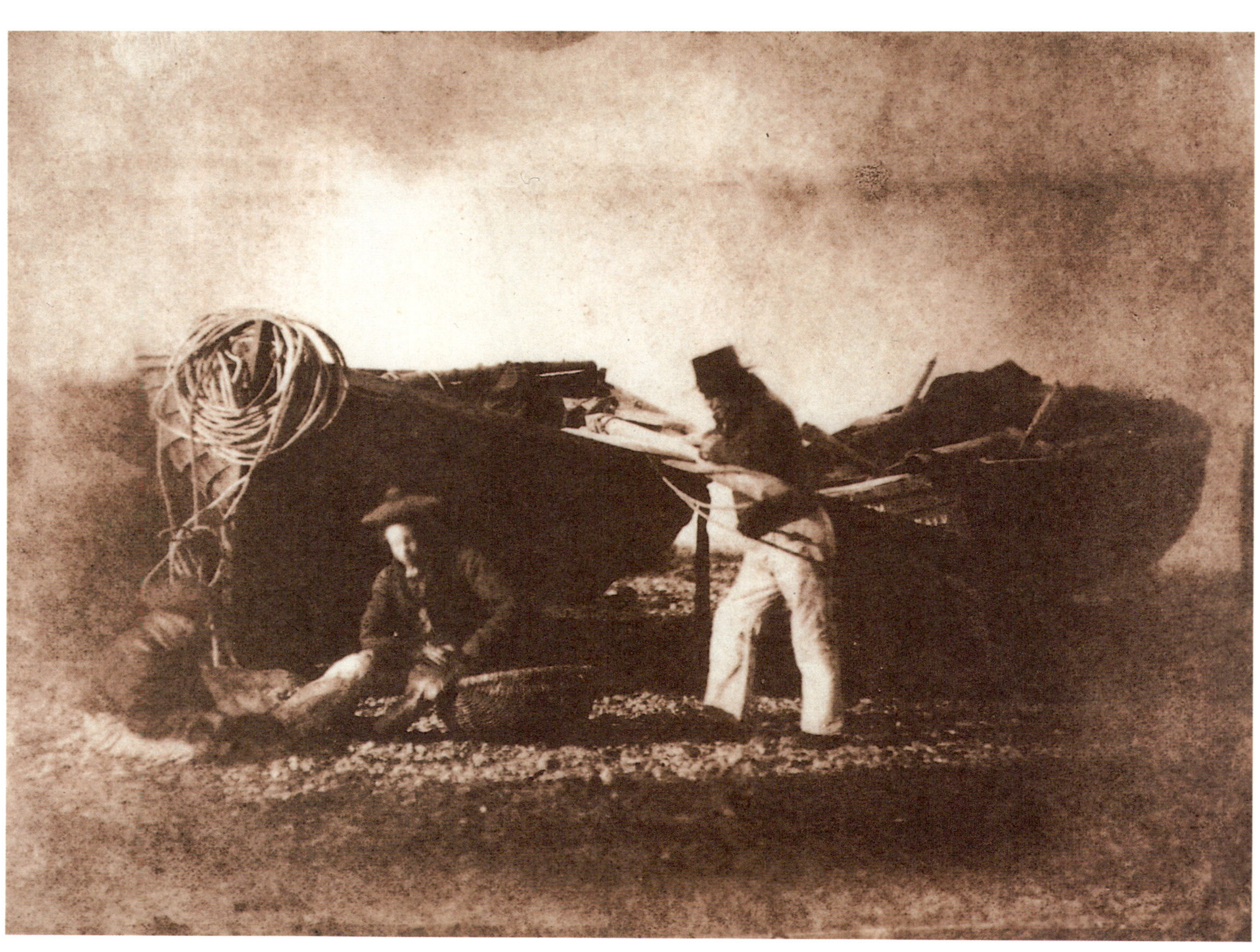

12

On the Beach at Newhaven

Modern print from Edinburgh Photographic Society negative, inscribed: '6 (or '9') Boats. Man & two boys / 82 / D2'
PGPEPS 74

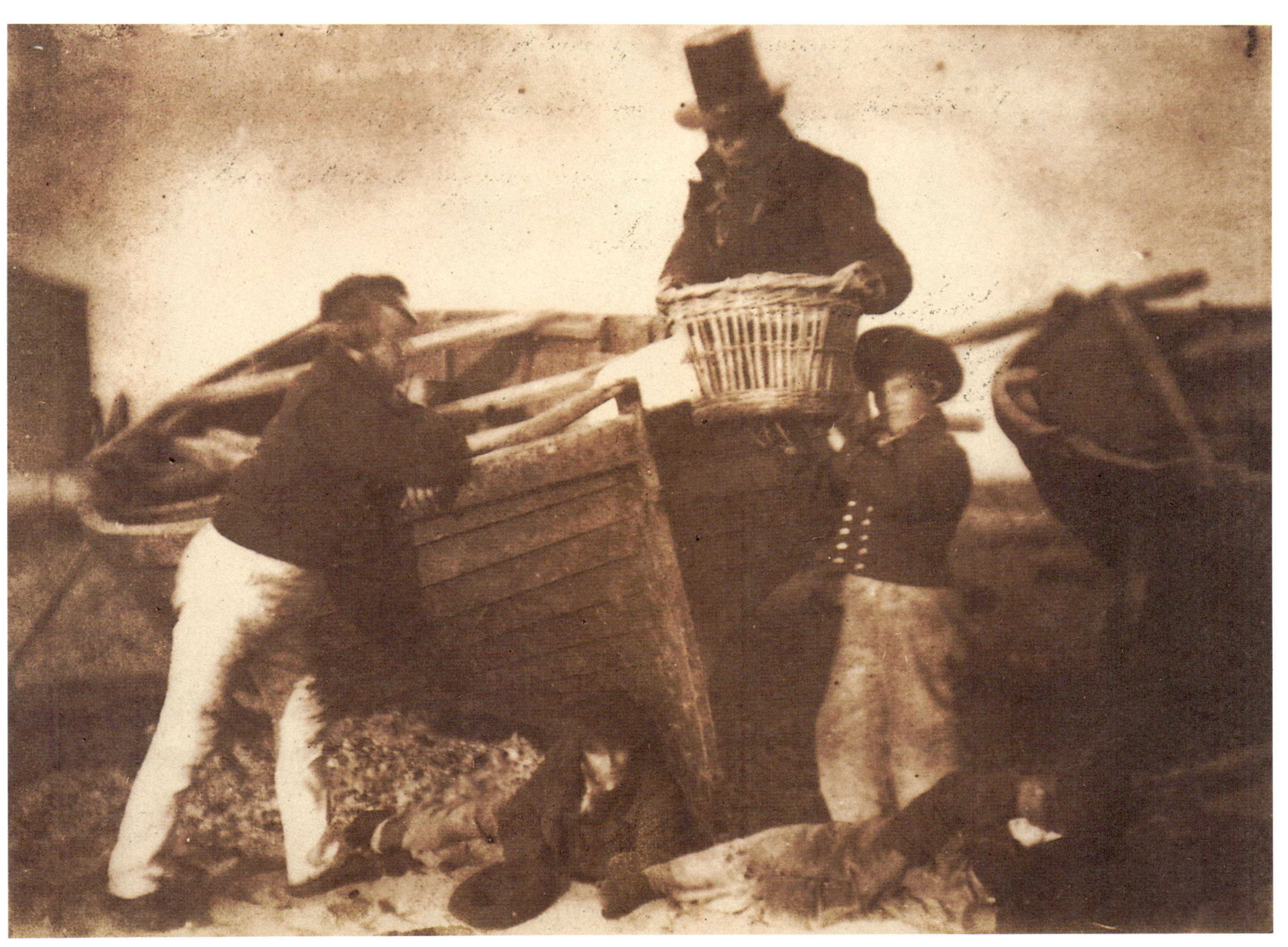

13

Newhaven Group

Harry Ransom Humanities Research Center, Clarkson Stanfield Album 090

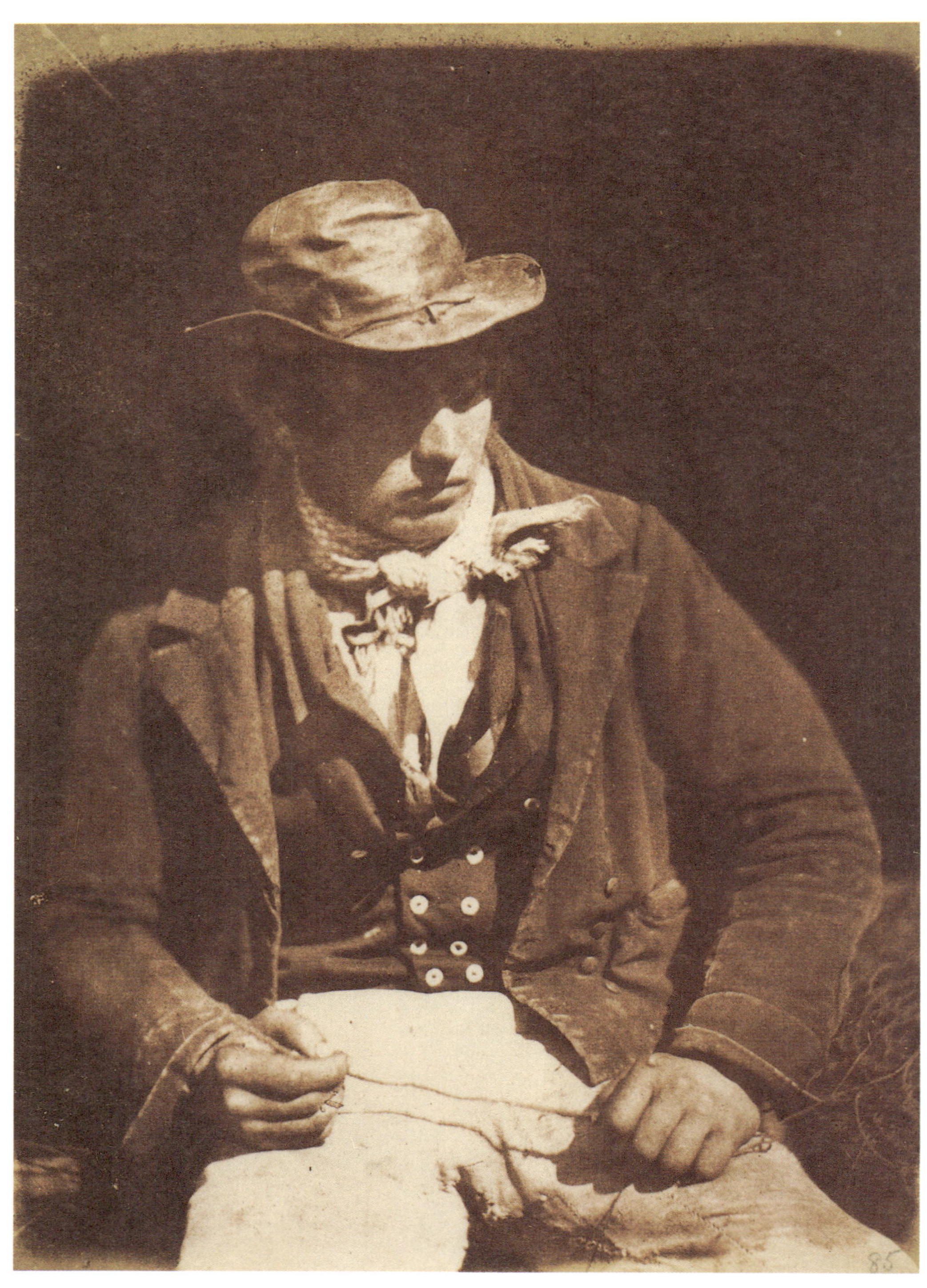

14
Willie Liston 'Redding [preparing] the Line'
Scottish National Portrait Gallery
PGPHA 300

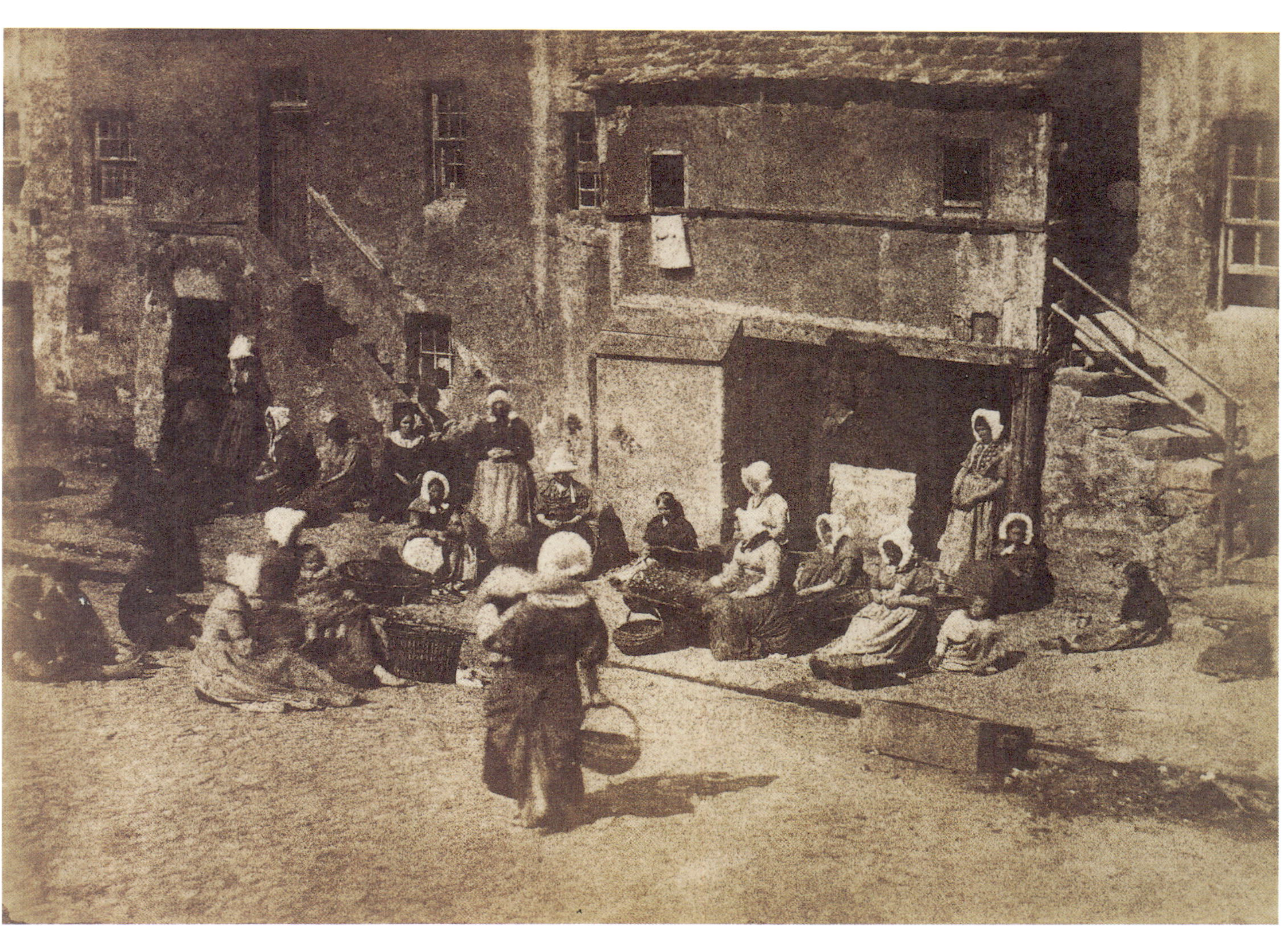

15
St Andrews, Fishergate, Women and Children Baiting the Lines

Scottish National Portrait Gallery
PGPHA 299

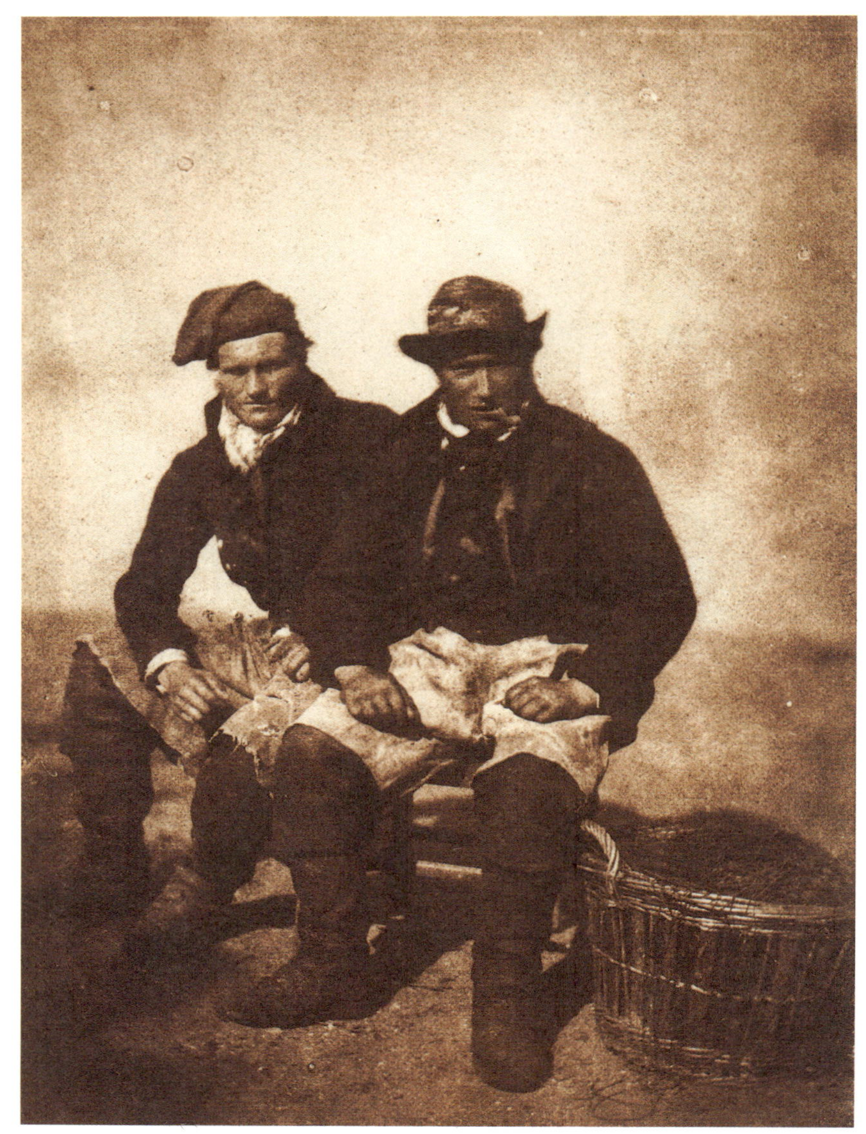

16

Two Newhaven Fishermen, David Young on the left

probably taken in 1843

'"We coost our line in Largo Bay
And fishes we caught nine
There's three to fry and three to buy
And three to bait the line" The Boatie Rows'

Quotation from James Wilson Album
Scottish National Portrait Gallery, Notman Collection

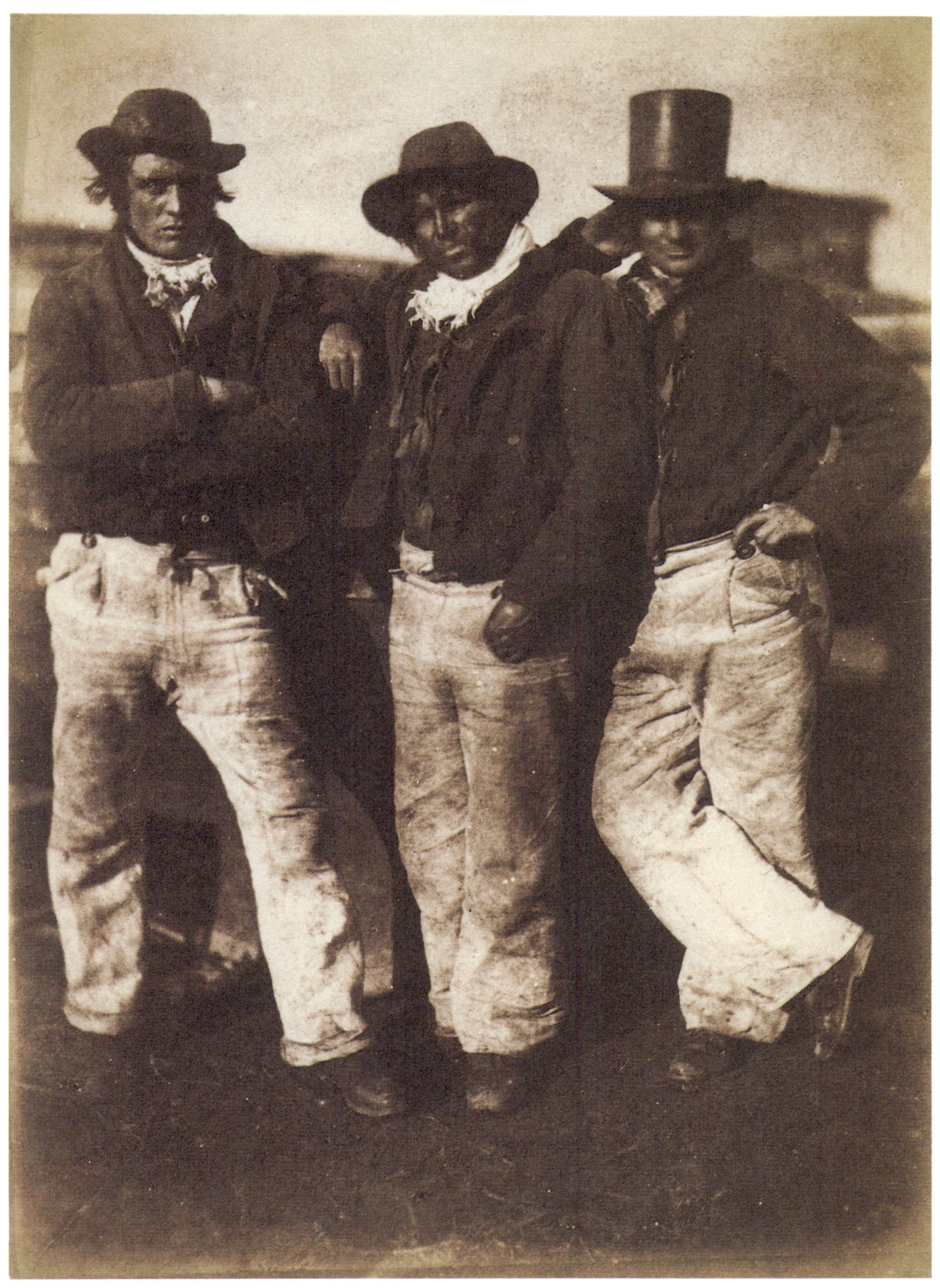

17

Newhaven Fishermen: Alexander Rutherford, William Ramsay and John Liston
'Fishermen Ashore'

Title from Royal Academy Album
Scottish National Portrait Gallery
PGPHA 302

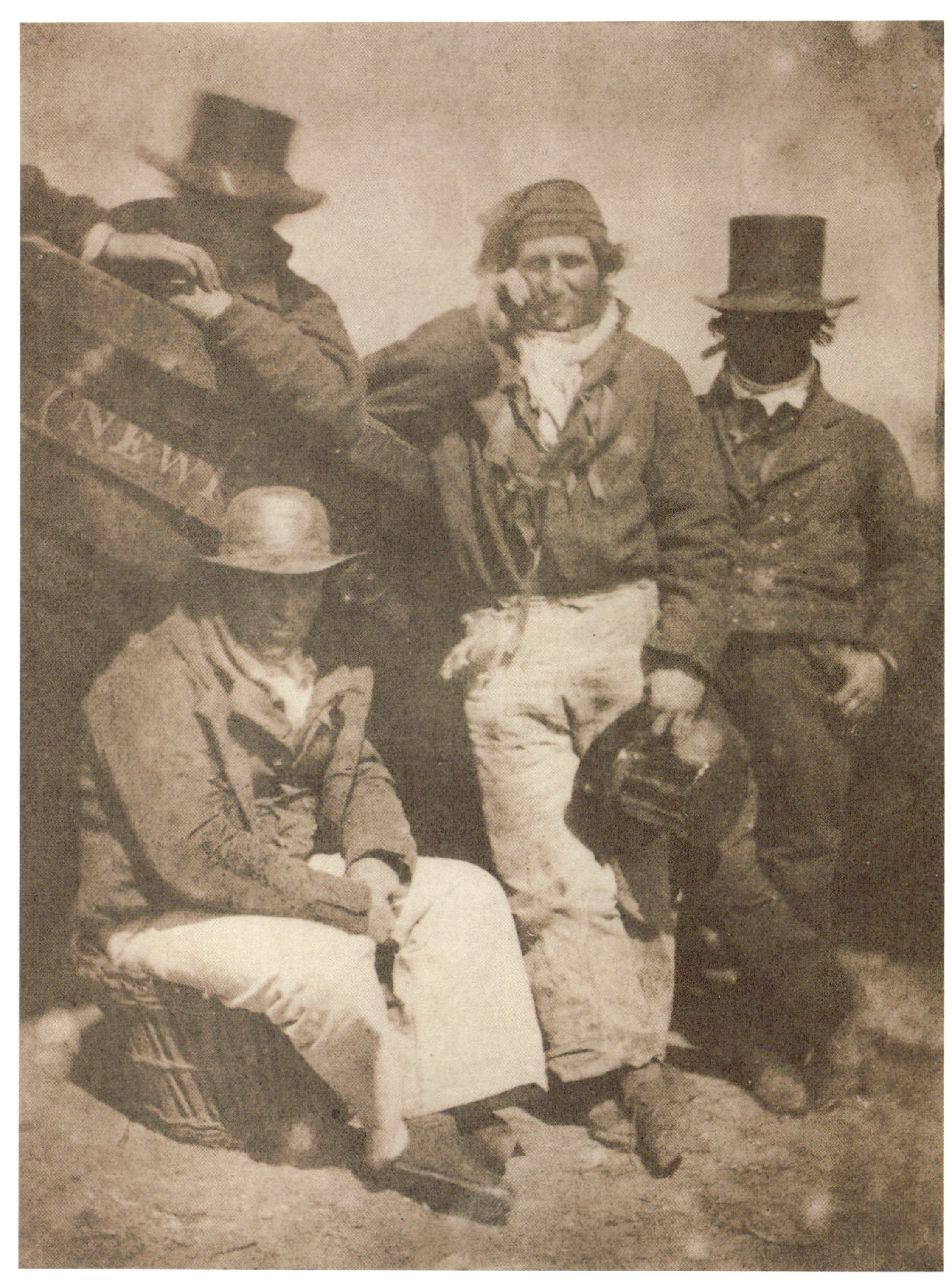

18

Newhaven Fishermen

Modern print from Glasgow University negative, Dougan Collection

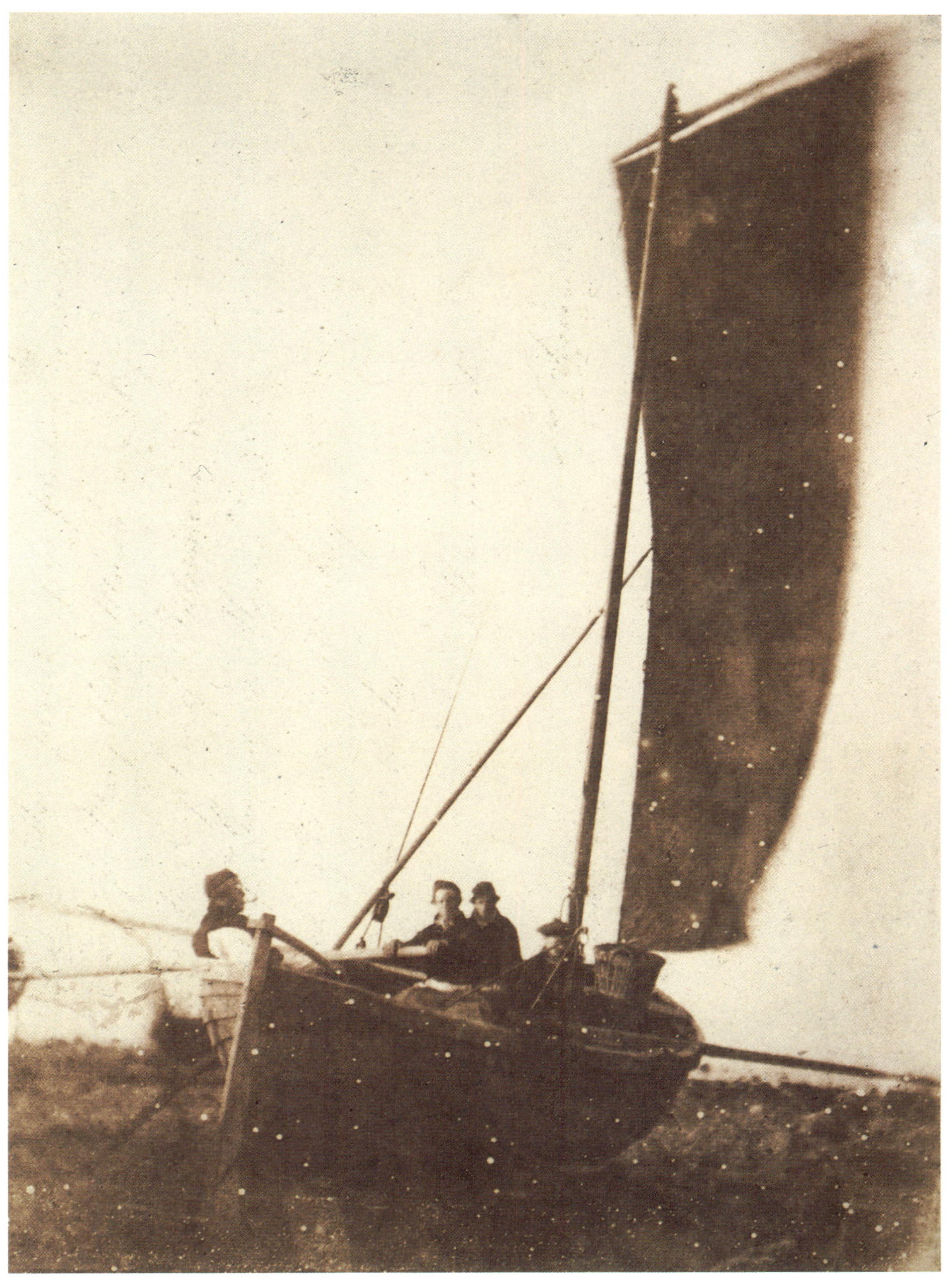

19

'An Oyster Boat'

Harry Ransom Humanities Research Center, Clarkson Stanfield Album 078B

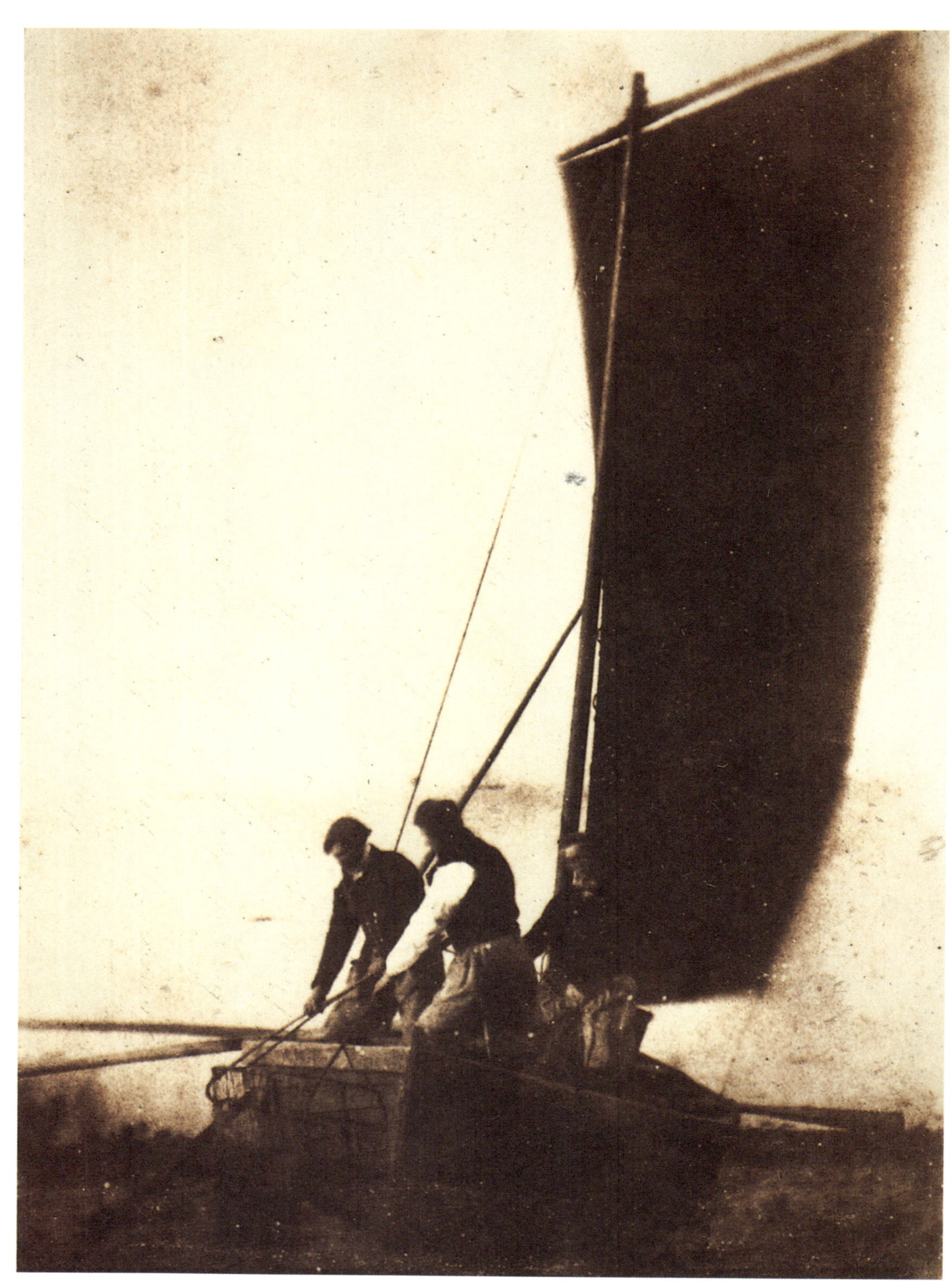

20
'Oyster Dredging'
Harry Ransom Humanities Research Center, Clarkson Stanfield Album 077

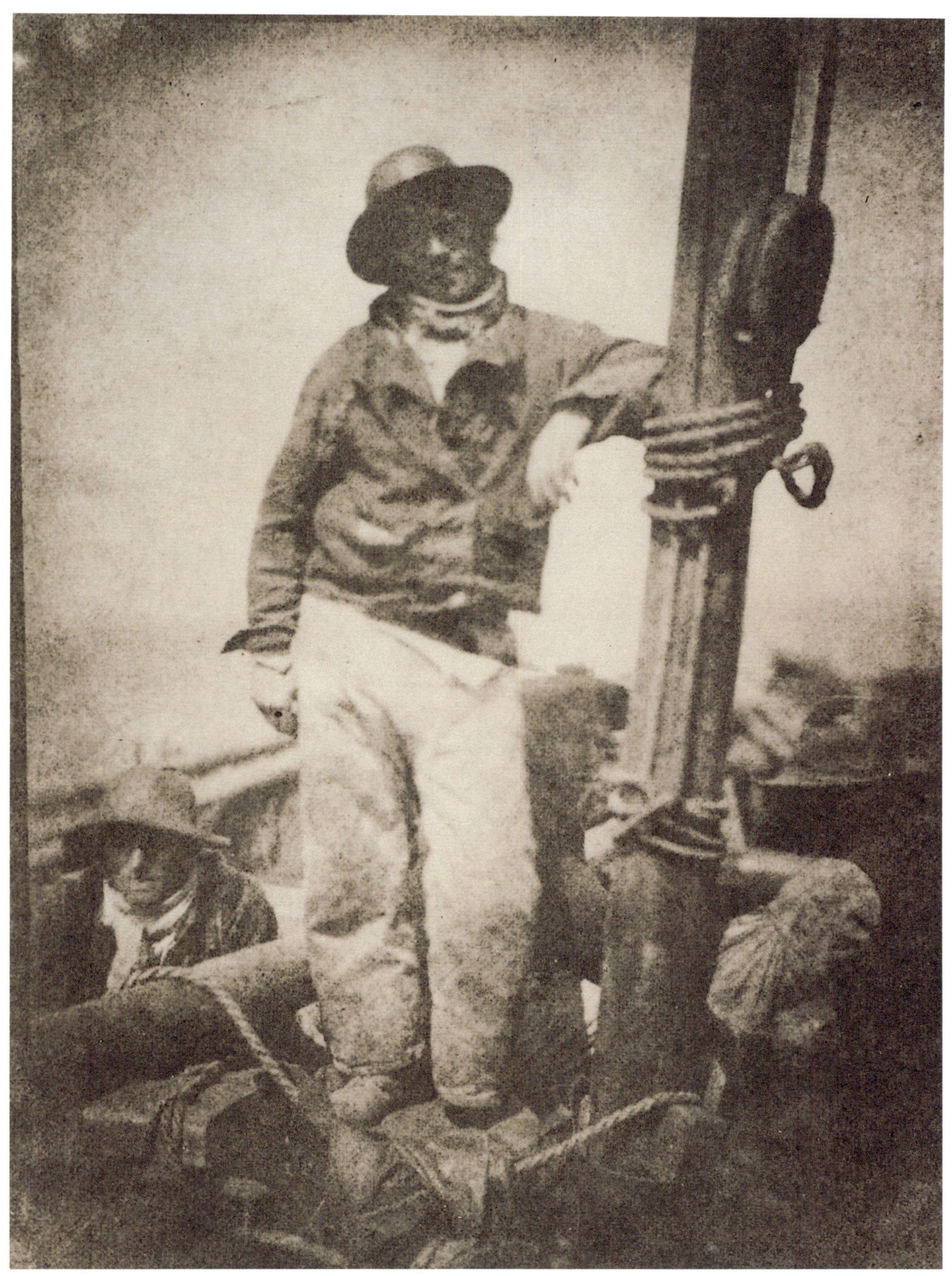

21

Men on Board a Fishing Boat

Modern print from Edinburgh Photographic Society negative, inscribed: '52 June 21 / 45'

PGPEPS 60

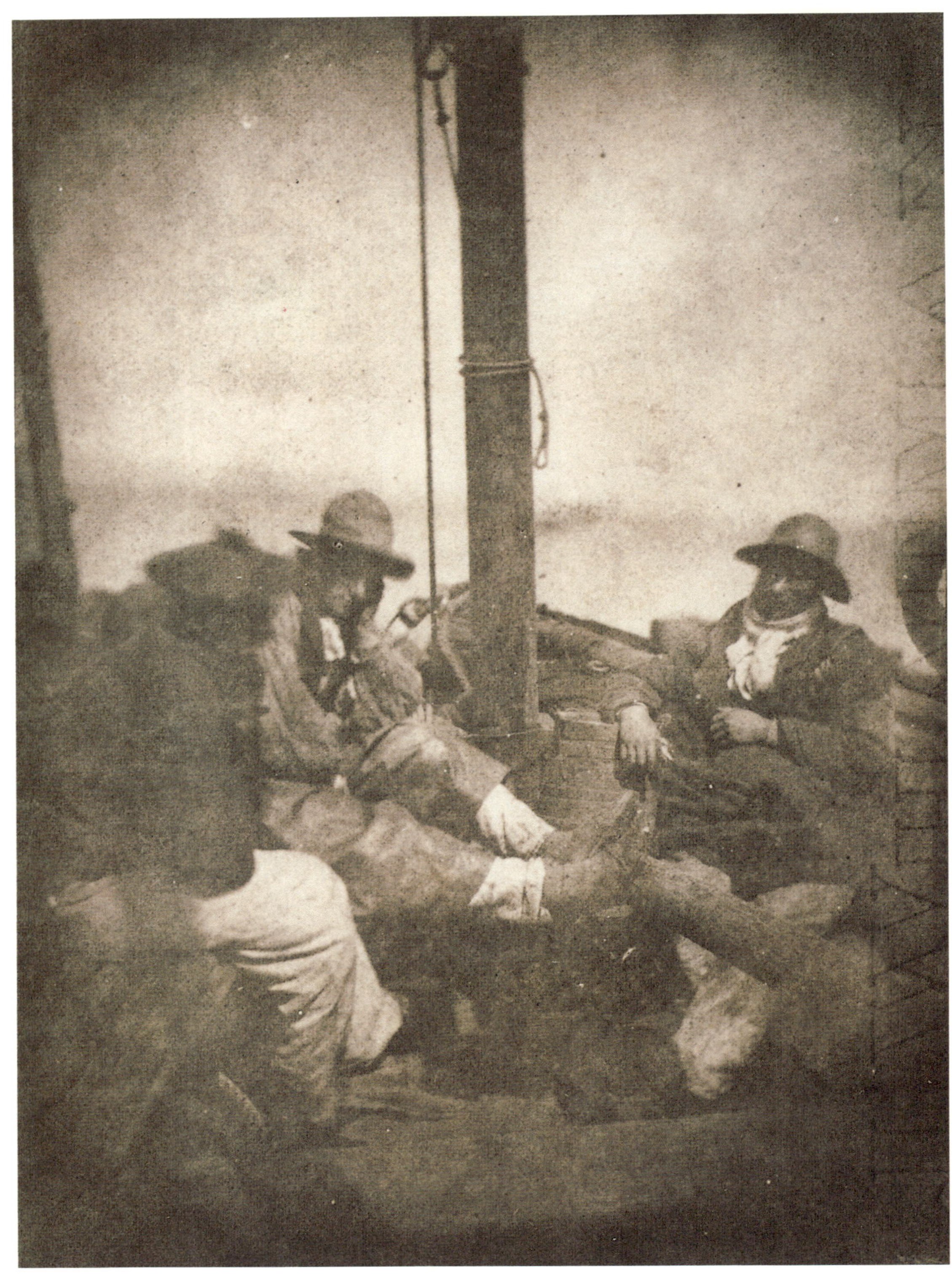

22

Men on Board a Fishing Boat

Modern print from Edinburgh Photographic Society negative, inscribed: '206 (or 4) / ex4ho du / 57
Group of fishermen in boat June 21 / 45 / Faint & Yellow'
FGPEPS 59

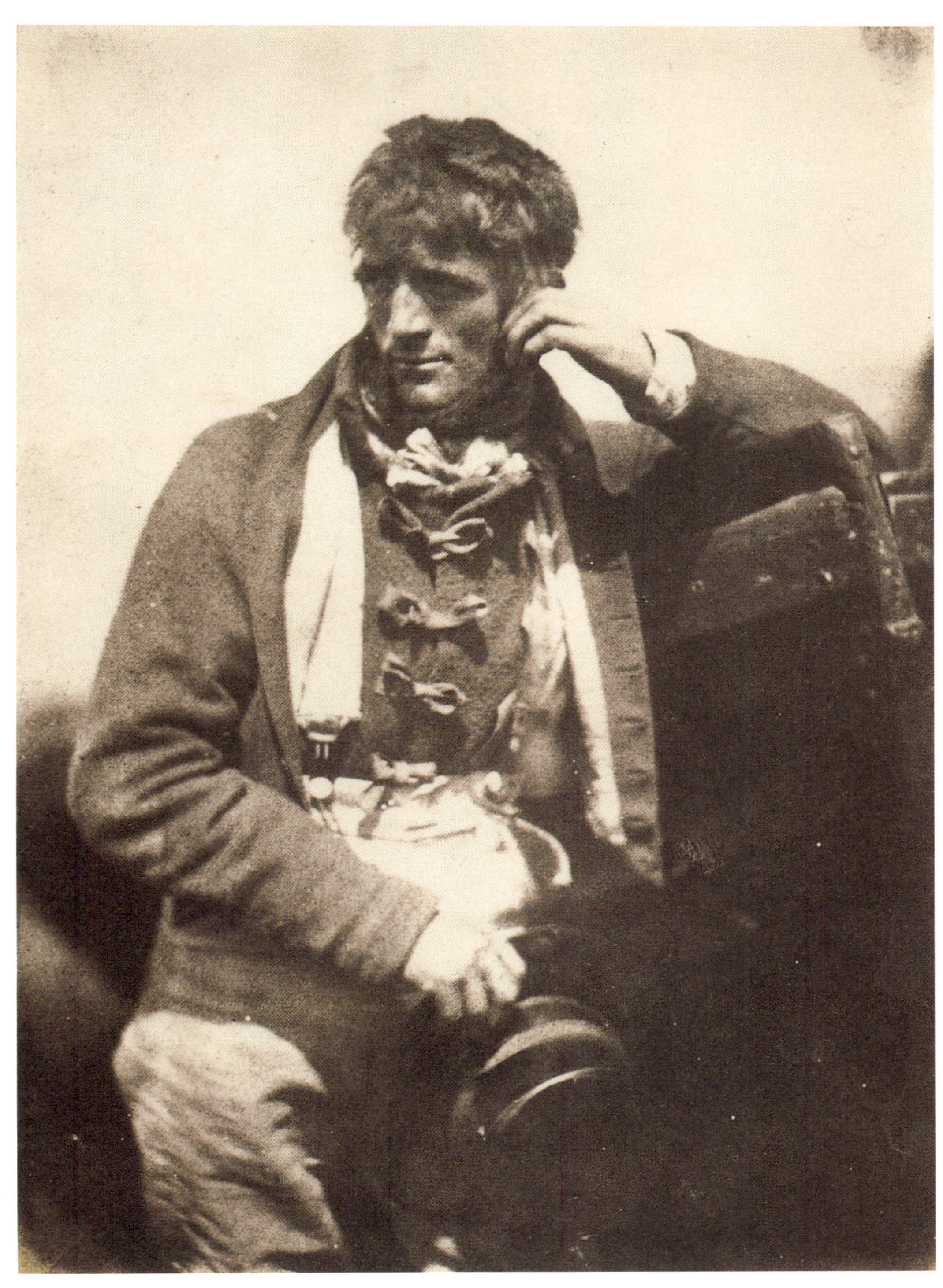

23

'A Newhaven Pilot'

Mrs Robertson, Henry Bicknell Album

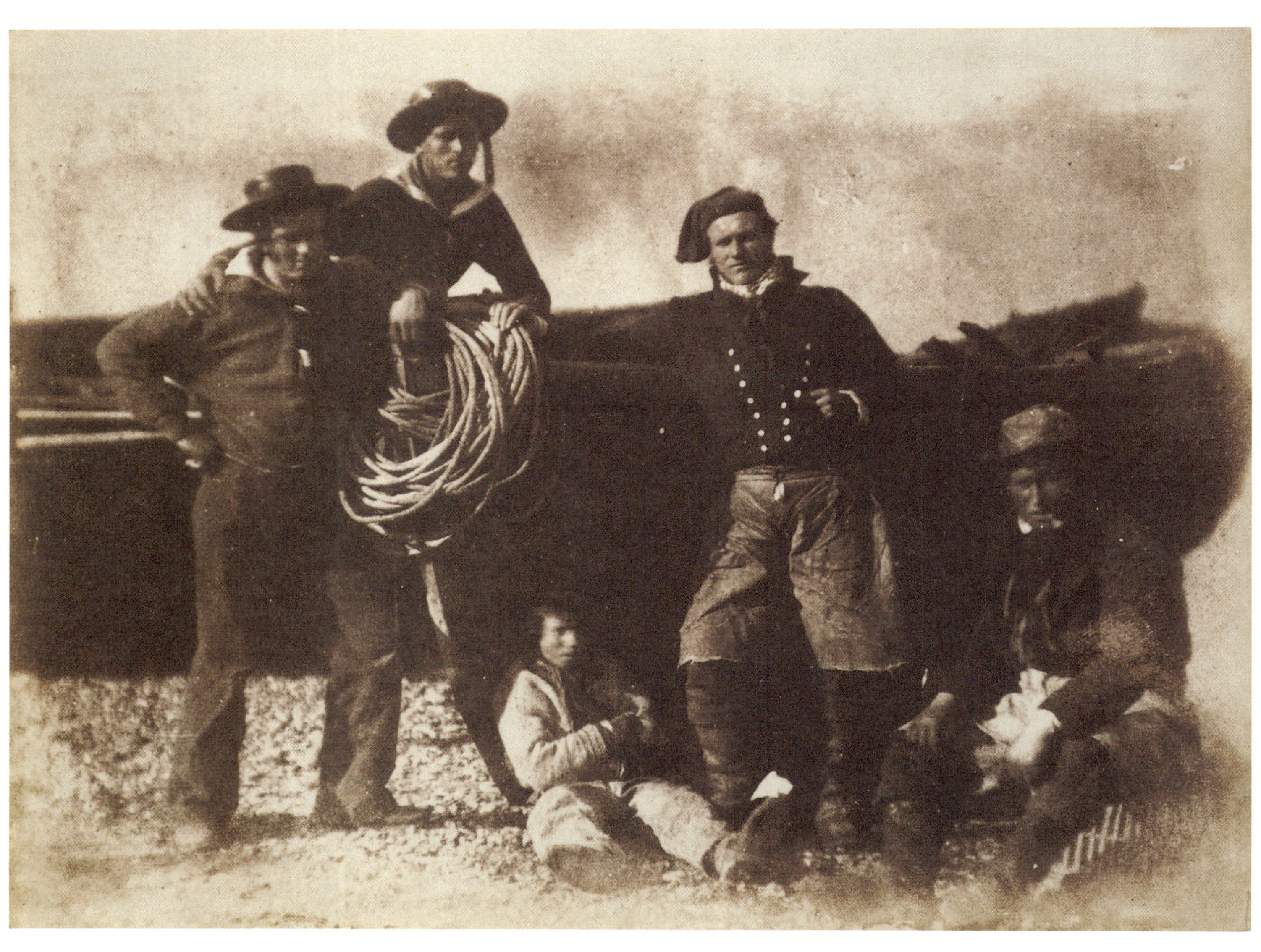

24
'English Yachtsmen and Newhaven Fishermen' including David Young

Scottish National Portrait Gallery
PGPHA 304

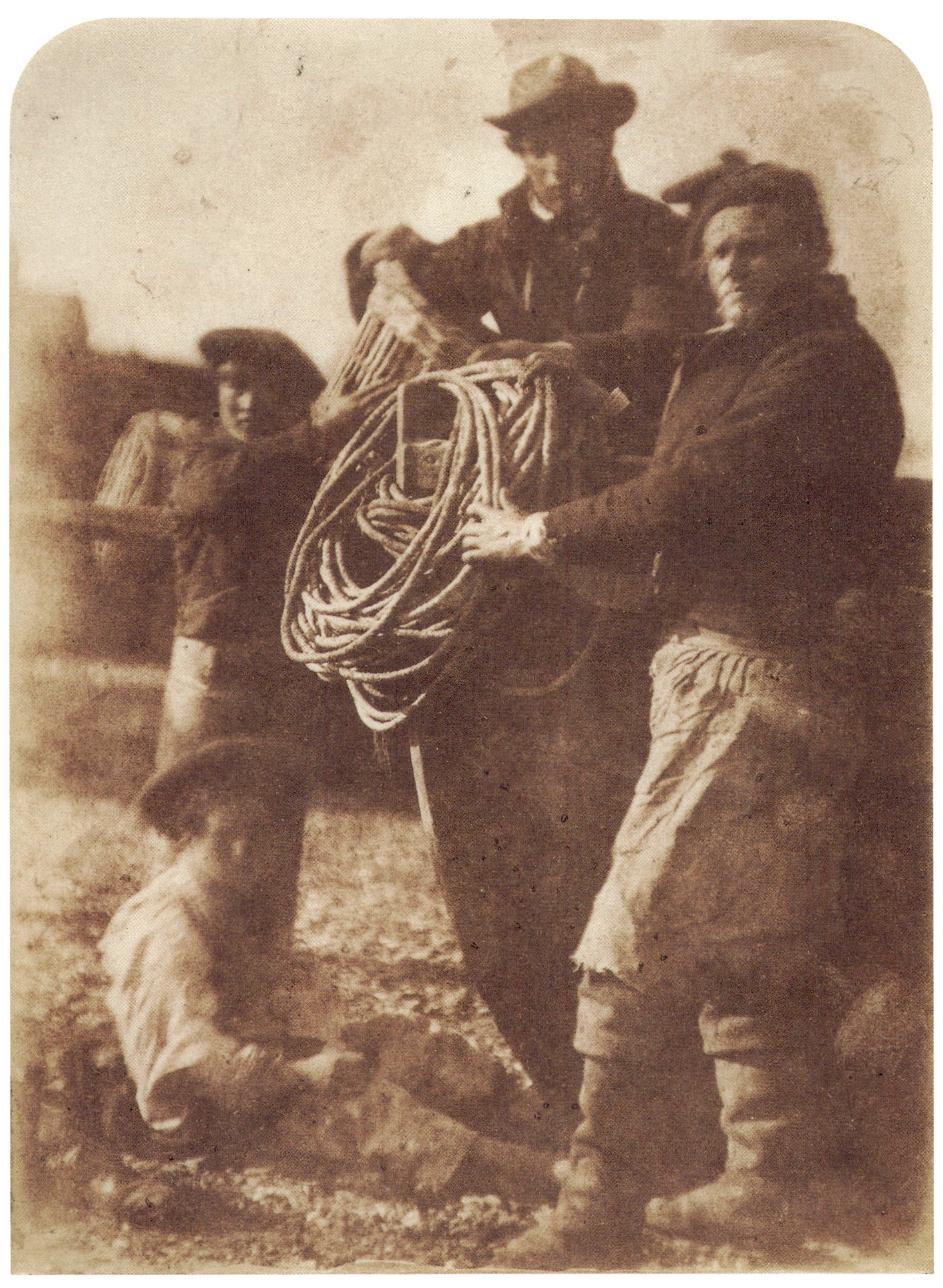

25

'Just Landed'

Scottish National Portrait Gallery, Notman Collection

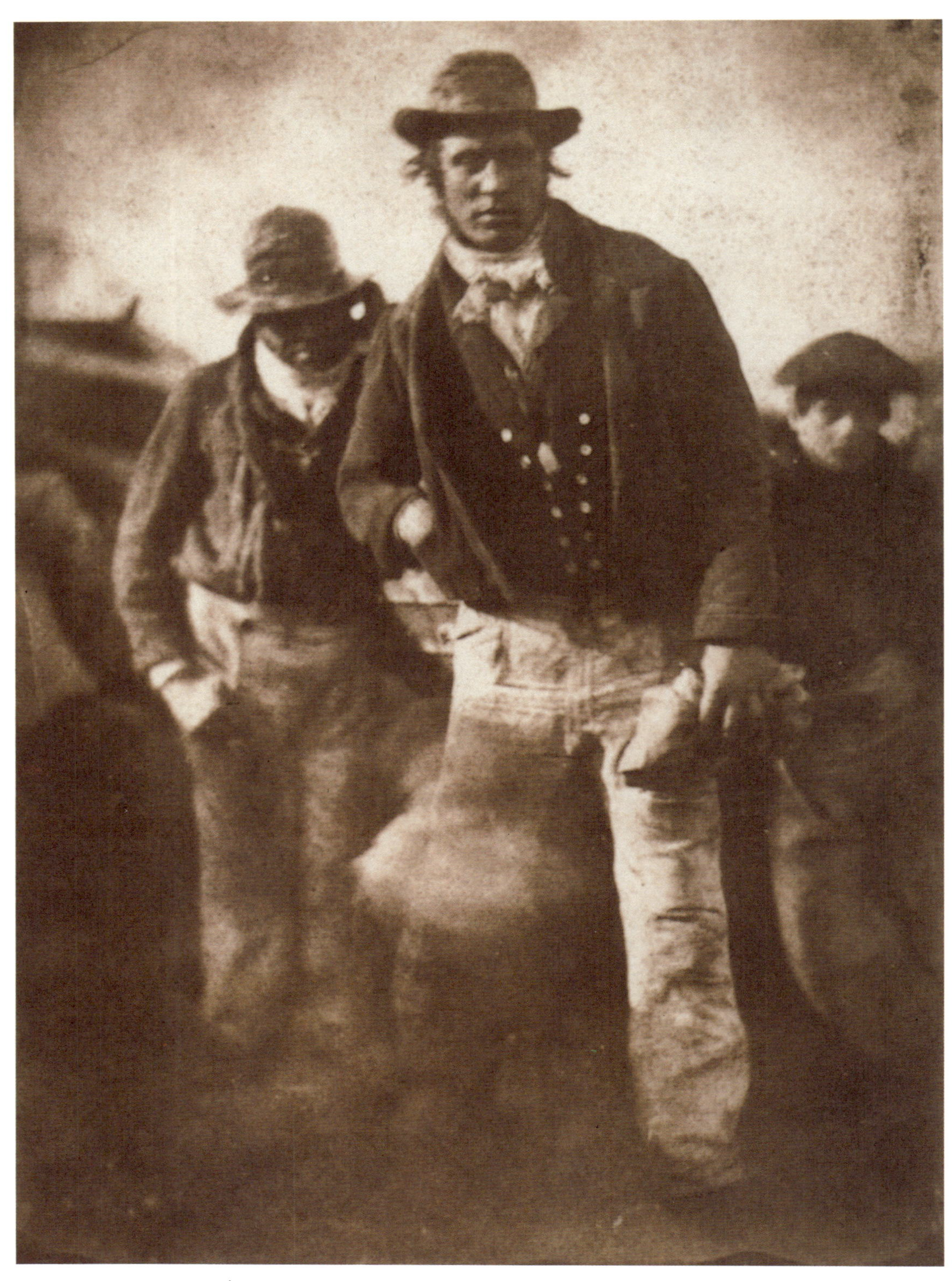

26

Group with William Ramsay on the left and Andrew Rutherford centre

Modern print from Edinburgh Photographic Society negative, inscribed: 'no gal lit wax / 87'

PGPEPS 72

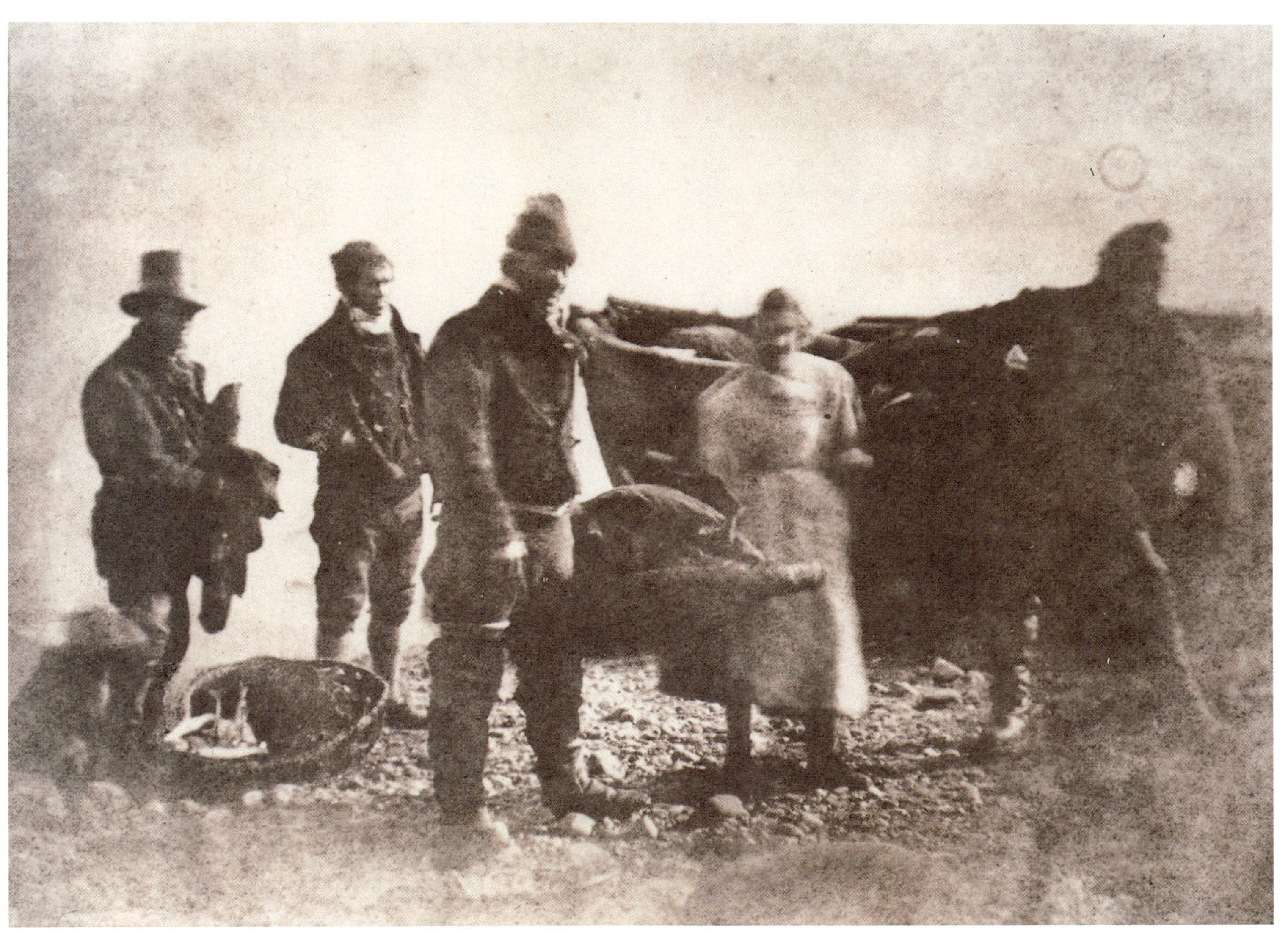

27

Bringing in the Catch

Modern print from Edinburgh Photographic Society negative, inscribed: '24 / 89'

PGPEPS 70

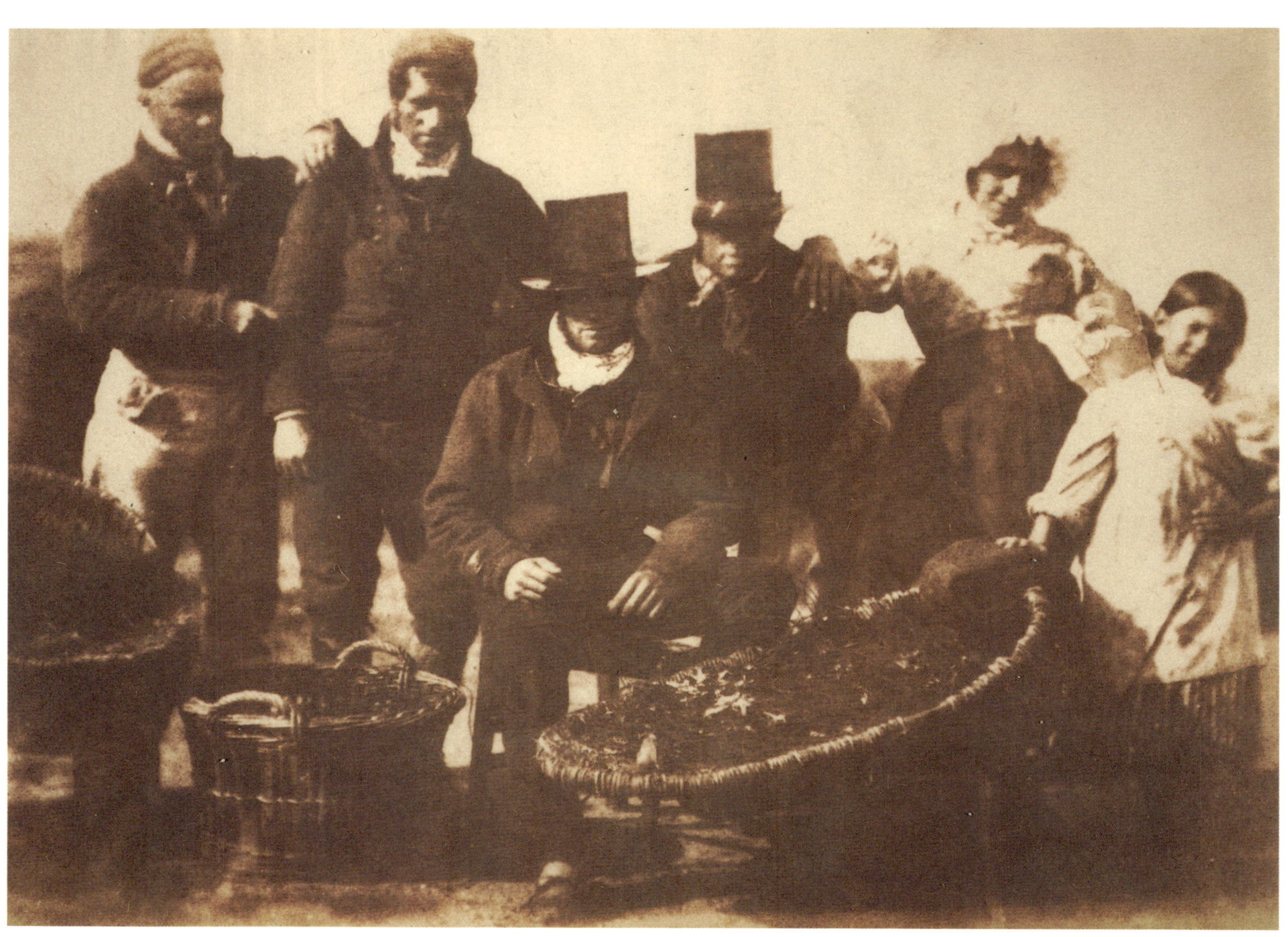

28

Newhaven Group

Scottish National Portrait Gallery
PGPHA 309

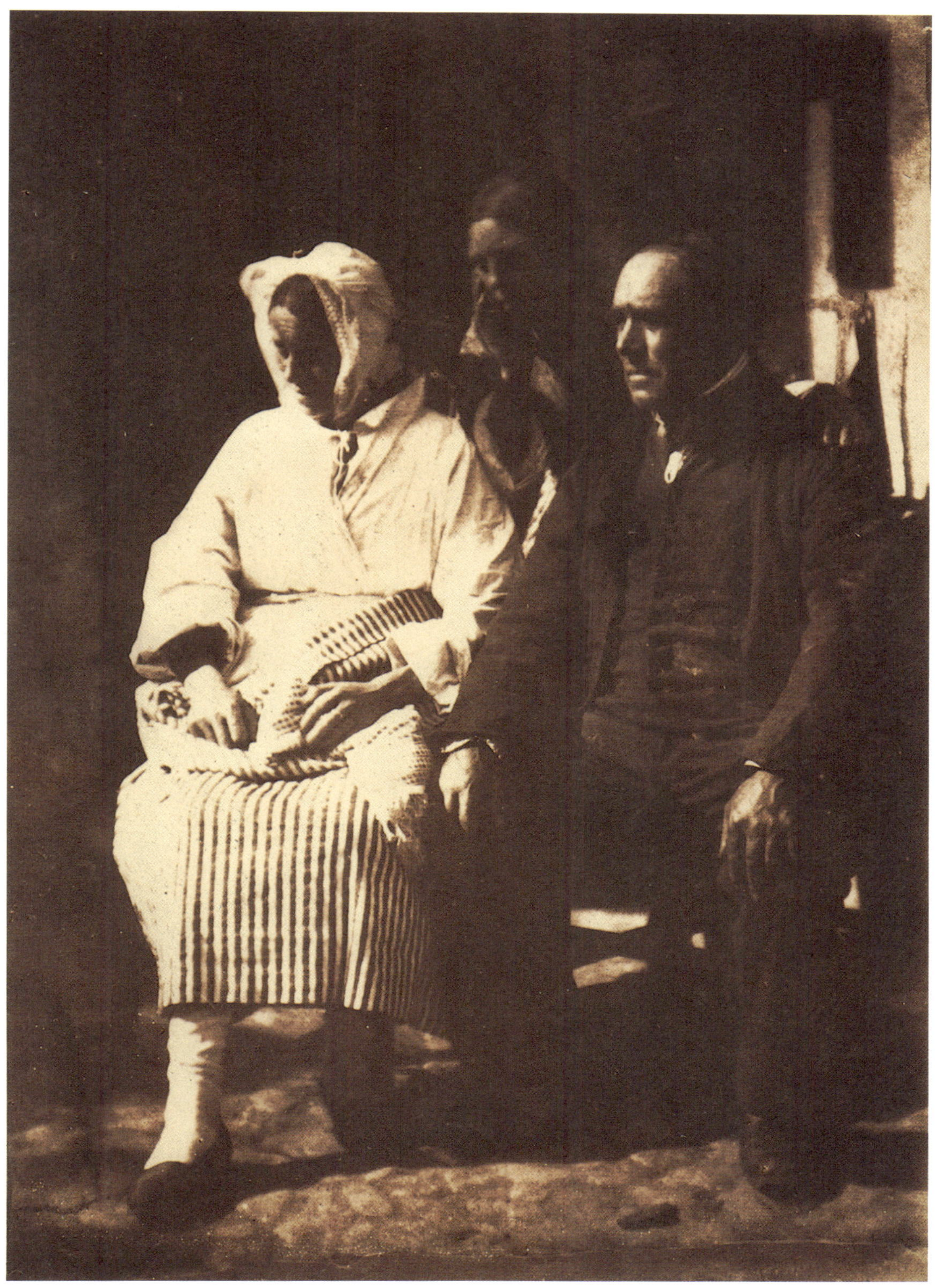

29

Newhaven Group with Mr Laidlaw on the right
'The Elder, Newhaven'

Harry Ransom Humanities Research Center, Clarkson Stanfield Album 079

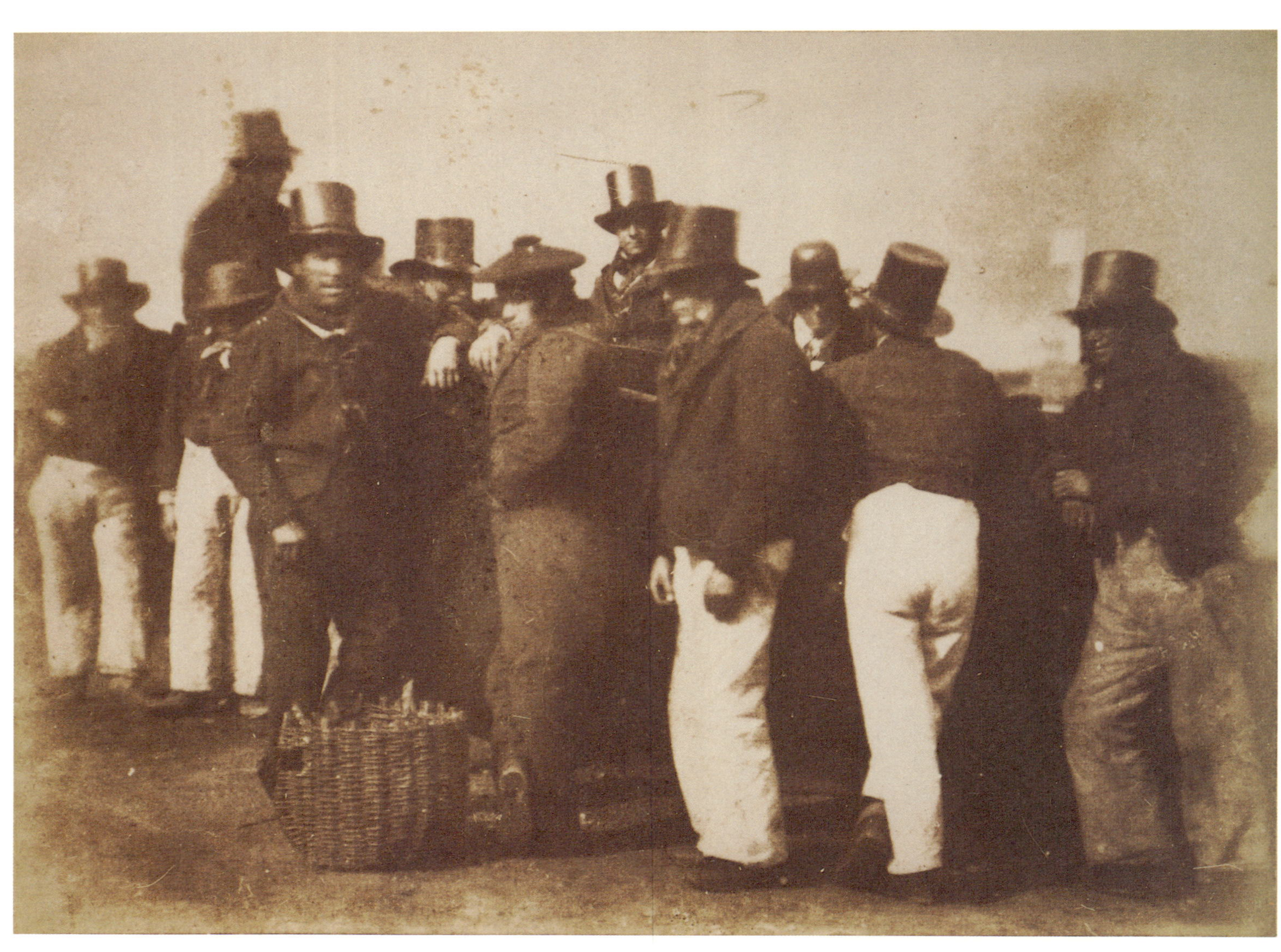

30

Resting or Waiting Fishermen, 'Dolce Far Niente'

Title from Royal Academy Album
Scottish National Portrait Gallery
PGPHA 306

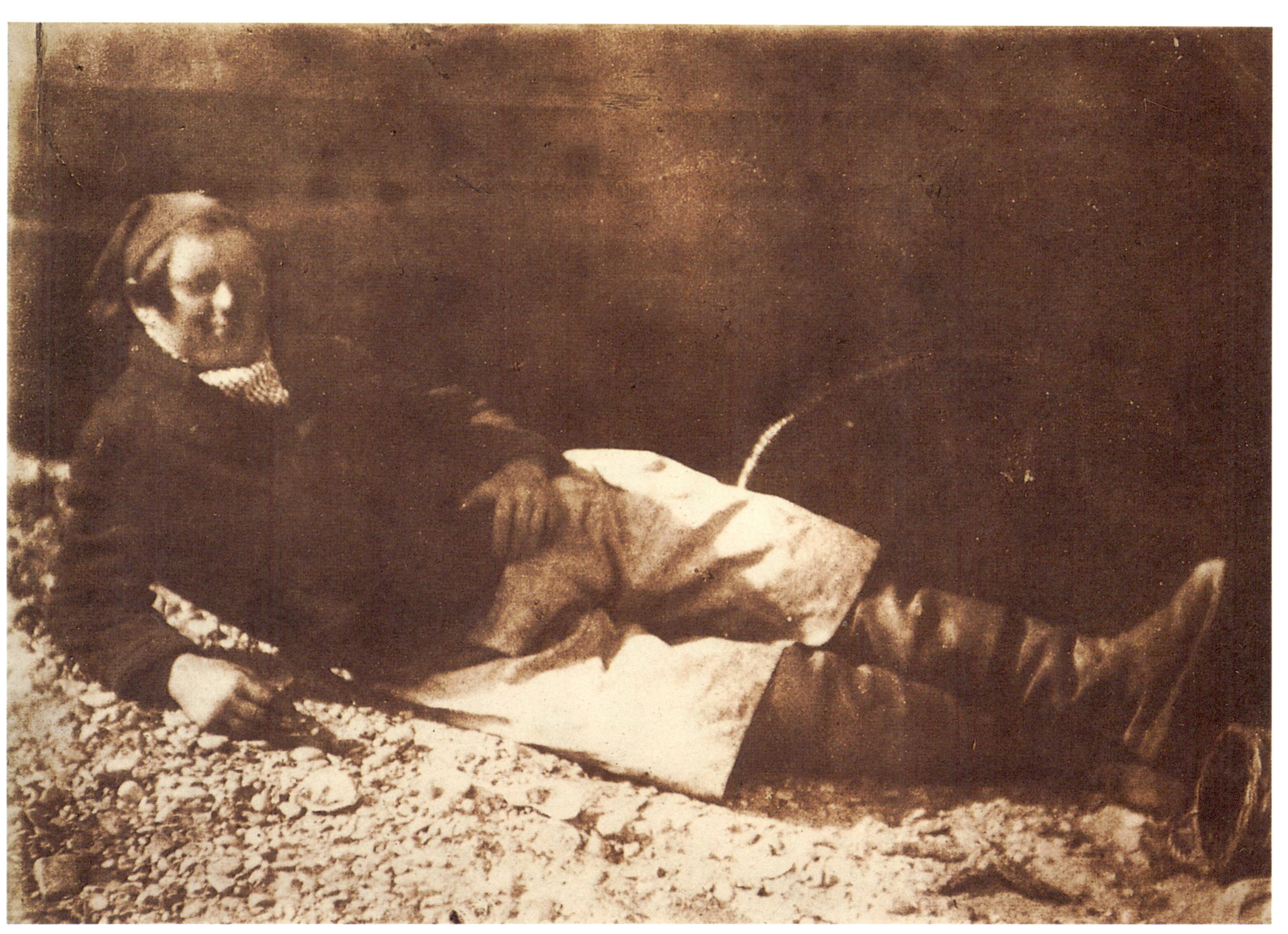

31

Resting Fisherman

Harry Ransom Humanities Research Center, Clarkson Stanfield Album 093B

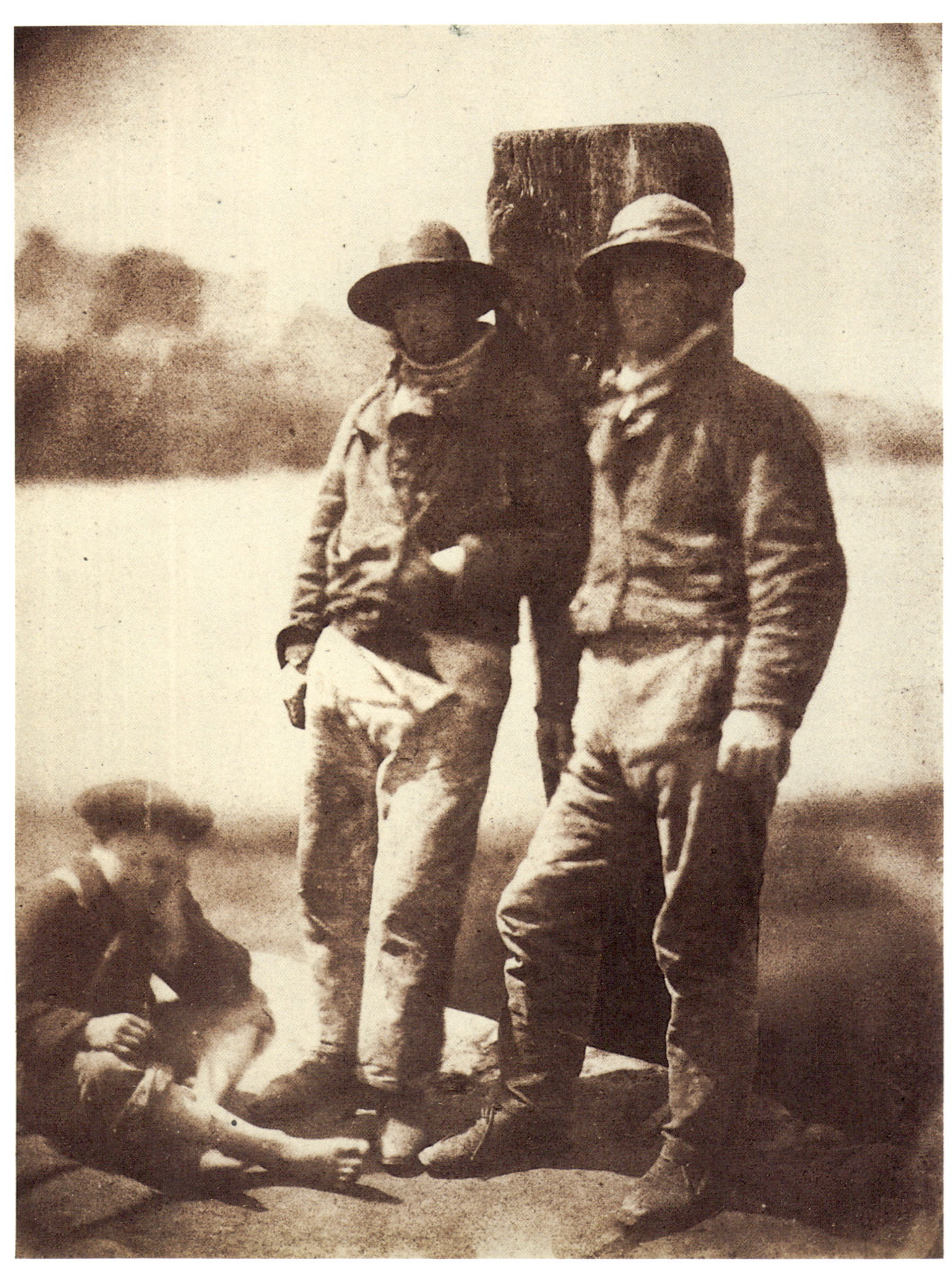

32

'Prestonpans Fishermen'

Harry Ransom Humanities Research Center, Clarkson Stanfield Album 081

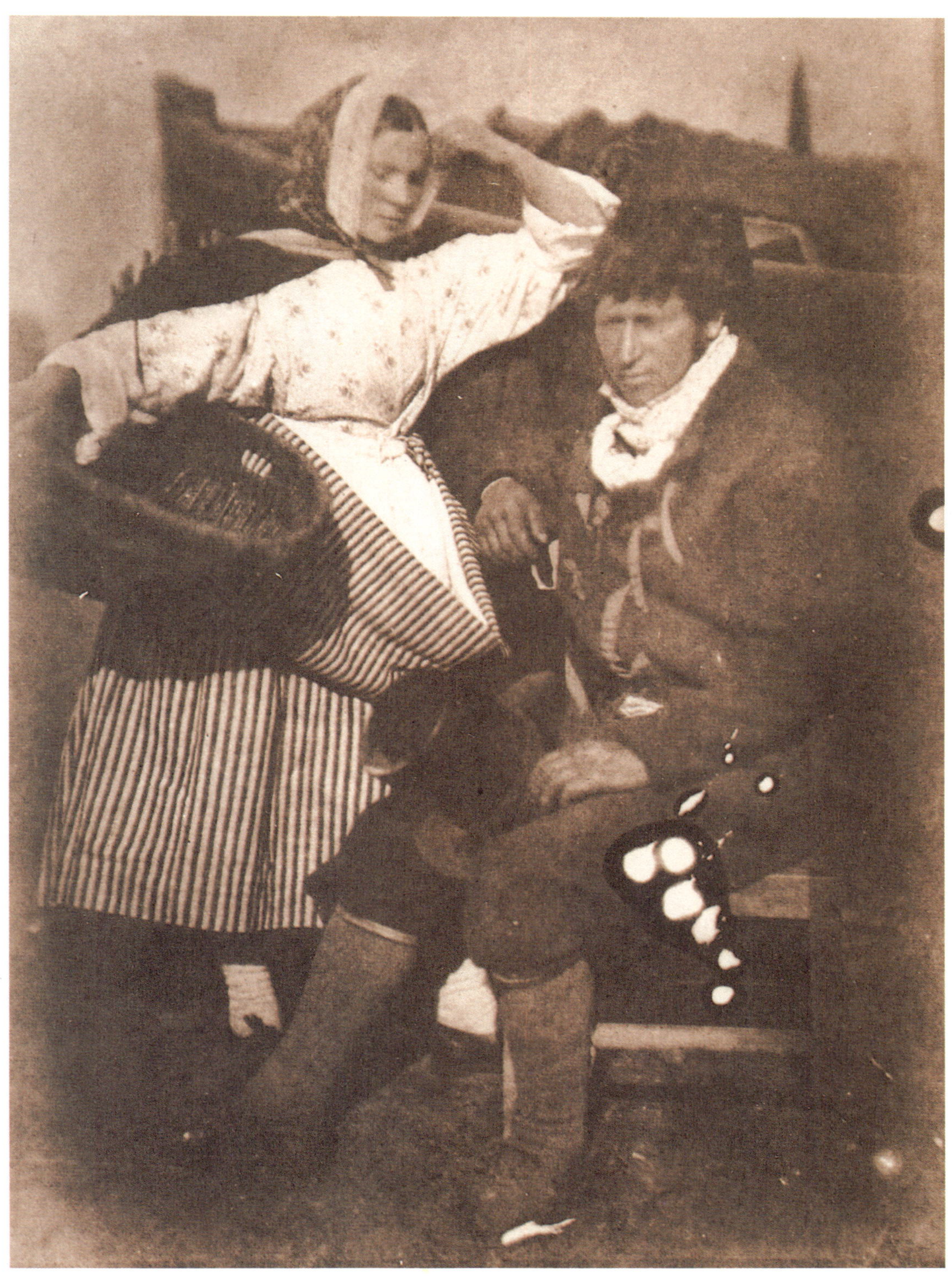

33

Newhaven Fisherman and Wife

Modern print from Edinburgh Photographic Society negative, inscribed: 'D2 / 62',
PGPEPS 53

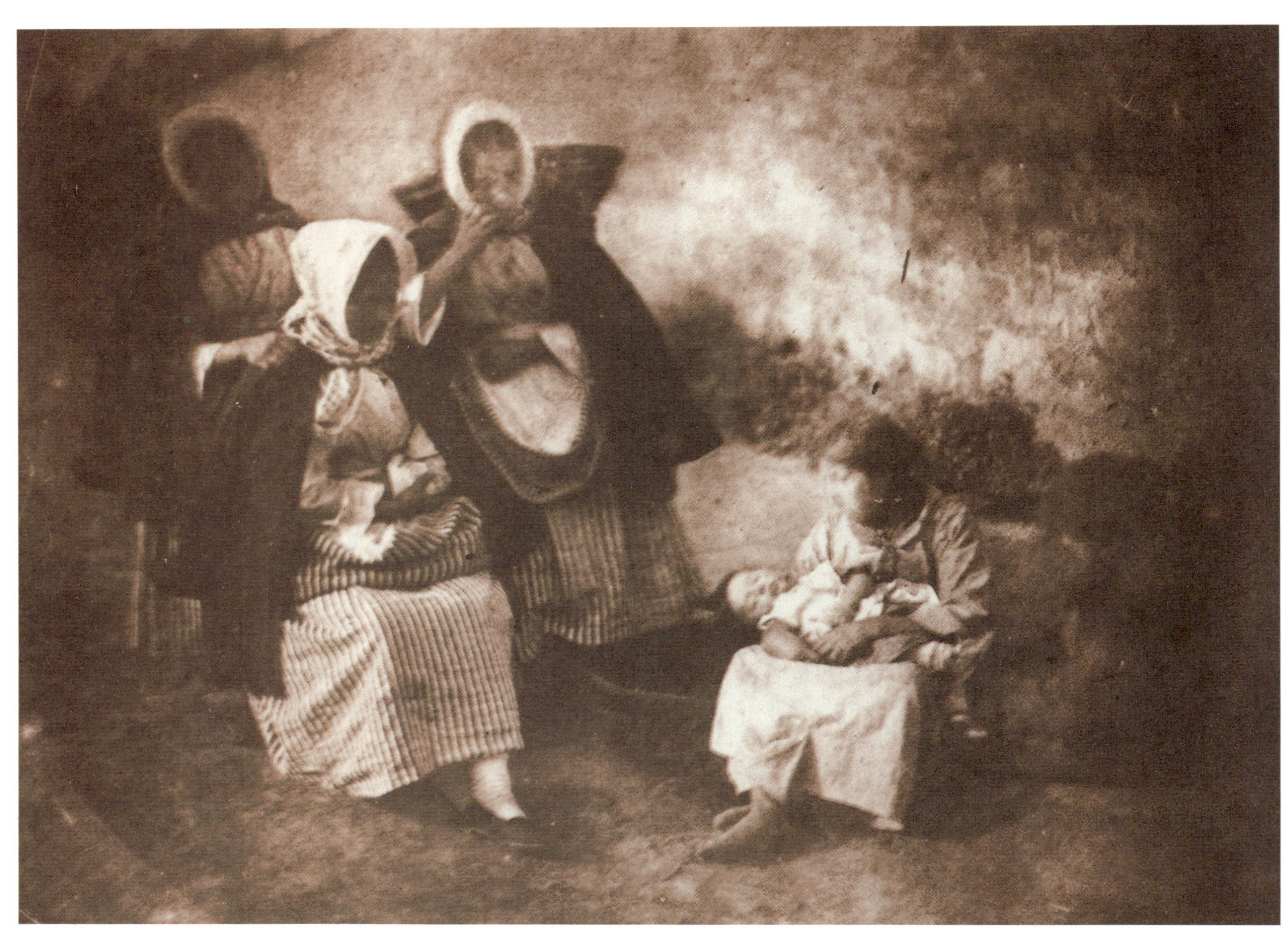

34

Newhaven Fishwives, probably Dressed for Market, Leaving a Sleeping Infant with a Younger Girl

Modern print from Glasgow University negative

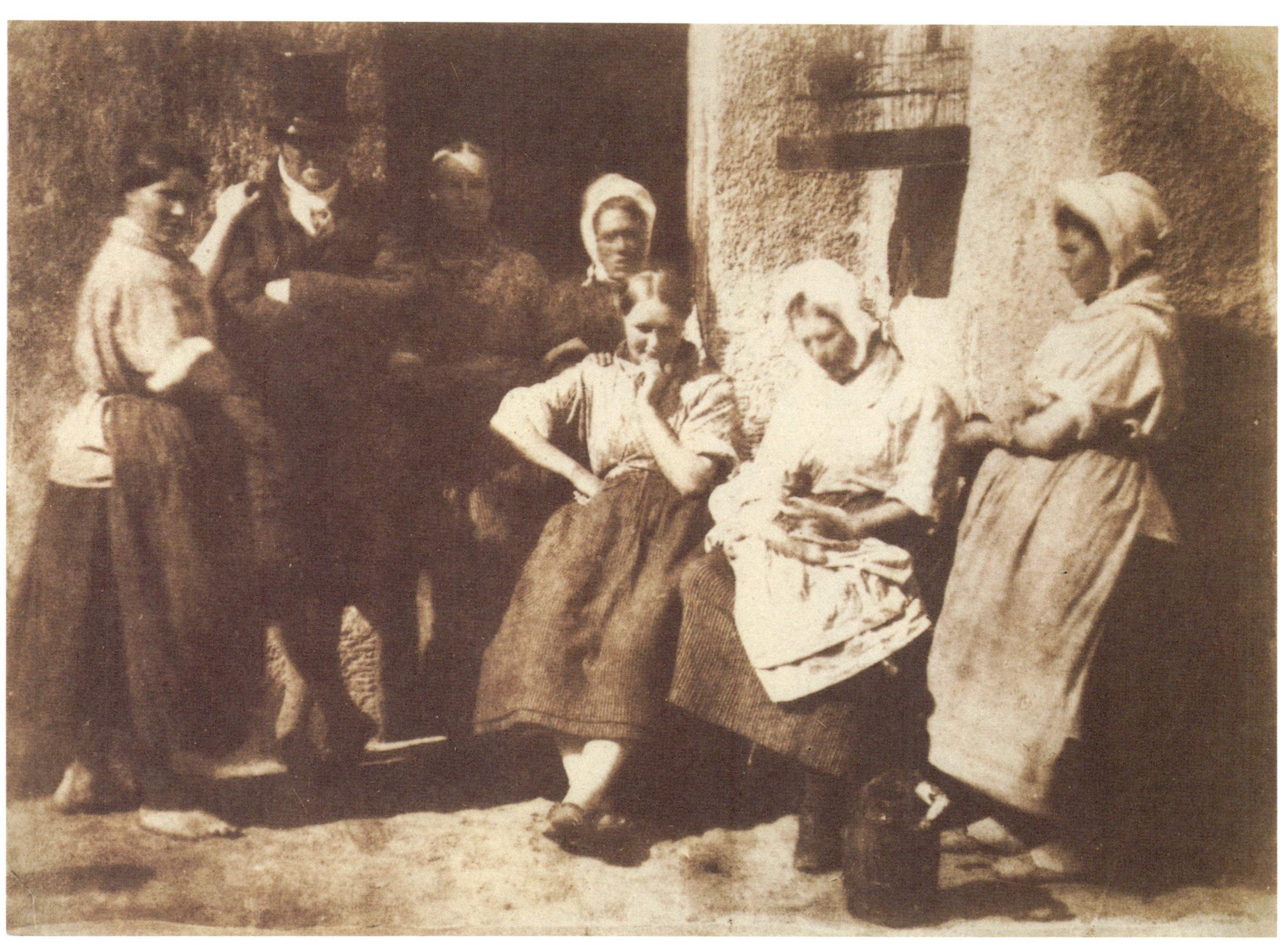

35
'A Newhaven Pilot's Cottage Door'

Scottish National Portrait Gallery
PGPHA 311

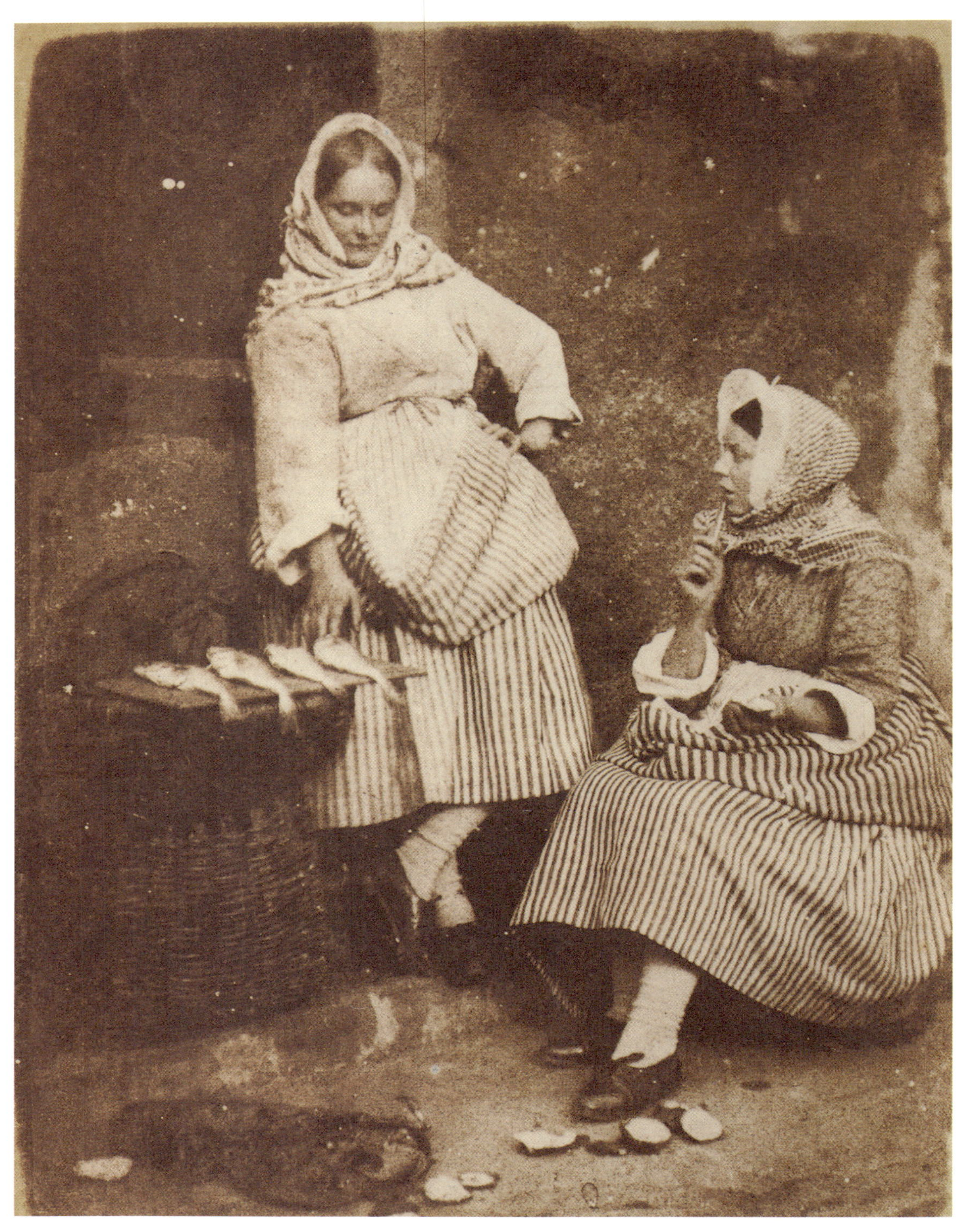

36

Jeanie Wilson and Annie Linton, 'They were twa bonnie lasses'

Title in James Wilson Album
Mrs Robertson, Henry Bicknell Album

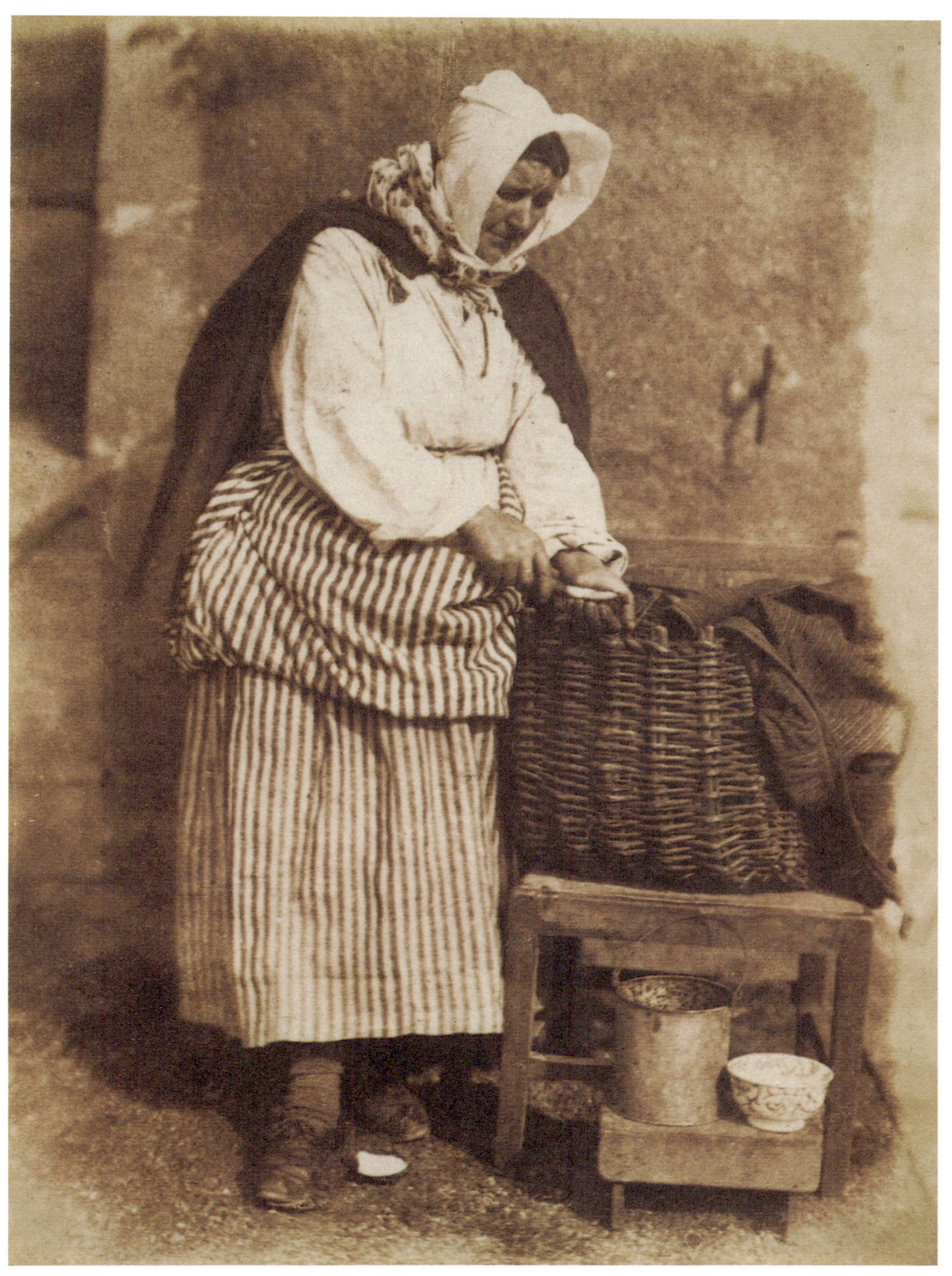

37

Mrs Barbara (Johnstone) Flucker Opening Oysters

Scottish National Portrait Gallery
PGPHA 308

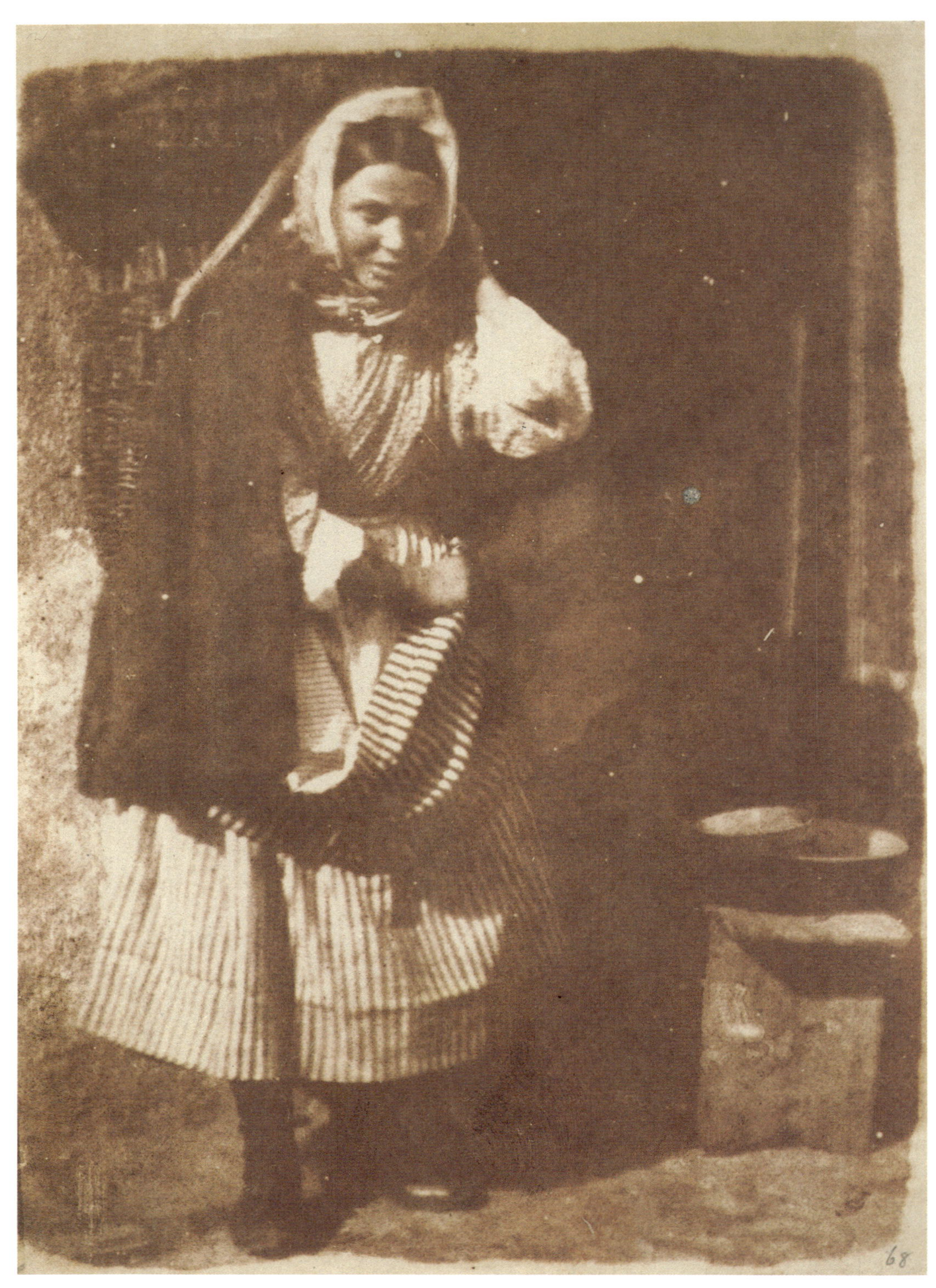

38

Annie Linton Carrying a Loaded Creel

Scottish National Portrait Gallery, Charles Finlay Album
PGPHA 318

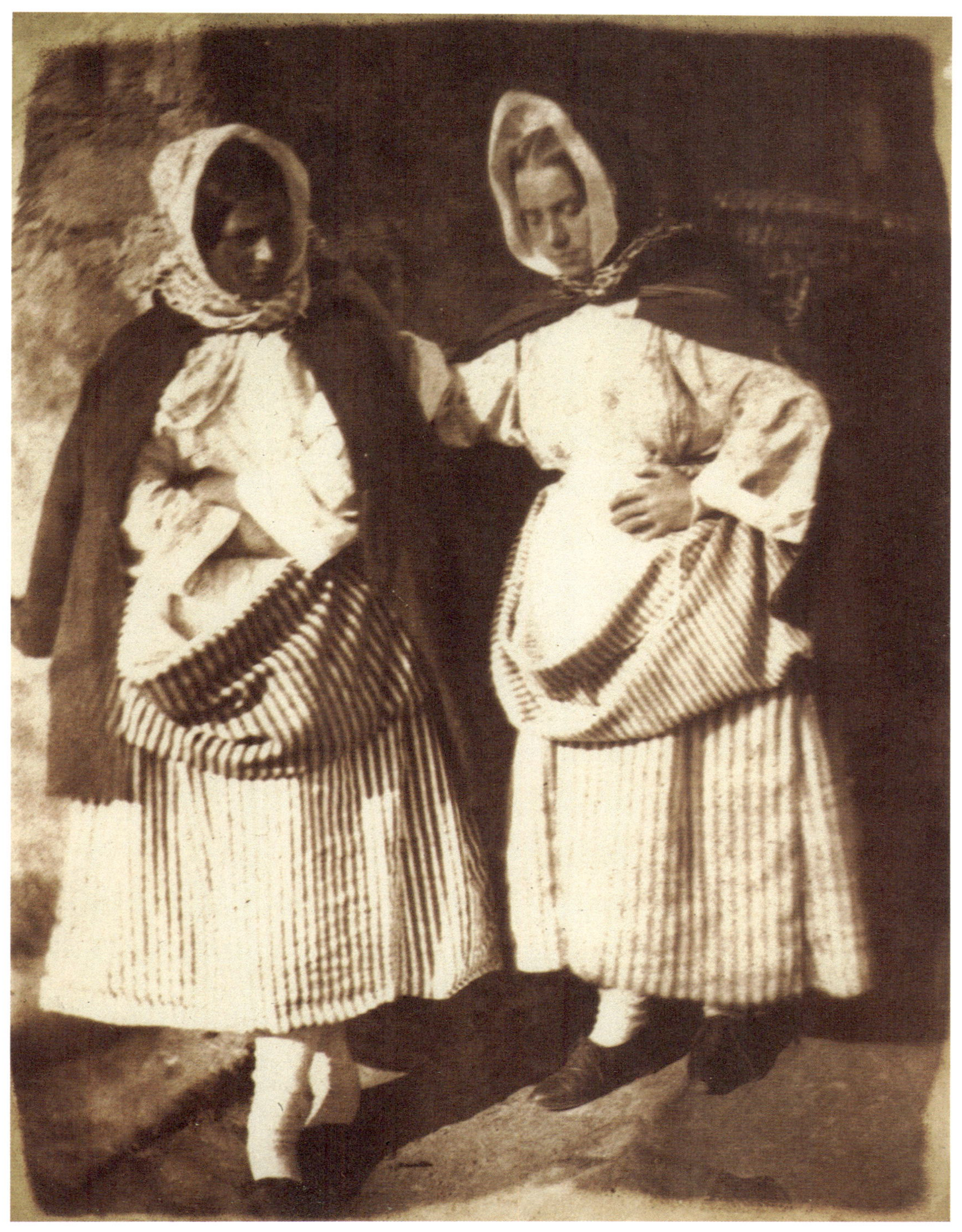

39

Two Fishwives, Mrs Elizabeth (Johnstone) Hall on the left

Scottish National Portrait Gallery

PGPHA 292

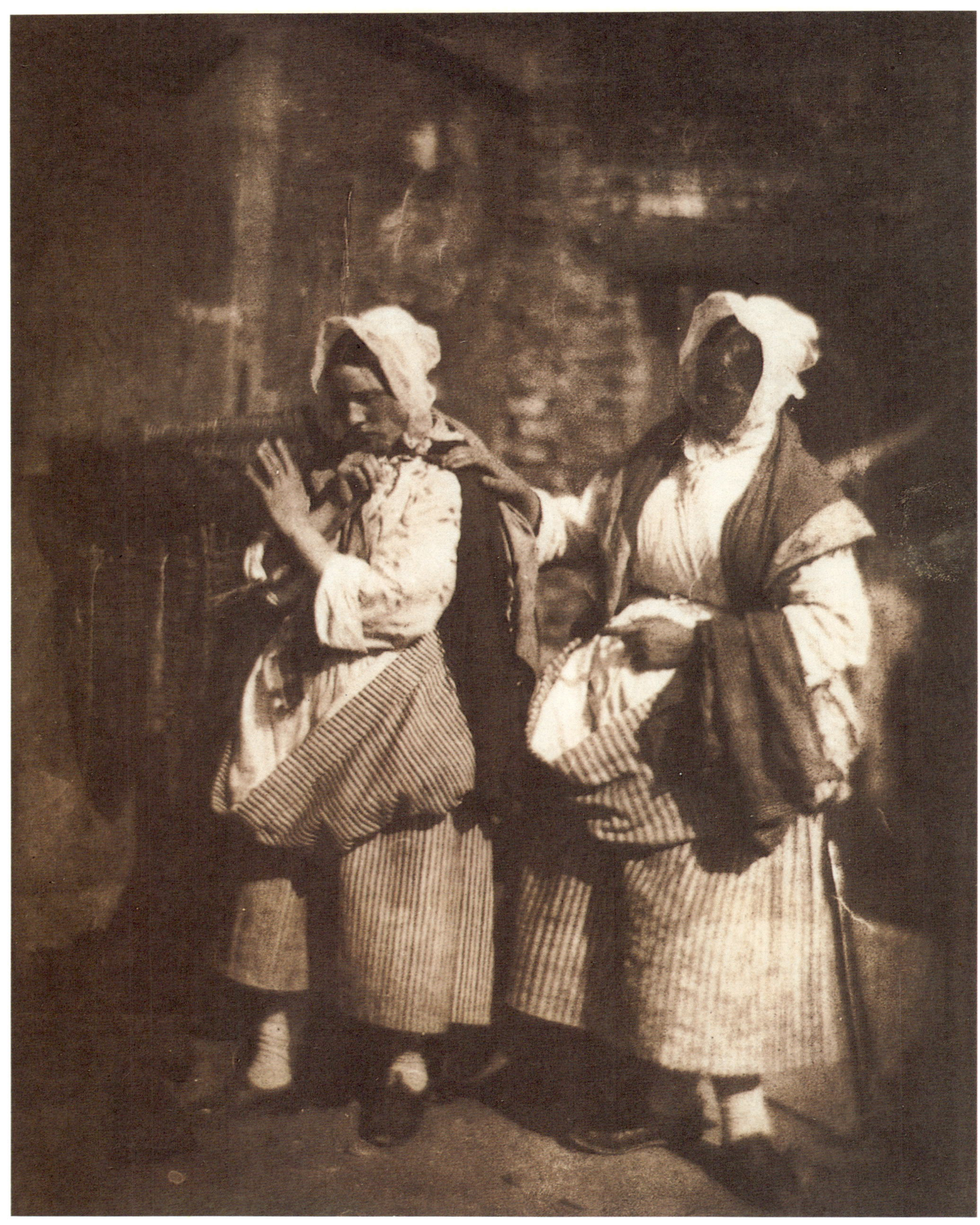

40

Two Fishwives, Mrs Elizabeth (Johnstone) Hall on the right

Modern print from Glasgow University negative, Dougan Collection

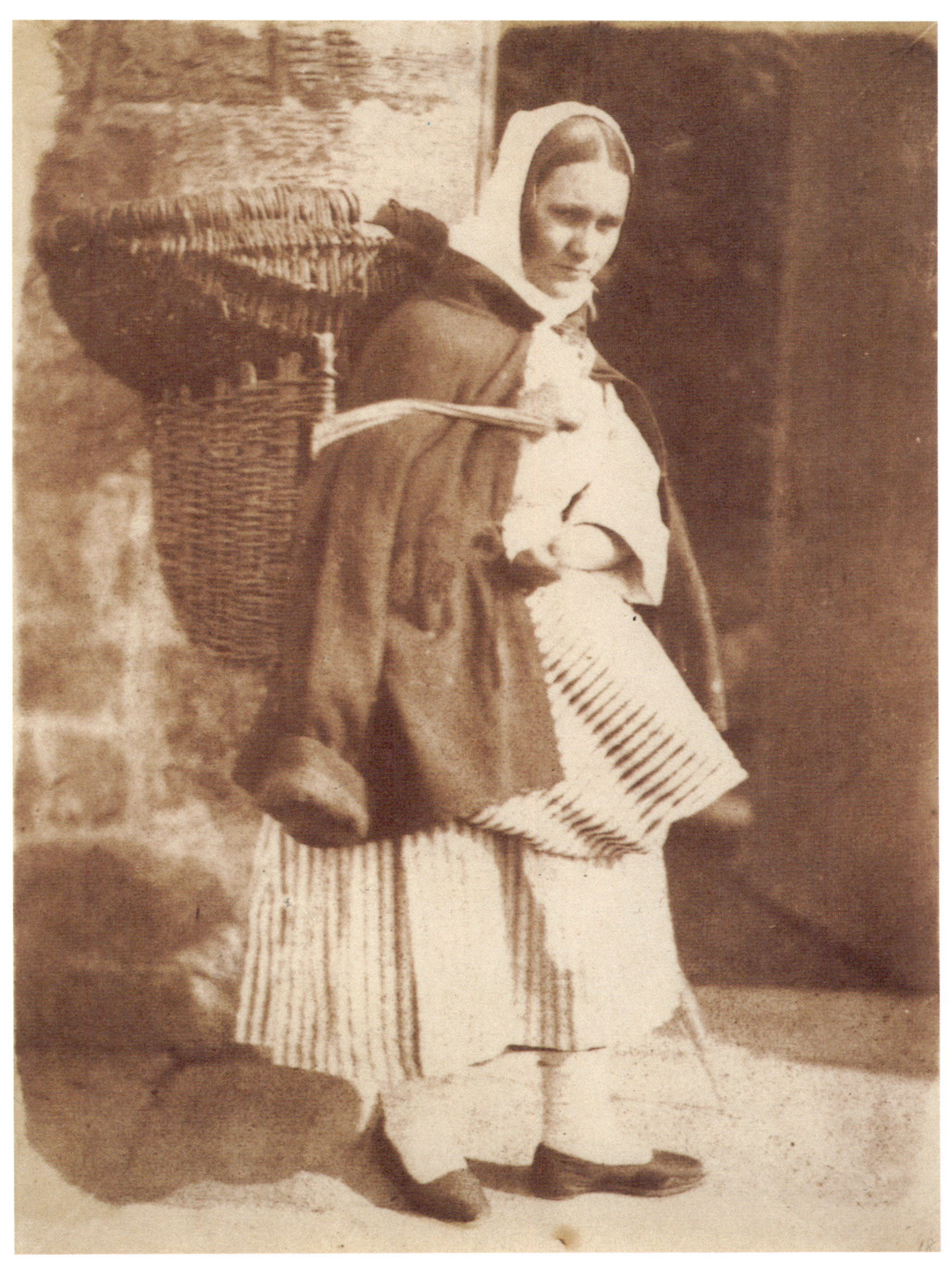

41

Newhaven Fishwife, 'Home from Market'

Title from Royal Academy Album
Scottish National Portrait Gallery
PGPHA 307

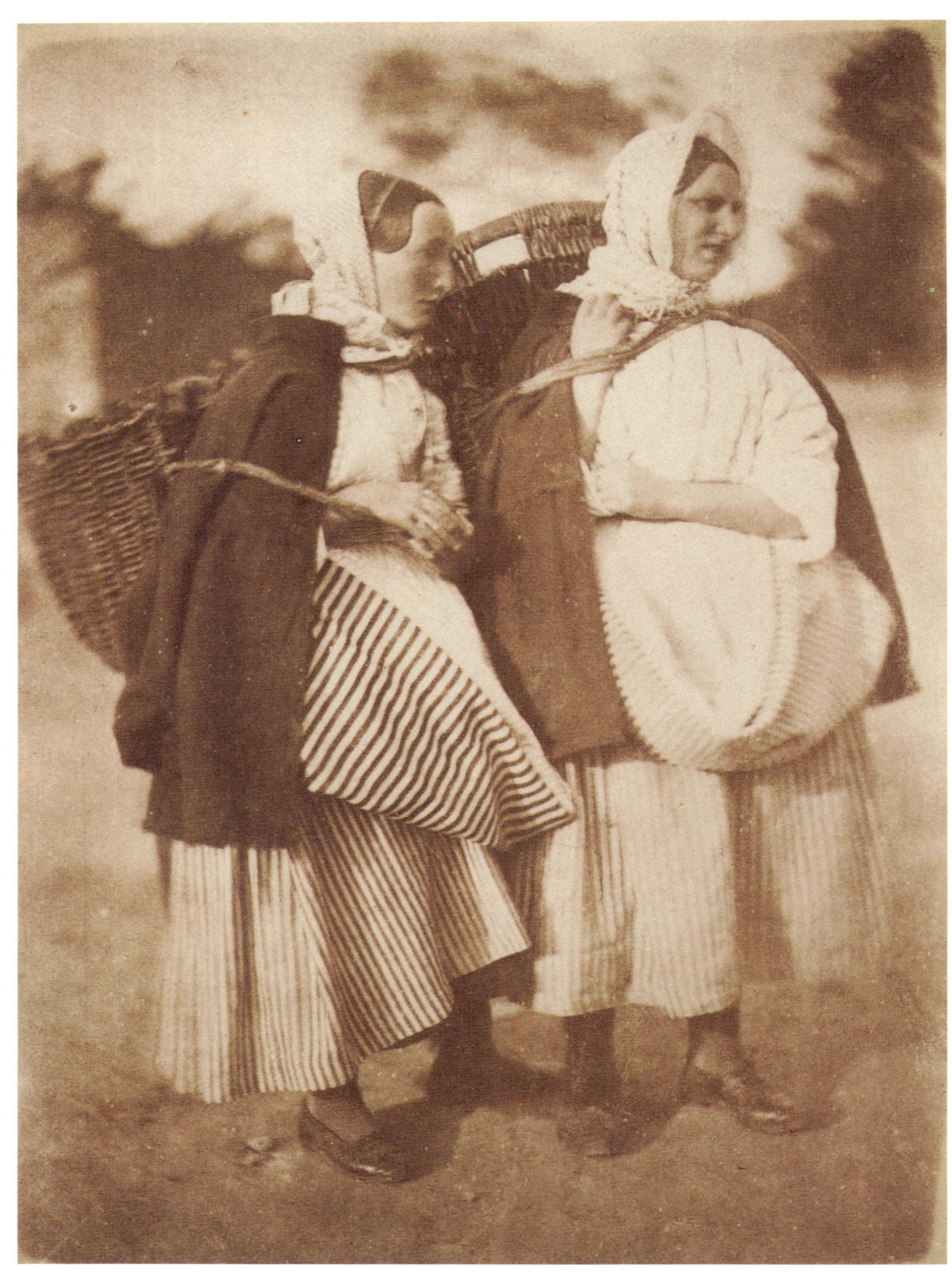

42

Newhaven Fishwives, 'To Hail the Bark that Never can Return'

Title from James Wilson Album
Mrs Robertson, Henry Bicknell Album

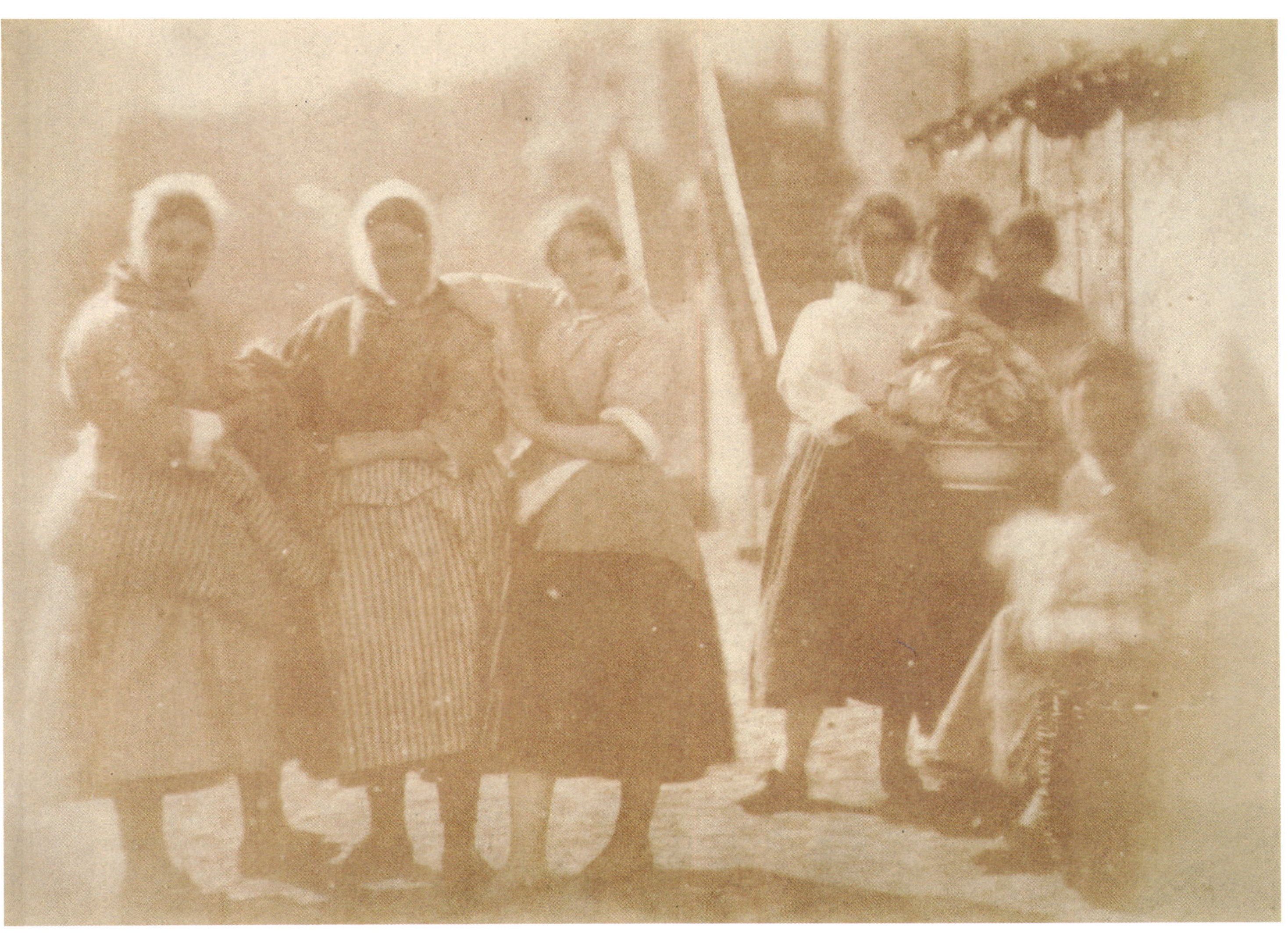

43

'A Lane in Newhaven', Fishwives at Home

'The Dredging Sang, Newhaven
"The herring loves the merry moonlicht,
The mackerel loves the wind;
But the oyster loves the dredging sang
For it comes o' the gentle kind"'

Quotation from James Wilson Album
Scottish National Portrait Gallery
PGPHA 295

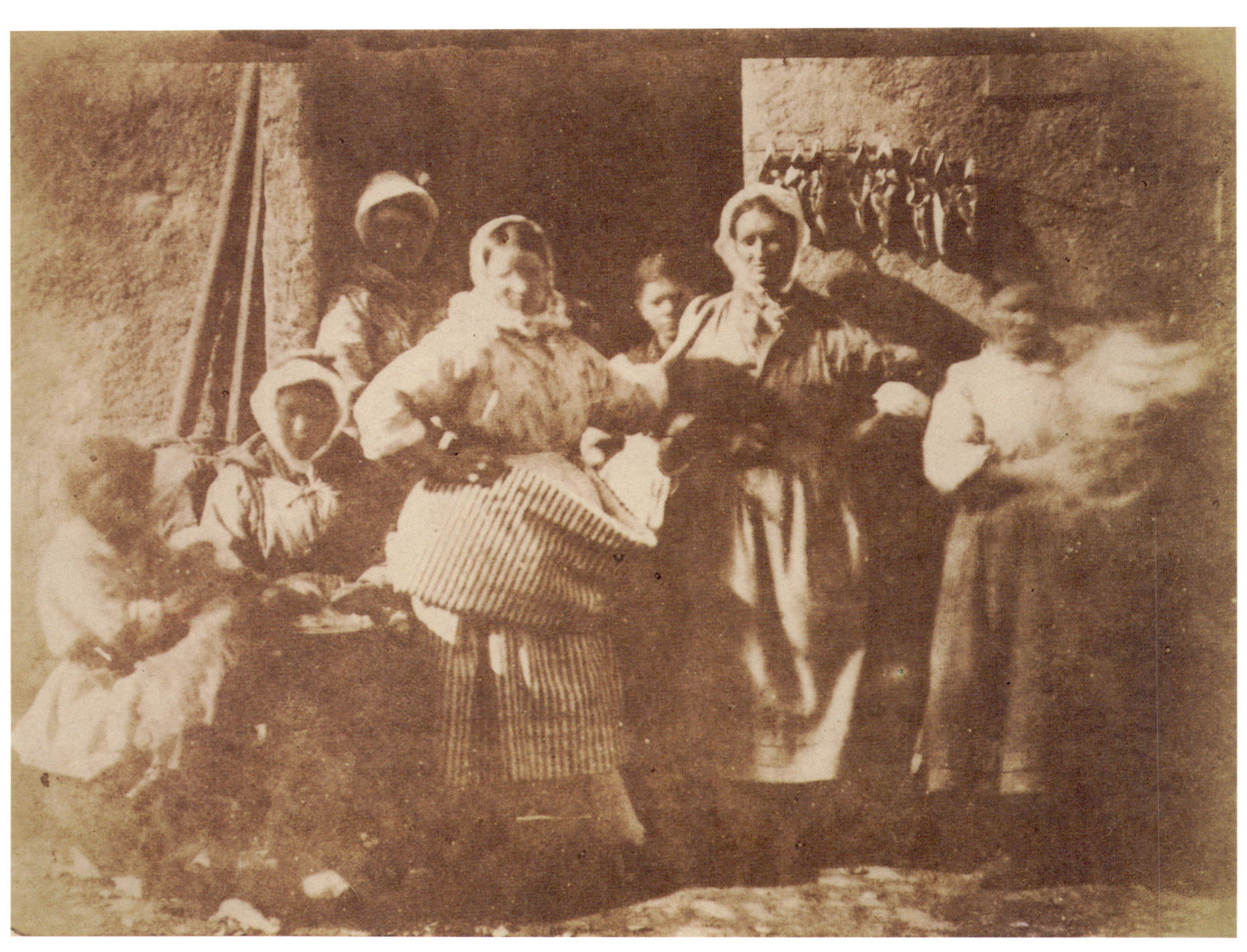

44
Newhaven Fishwives by a Cottage Door, 1843
Scottish National Portrait Gallery
PGPHA 310

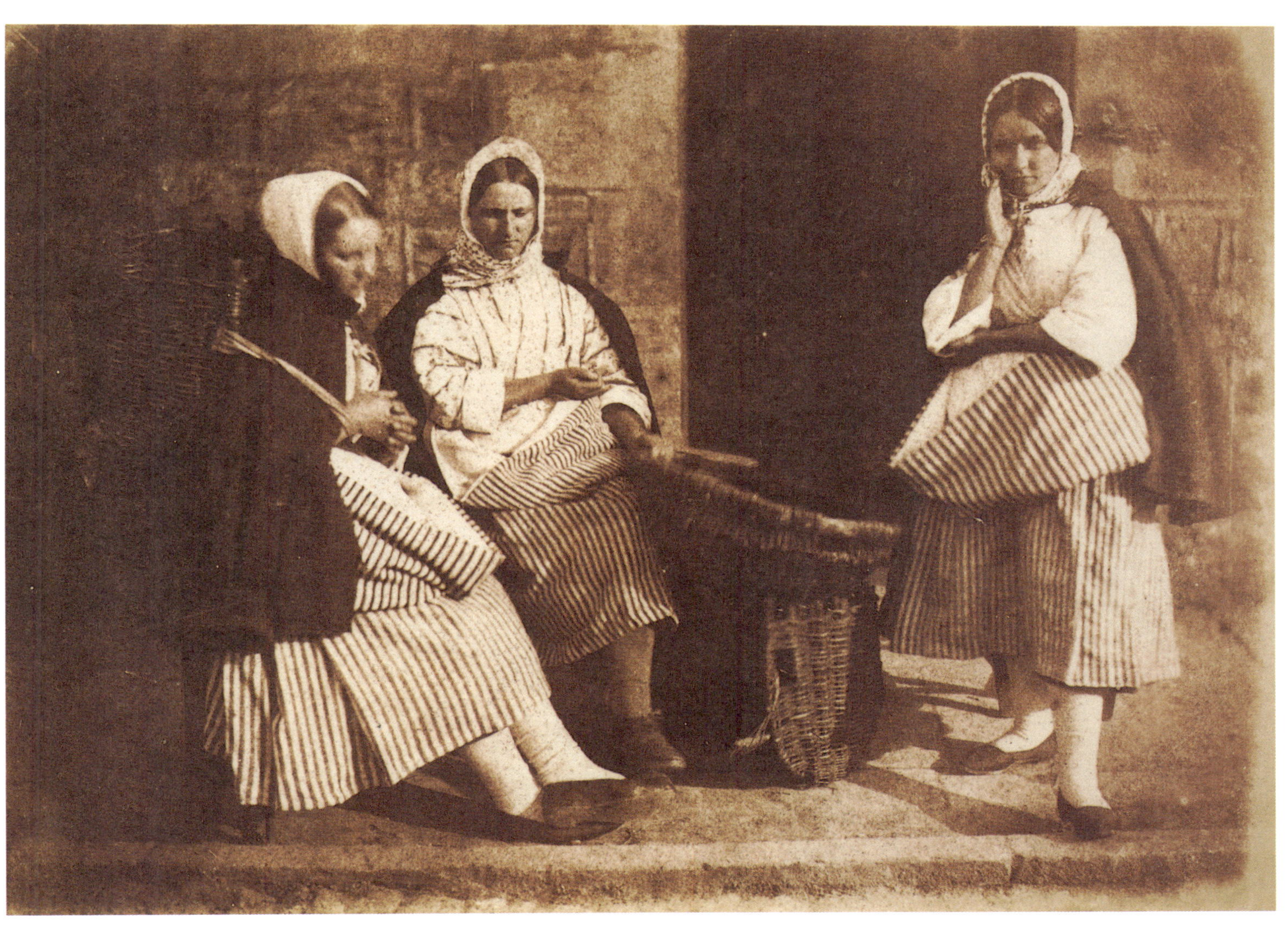

45

Newhaven Fishwives

Scottish National Portrait Gallery, J. Irvine Smith Album
PGPHA 313

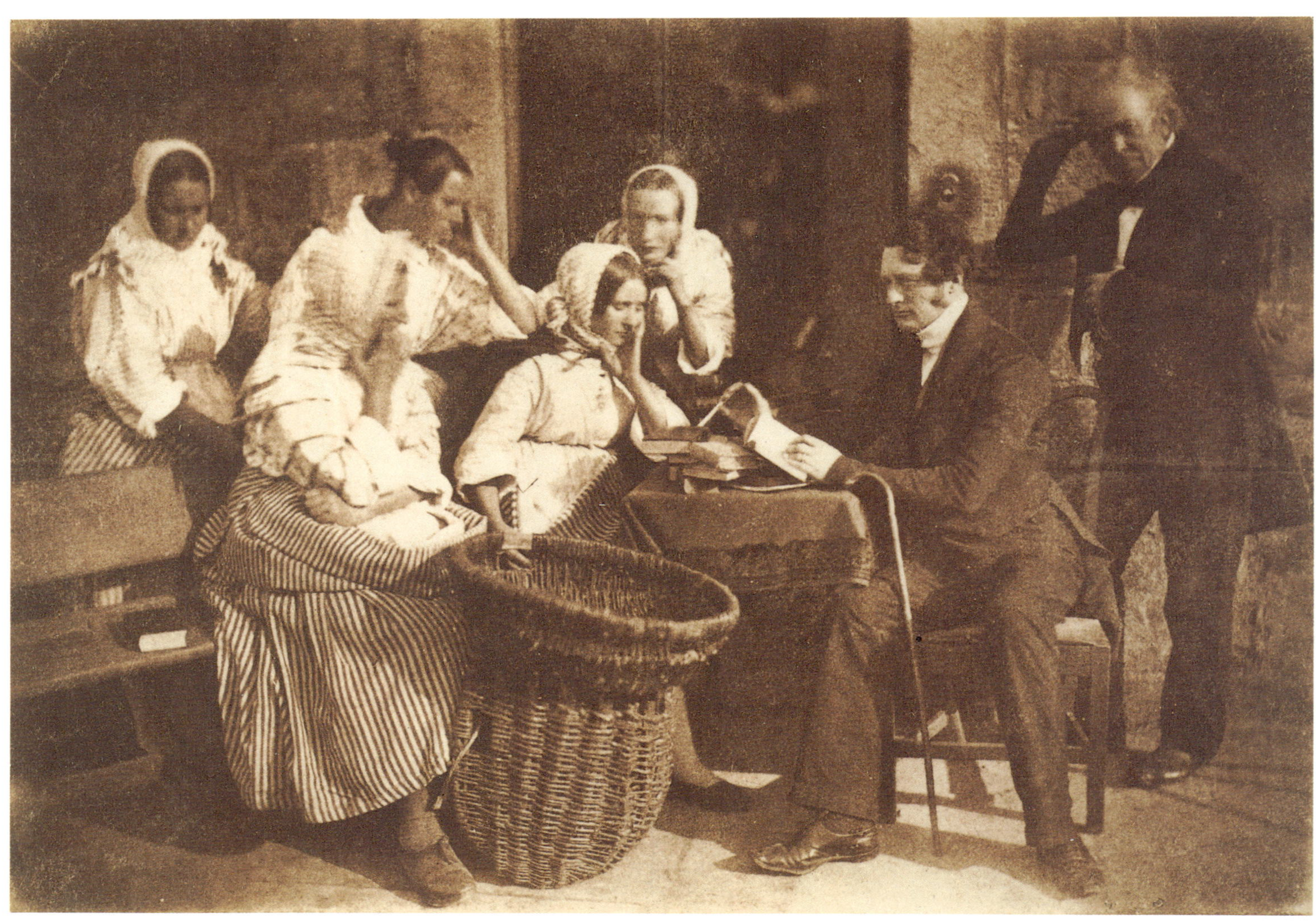

46

Newhaven Group

including Mrs Carnie Noble, Bessie Crombie, Mary Combe, Mrs Margaret (Dryburgh) Lyall,
Rev Dr James Fairbairn and James Gall, taken on 16 July 1845.

'The Pastor's Visit "He speaks of those who go down to the sea in ships and do business in the great waters" Job'

Quotation from James Wilson Album
Scottish National Portrait Gallery
PGPHA 293

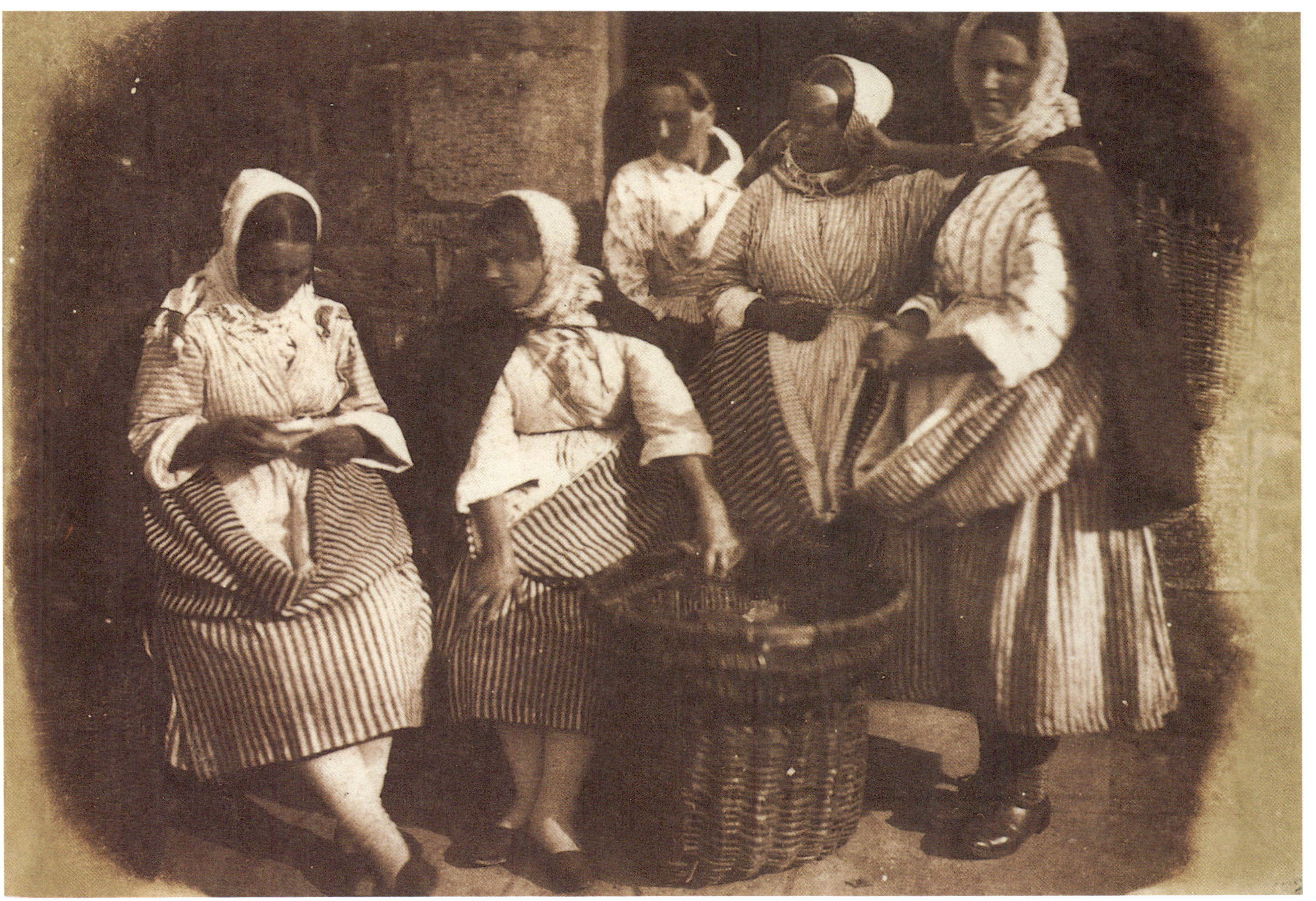

47

Newhaven Group

including Mrs Margaret (Dryburgh) Lyall, Marion Finlay and Mrs Grace (Finlay) Ramsay.

'And certain stars shot madly from their spheres
To hear the Seamaids music'

Quotation from *A Midsummer Night's Dream*, used in James Wilson Album
Scottish National Portrait Gallery, Charles Finlay Album
PGPHA 316

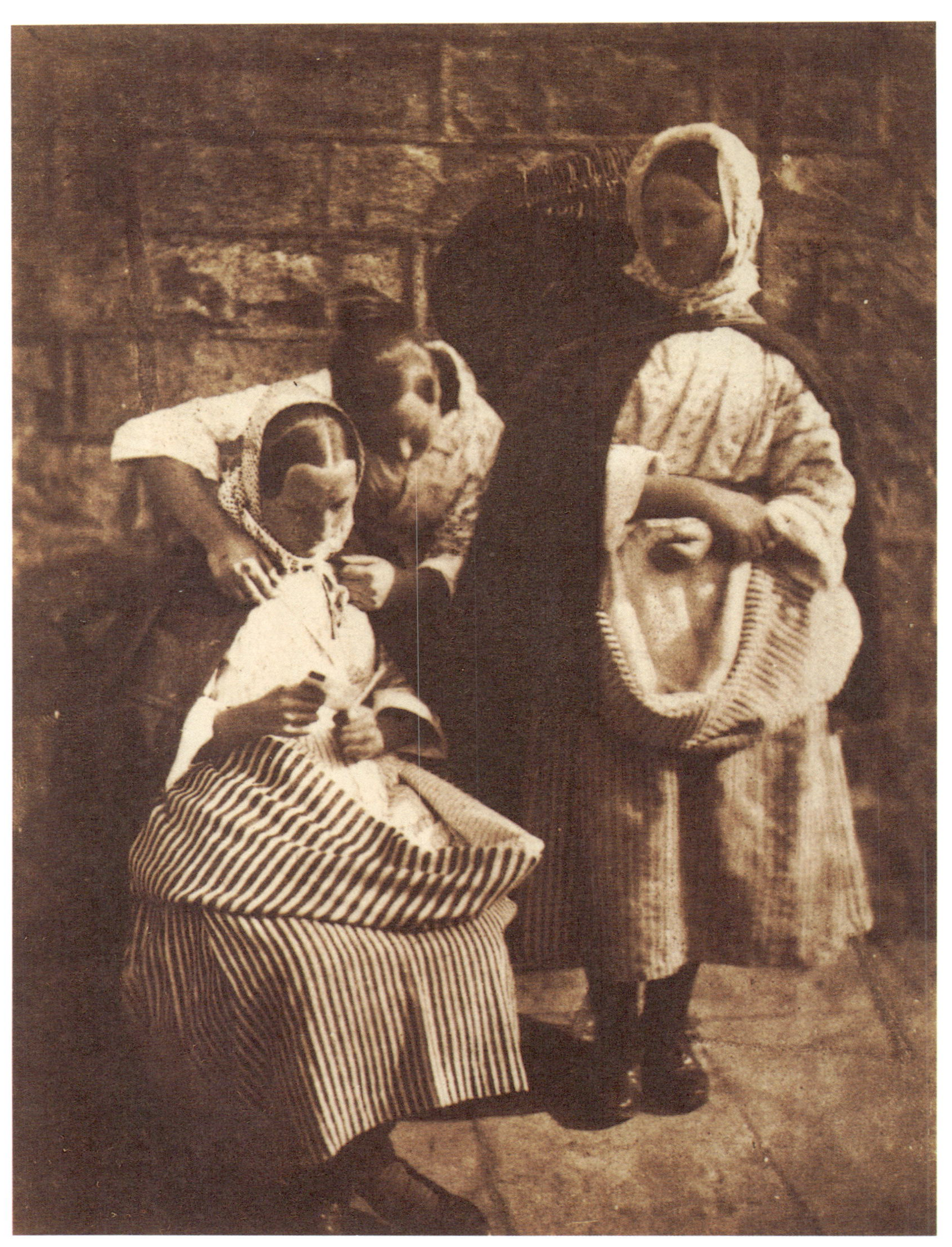

48

Marion Finlay, Mrs Margaret (Dryburgh) Lyall and Mrs Grace (Finlay) Ramsay

'The Letter—Newhaven "Frae Jamie at the sea"'

Quotation from James Wilson Album
Scottish National Portrait Gallery
PGPHA 298

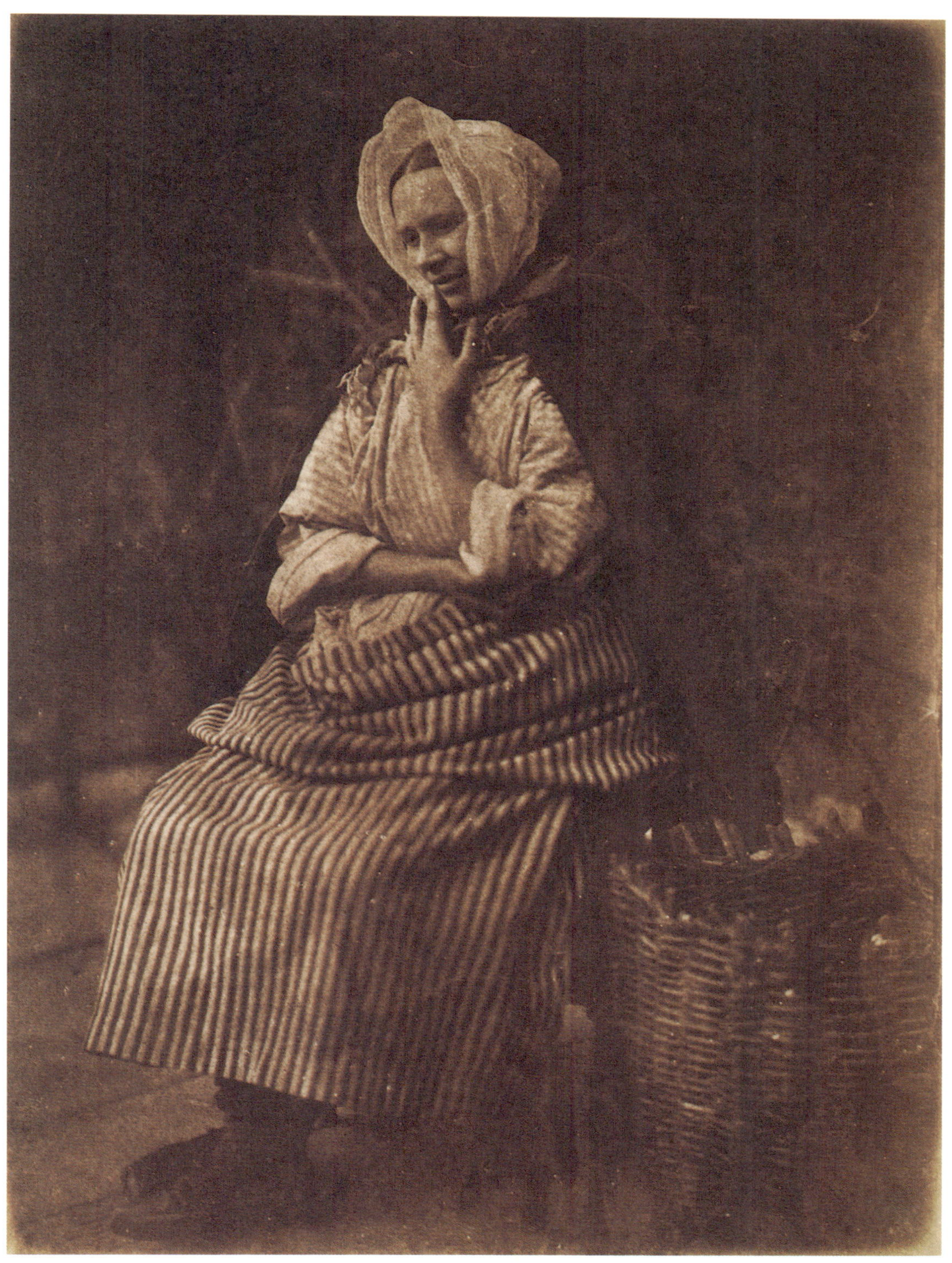

49

Jeanie Wilson

'A Love Reverie. Mrs Wilson sings
"When Jamie vowed he would be mine
And won frae me my heart
Oh meikle lichter grew my creel
We said we'd never part" The Boatie Rows'

Quotation from James Wilson Album
Scottish National Portrait Gallery
PGPHA 317

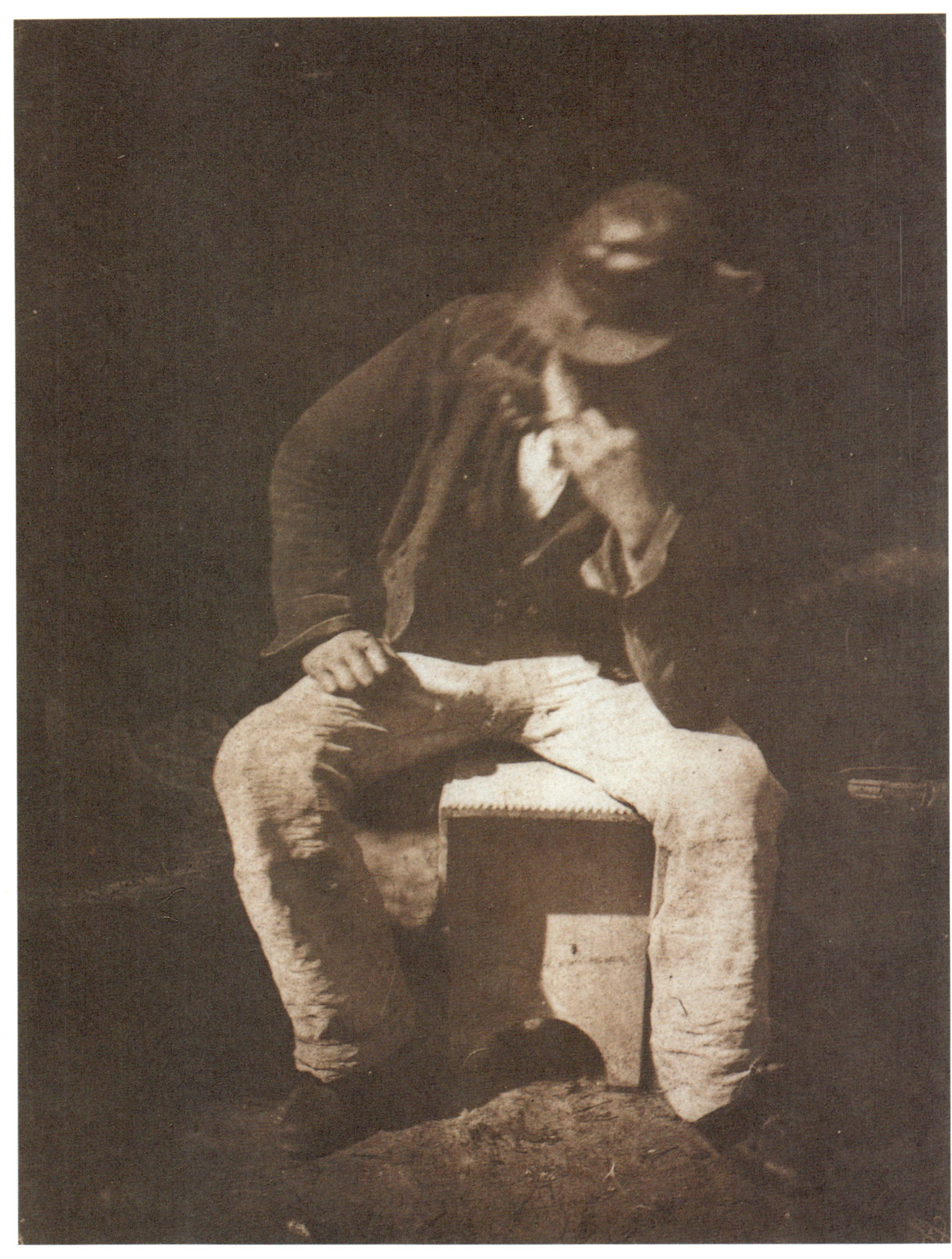

50

Willie Liston Thinking

Modern print from Edinburgh Photographic Society negative, inscribed: 'no gal / 13 (?) / 88'

PGPEPS 73

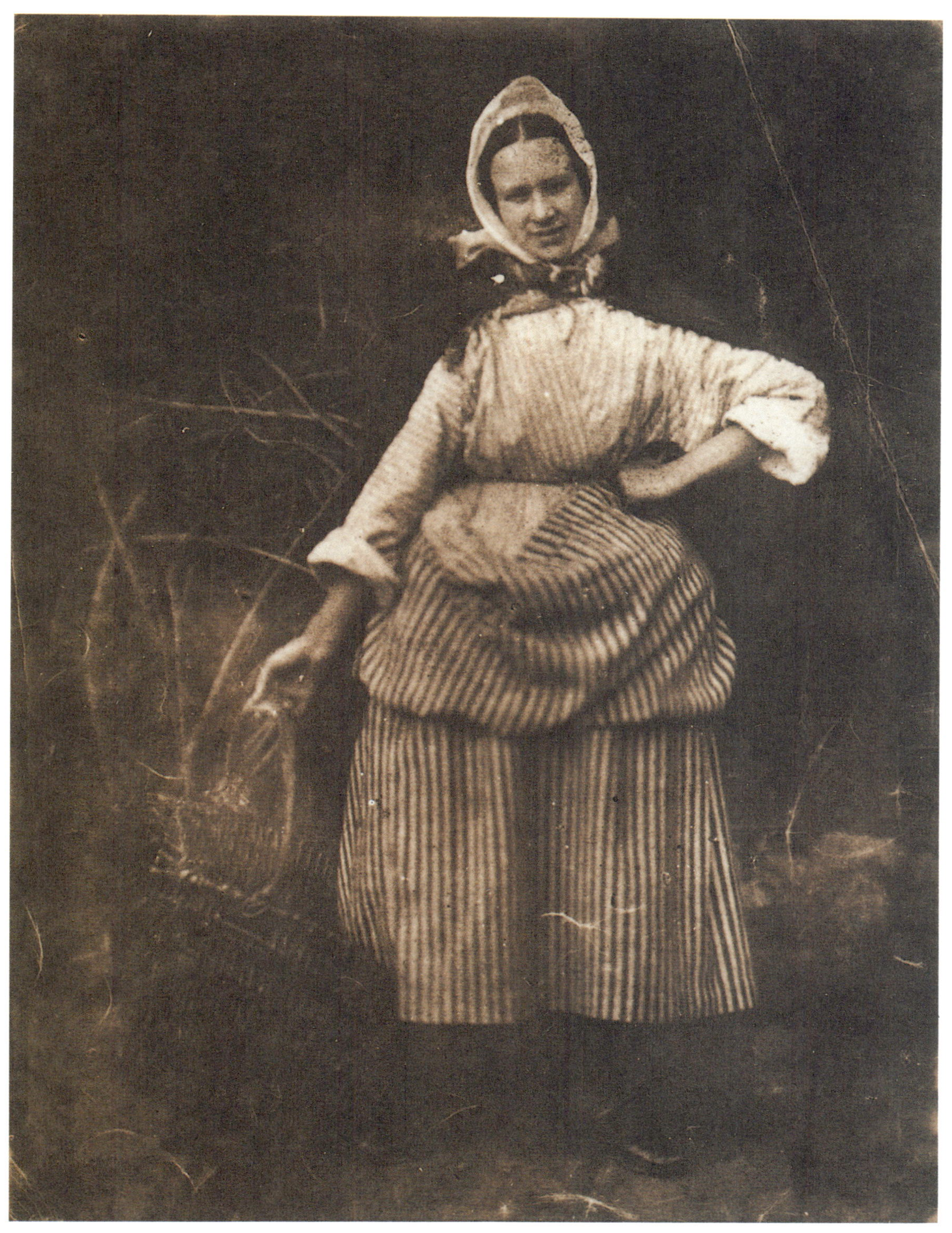

51

Newhaven Fishwife

Modern print from Edinburgh Photographic Society negative, inscribed: 'ex1h / 306 / 57',
PGPEPS 46

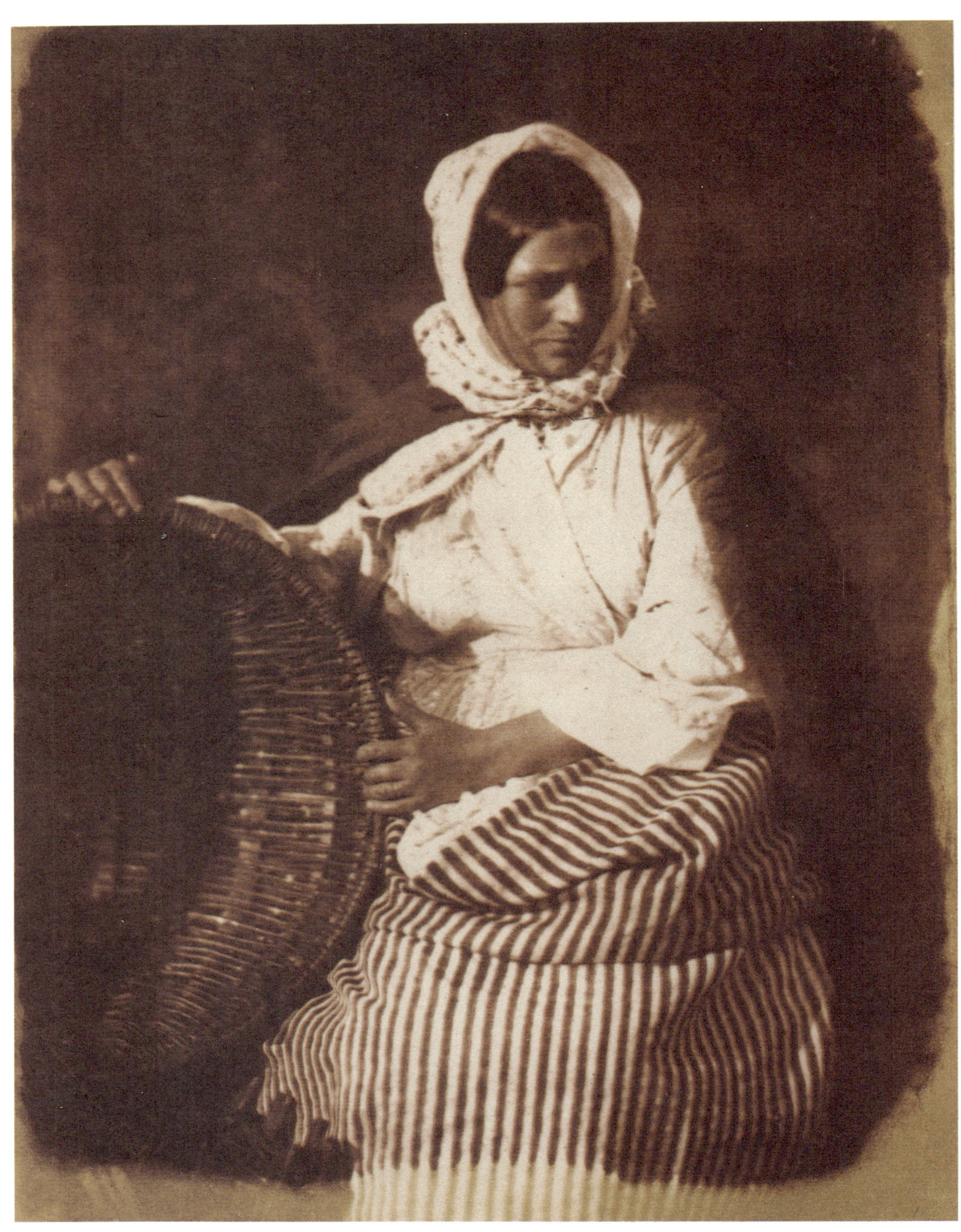

52

Mrs Elizabeth (Johnstone) Hall

'A Newhaven Beauty. "It's no fish ye're buying, it's men's lives"'

Quotation from James Wilson Album
Scottish National Portrait Gallery
PGPHA 301

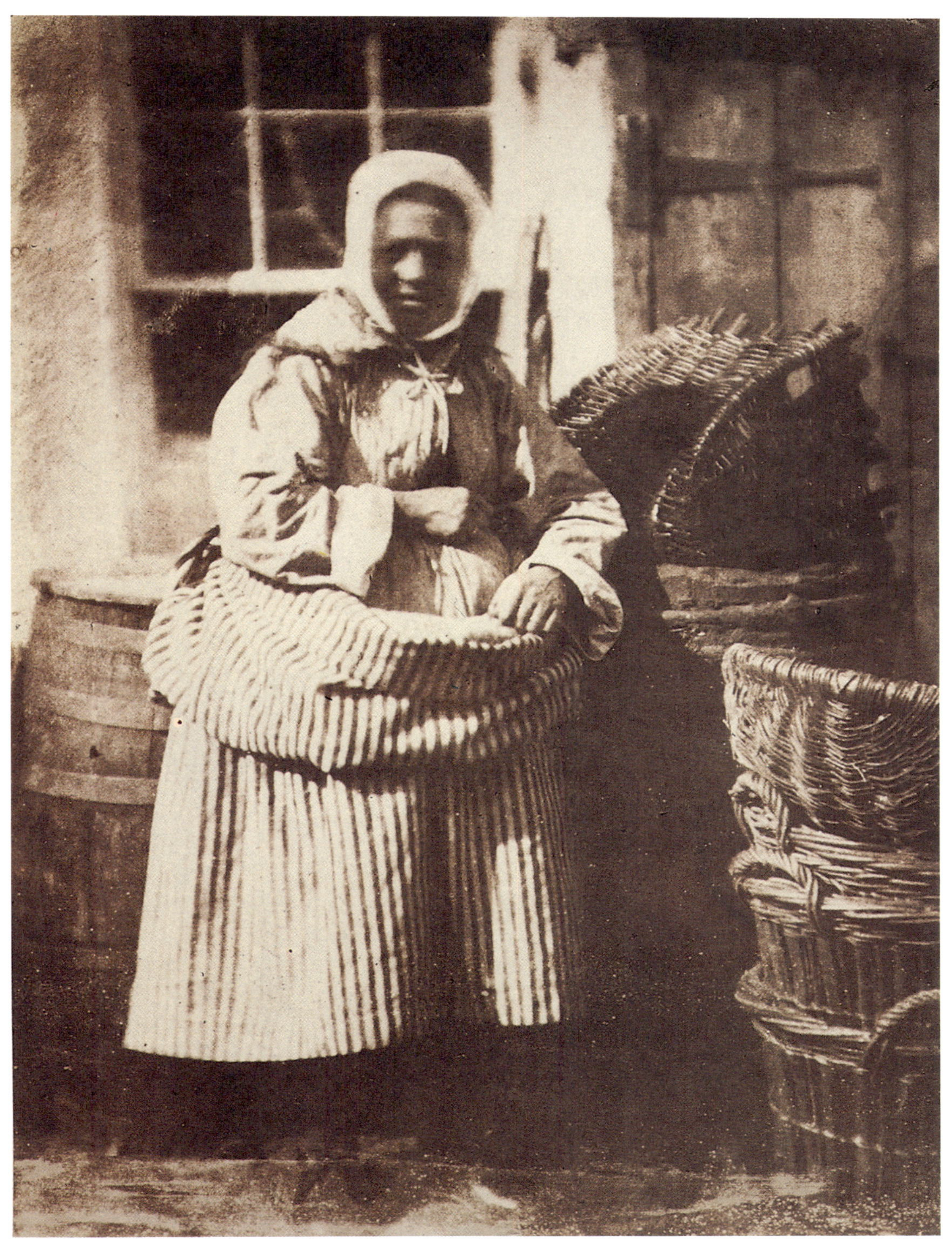

53

'Aunty Nell, A Newhaven Fishwife'

Harry Ransom Humanities Research Center, Clarkson Stanfield Album 086

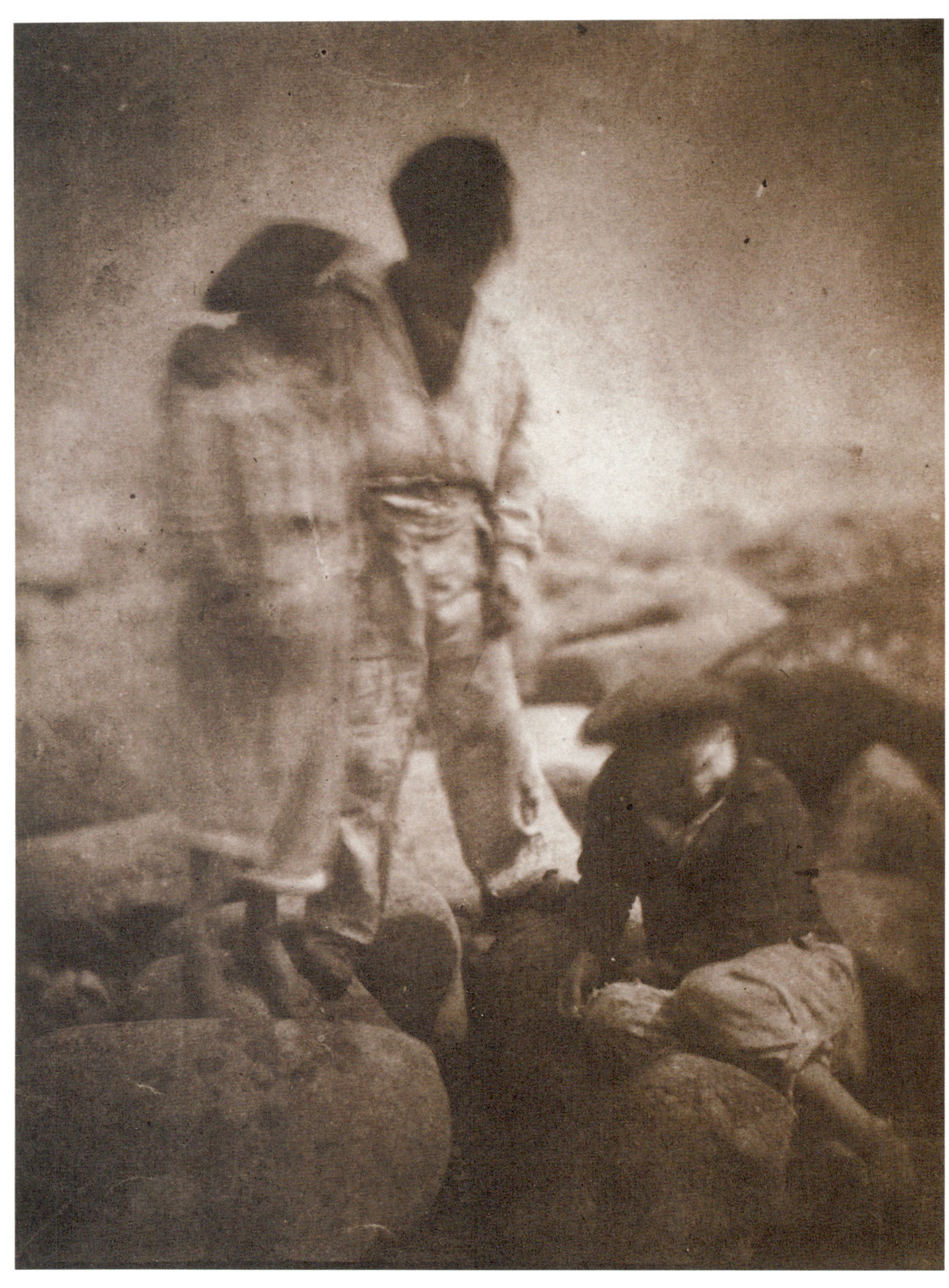

54

Fisherboys

Modern print from Glasgow University negative, Dougan Collection

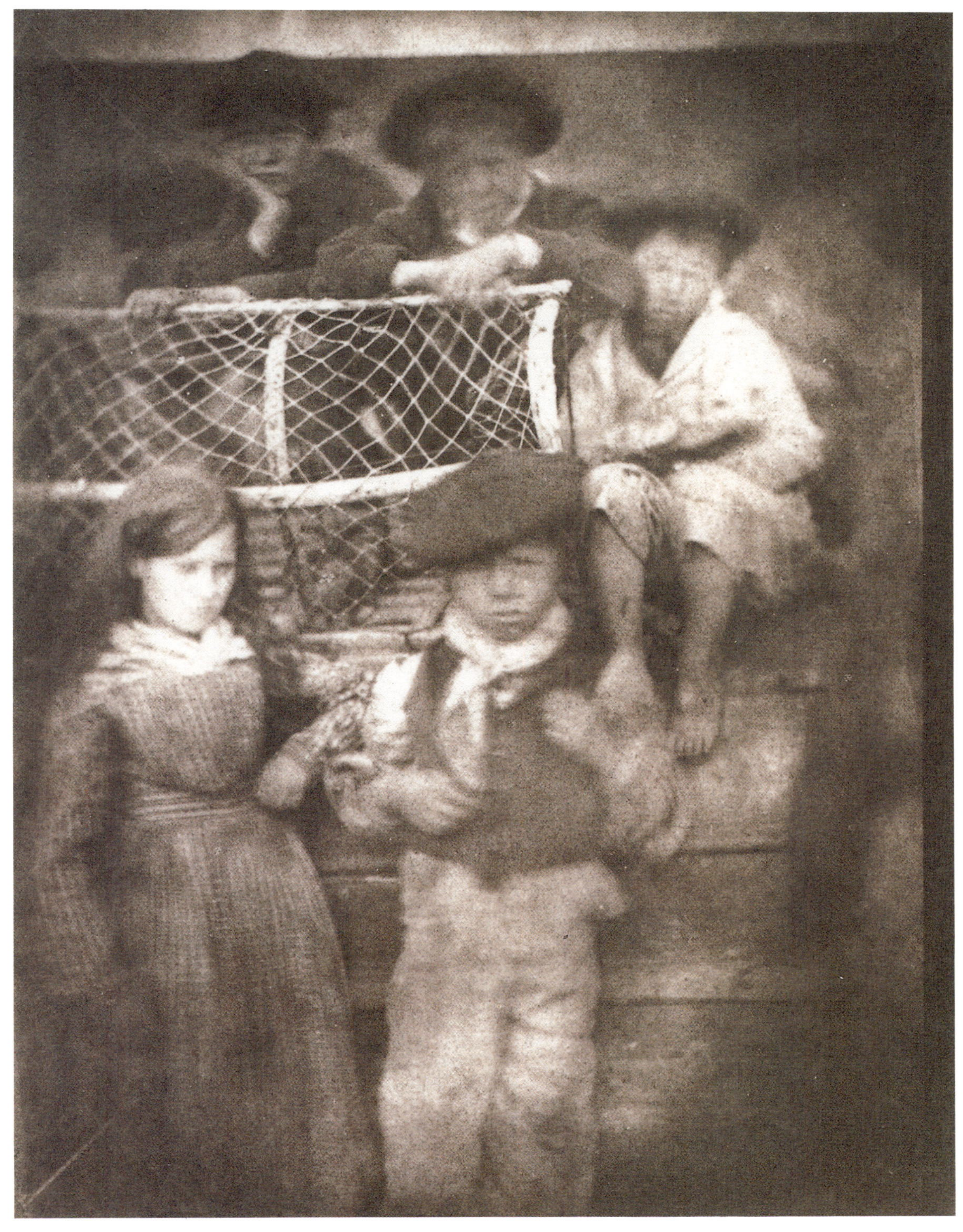

55

Newhaven Children

Modern print from Edinburgh Photographic Society negative, inscribed: '15 / 61'
PGPEPS 51

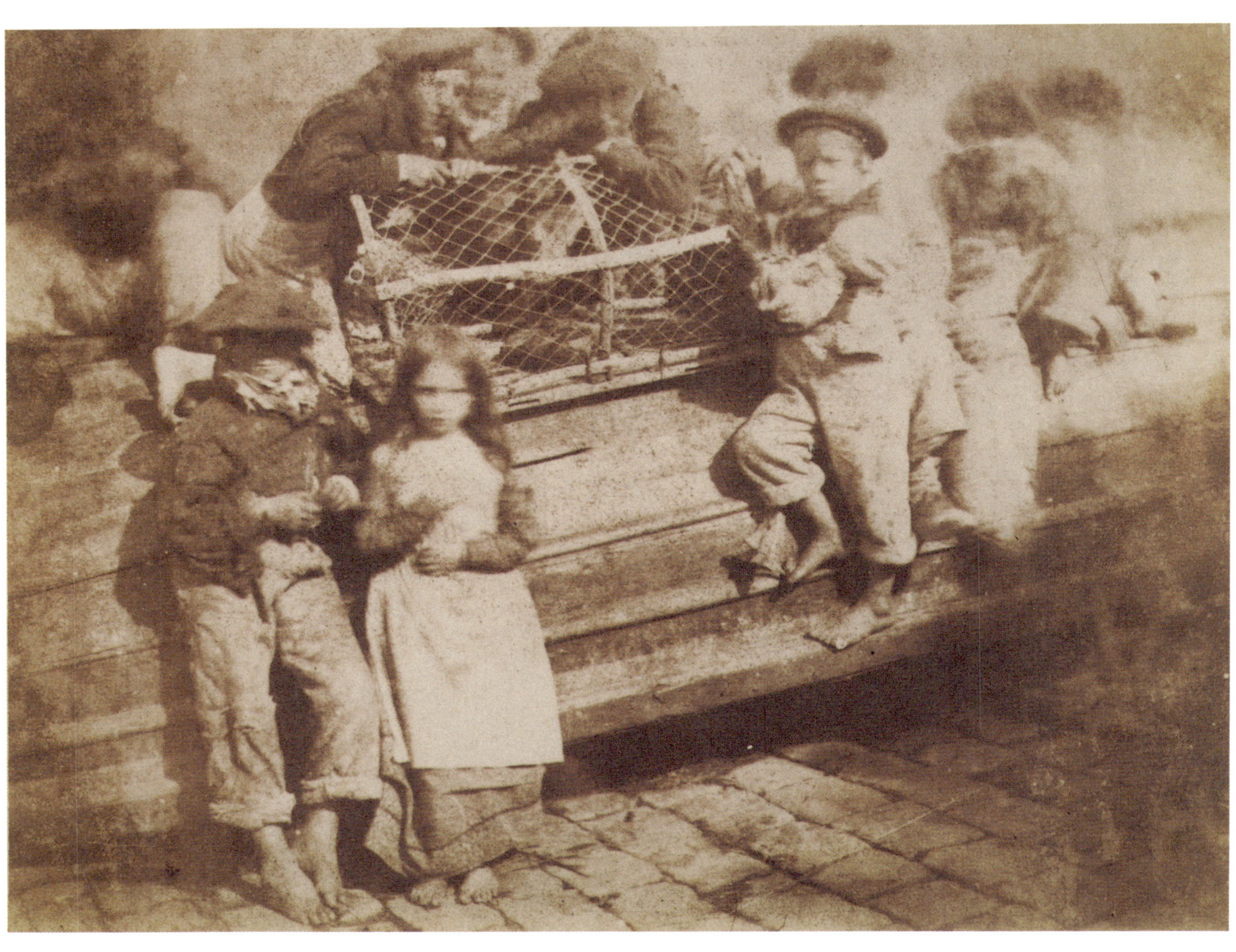

56

Newhaven Children, 'Fisherladdies'

Scottish National Portrait Gallery
PGPHA 263

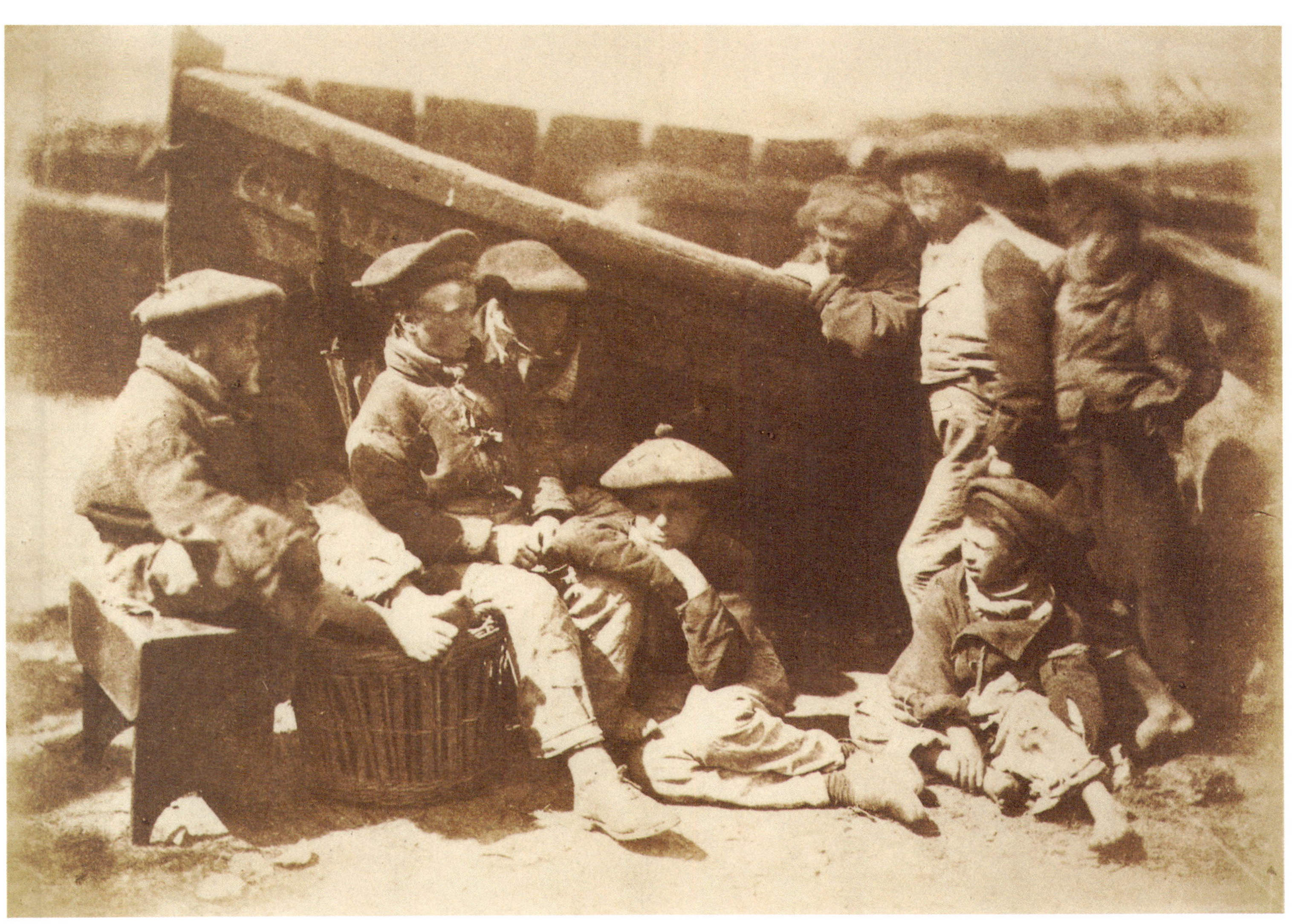

57

Newhaven Boys

'Newhaven Fisher Callants' 'Our Coast-Guards To Be'

Titles from Royal Academy and James Wilson Albums
Scottish National Portrait Gallery
PGPHA 305

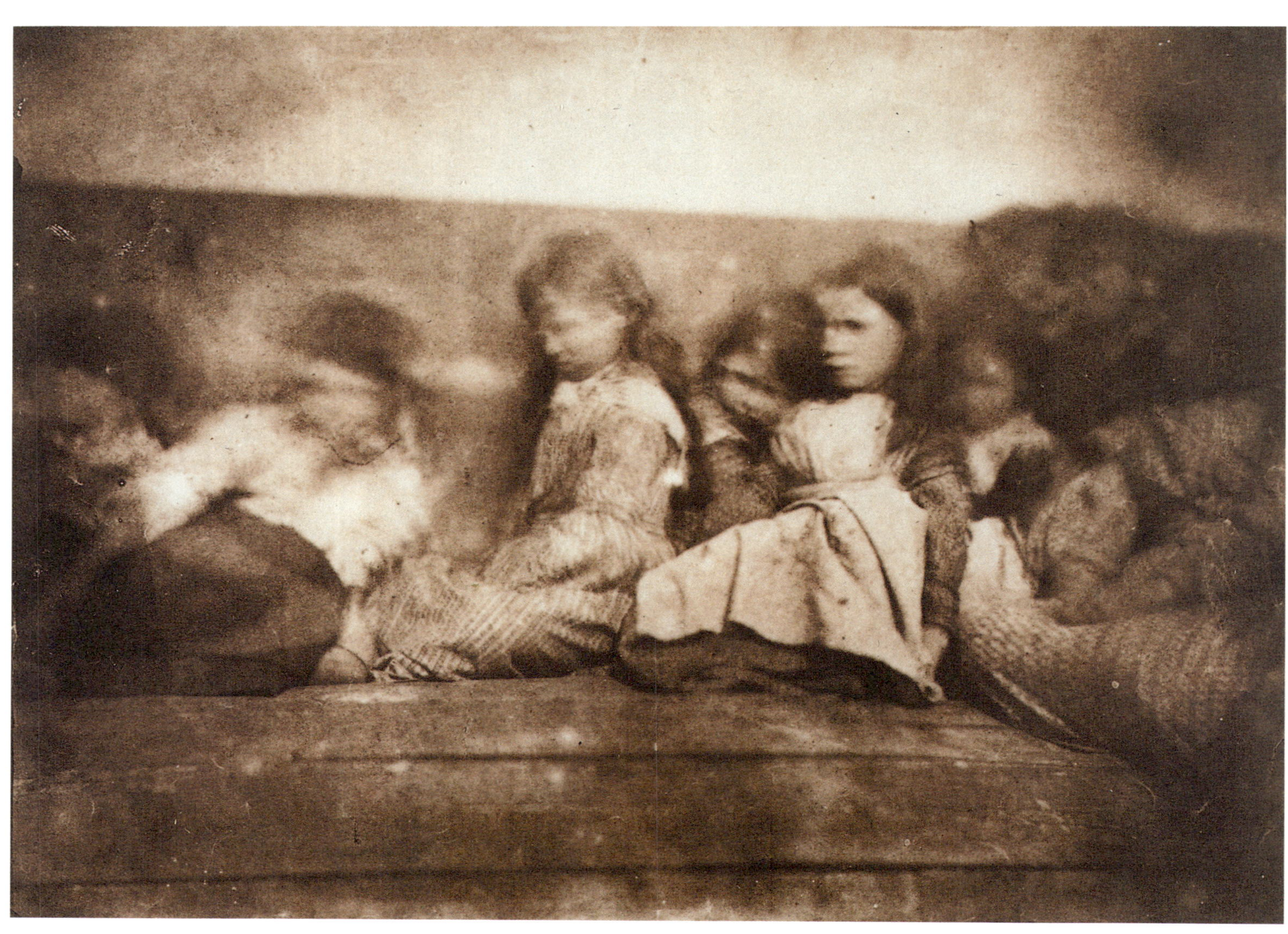

58

Group of Girls

Modern print from Glasgow University negative, Dougan Collection

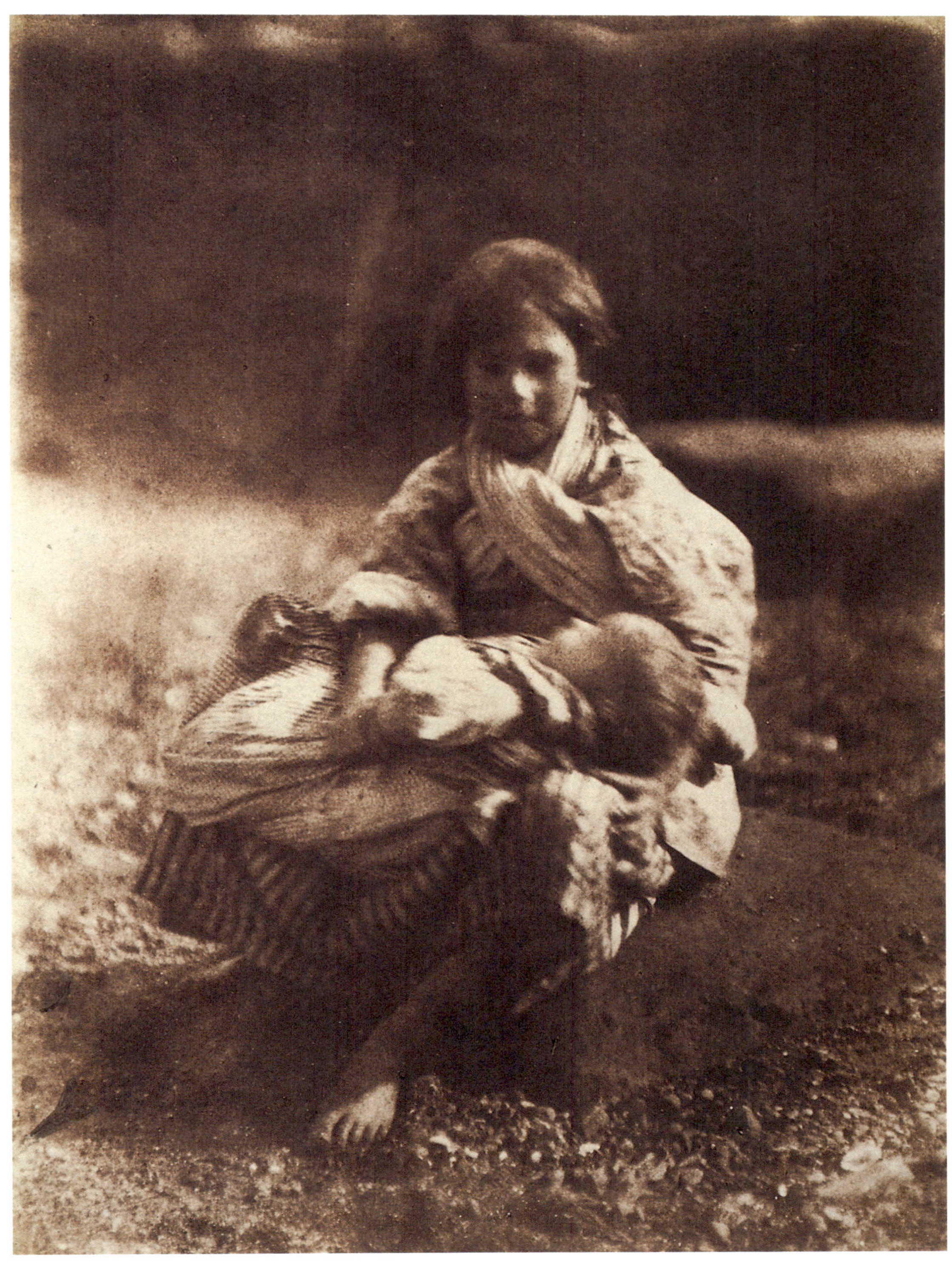

59

'Fisher Lassie and Child'

Harry Ransom Humanities Research Center, Clarkson Stanfield Album 080

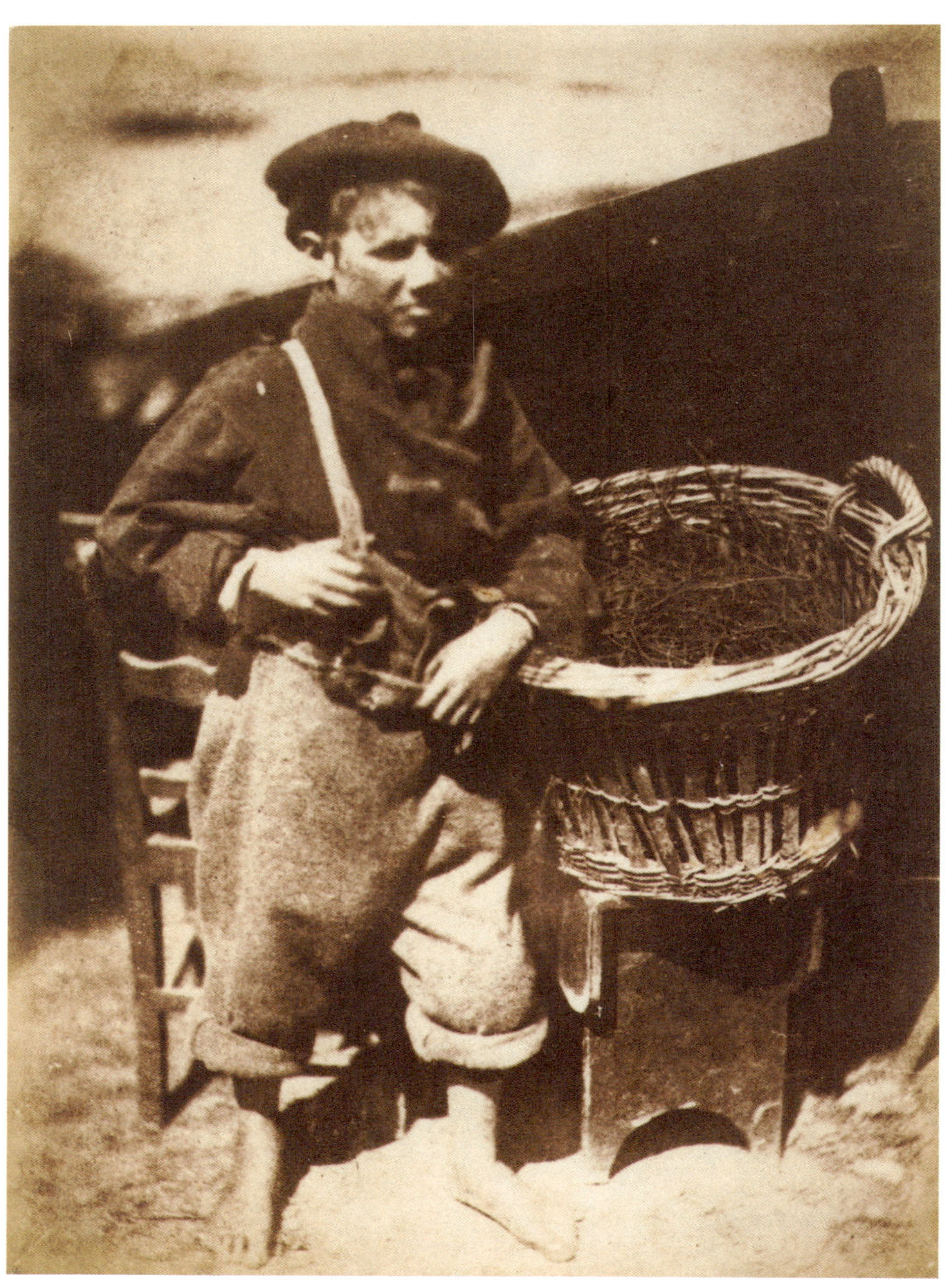

60

'The King Fisher, Newhaven'

"His father's breeks he hath girded on"

Quotation, a pun on the lines in 'The Minstrel Boy': 'His father's sword he hath girded on', from John Scott Album
Scottish National Portrait Gallery
PGPHA 303

Index

Select Bibliography

Keith Bell, David Harris and Grant Arnold, *The Photographs of David Octavius Hill and Robert Adamson*, Saskatoon, (exhibition catalogue) 1987

David Bruce, *Sun Pictures: the Hill-Adamson Calotypes*, London, 1973

Colin Ford and Roy Strong, *An Early Victorian Album. The Photographic Masterpieces of David Octavius Hill and Robert Adamson*, London, 1976

Malcolm Gray, *The Fishing Industries of Scotland 1790–1914. A Study in Regional Adaption*, Oxford 1978

Tom McGowran, *Newhaven-on-Forth, Port of Grace*, Edinburgh, 1985

Katherine Michaelson, *A Centenary Exhibition of the Work of David Octavius Hill 1802–1870 and Robert Adamson 1821–1848*, Edinburgh (exhibition catalogue) 1970

A. D. Morrison-Low, 'Dr. John Adamson and Robert Adamson: An Early Partnership in Scottish Photography', *Photographic Collector*, vol. 4 no. 2 1983, p198–214

Papers of the Society of Free Fishermen of Newhaven, manuscripts in the Scottish Record Office, GD265

Charles Reade, *Christie Johnstone*, London, 1889

Graham Smith, 'Hill and Adamson at St Andrews: The Fishergate calotypes', *The Print Collector's Newsletter*, 10, 1979, p45–48

Sara Stevenson, *David Octavius Hill and Robert Adamson. Catalogue of their calotypes taken between 1843 and 1847 in the collection of the Scottish National Portrait Gallery*, Edinburgh, 1981

John Ward and Sara Stevenson, *Printed Light. The Scientific Art of William Henry Fox Talbot and David Octavius Hill with Robert Adamson*, Edinburgh, 1986

James Wilson, *A Voyage Round the Coasts of Scotland 1841*, Edinburgh 1842

James Wilson, *The Society of Free Fishermen of Newhaven*, Newhaven, 1951